Conservation and the consumer

Awareness about conservation issues is constantly growing, but how can levels of environmental concern be accurately quantified? An increasing amount of research is being carried out in the area of conservation and the environment which involves assessing response levels amongst the public as part of developing programmes for environmental planning. But just how *do* people define their level of 'greenness', how far are they actively involved and what influences them to take action?

This volume develops a way to measure accurately levels of environmental concern. By using various techniques, including facet theory, Paul Hackett devises a mapping sentence to define accurately environmental concern, looking at cognitive processes and levels of involvement. The author covers a variety of issues, from saving blue whales to the development of community forests and develops a model that relates environmental concerns to social values. This book will be of interest to all those concerned with researching consumer behaviour and environmental activity.

Paul Hackett is a Research Psychologist at the University of Wales, College of Medicine in Cardiff.

Consumer Research and Policy Series
Edited by Gordon Foxall

Conservation and the consumer

Understanding environmental concern

Paul Hackett

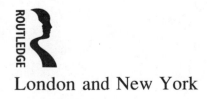

London and New York

First published in 1995
by Routledge
11 Fetter Lane, London EC4P 4EE

Simultaneously published in the USA and Canada
by Routledge
29 West 35th Street, New York, NY 10001

© 1995 Paul Hackett

Typeset in Times by
J&L Composition Ltd, Filey, North Yorkshire
Printed and bound in Great Britain by
TJ Press (Padstow) Ltd, Padstow, Cornwall

British Library Cataloguing in Publication Data
A catalogue record for this book is available from the British Library

Library of Congress Cataloging in Publication Data
Hackett, Paul, 1960–
    Conservation and the consumer: understanding environmental
concern / Paul Hackett.
        p.   cm. – (Consumer research and policy series)
    Includes bibliographical references and index.
    ISBN 0–415–08096–7
    1. Environmental policy.   2. Conservation of natural resources.
3. Economic development.   4. Social ecology.   I. Title.
II. Series.
GE170.H33   1994
363.7–dc20
                                                              94–24886
                                                                   CIP

ISBN 0–415–08096–7

This book is dedicated to my parents, to Karen and to the two relatively 'unspoilt' locations of Cleobury Mortimer and Sutton St Nicholas.

Contents

Figures

Tables

Acknowledgements

I wish to thank the many people who participated in this study: they are too numerous to mention individually. Those who spared the time to complete a questionnaire and those who took part in the initial interviews are particularly thanked. Many organisations also co-operated in the research, and to these I express my gratitude: British Trust for Conservation Volunteers (Leeds), Urban Wildlife Group (Birmingham), Urban Base (Birmingham), Think Green Network (Birmingham), CLAWS (London), Centre for Urban Ecology (Birmingham), Friends of the Earth (London), Clouston Landscape Architects (Birmingham), Royal Society for the Protection of Birds (Droitwich and Sandwell Valley). I would also like to thank Dr Guy Cumberbatch, University of Aston, and Professor Alan Hedge, Cornell University.
My special thanks go to Karen and to my parents.

1 Introduction

In a recent survey 56 per cent of respondents reported feeling that the changes that have occurred in the British countryside had been for the worse. Sixty per cent of this sample also expressed a desire for the countryside to be afforded some form of protection from deleterious changes which have been, or may in the future be, occurring there (Jowell *et al.*, 1988). These figures show that a significant proportion of the British adult population expresses concern over the quality of the natural environment and the activities and changes taking place there. Moreover, when these figures are compared with previous studies carried out by Jowell and his colleagues between 1984 and 1987, they show environmental concern to be growing.

Major changes are occurring in the world's environment (Mannion and Bowlby, 1992) at all physical scales and in all geographical regions: at the global and international environmental scales (Wilson, 1984a; United Nations Environmental Program, 1991) and more locally within the British countryside (Blunden and Curry 1985a, 1985b). Accompanying these changes, sustained public concern for the quality of the natural environment has developed (Jowell *et al.*, 1987). In a survey conducted in 1983, Jowell and his associates (1984) found that across a number of different environmental issues, an average of 76 per cent of their sample regarded waste in the environment to be a serious or very serious issue. By 1986, this proportion had risen slightly to 80 per cent. This concern about the seriousness of environmental pollution is reflected in concern regarding changes in the British countryside. Here the same authors found in 1985 that 68 per cent of respondents expressed some degree of concern over countryside changes, whilst in 1986 this proportion had grown to 75 per cent.

Commenting upon the changes in public opinion in Britain, Young

(1988) wrote: 'We are witnessing some significant long-term shifts in public opinion as a result of which the countryside is likely to become a political issue in a deeper and more profound sense than ever before' (Young, 1988: 3).

Other studies have discovered a similar level of awareness of environmental issues to be present in the British public (MORI, 1987; NOP, 1987). For example, when asked how important the environment will be as a political issue over the next five years, 56 per cent replied very important, 38 per cent replied fairly important, whilst only 9 per cent thought that it would not be an important political issue (Harris, 1988). Accompanying this growth in interest in environmental matters and concern about changes in the countryside, there has been an increase in the number of groups or organisations working in environmental protection (see Barker, 1986; Porritt and Warner, 1988; Button, 1988a, 1988b). The environmental movement has also had an effect upon the consumer in general (Bruhn, 1979) and the environmentally aware consumer has been clearly identified (e.g., Hackett, 1992d). An effect upon the consumer has been brought about through requesting the purchaser to buy only products that have no deleterious effects upon the environment at the stage of their production, consumption, or when disposing of their waste by-products (e.g., Button 1988b; Elkington and Hailes, 1988).

There has also been a steady stream of research reports that have taken social aspects of environmental conservation and environmental usage as their subject matter (e.g., Millward and Bradley, 1986; Miller and Tranter, 1988; CEC, 1980; Countryside Commission, 1985, 1986a, 1986b, 1986c, 1987, 1988a). However, social scientists in general, and psychologists in particular, have been slow to become involved in this area of research. This is in spite of this lack of involvement being noted in the literature and a call on several occasions for a greater level of psychological interest (e.g., Fairweather, 1972; Lounsbury and Tornatsky, 1977; Heale, 1986).

SOCIAL SCIENCE ENVIRONMENTAL CONCERN RESEARCH

Psychological and other social science research has viewed many aspects of human responses to the quality of the natural environment. However, relatively few studies have investigated the structure of attitudes which may underlie the personal beliefs and behaviours associated with changes in the natural environment, and/or actions that are aimed at conserving the natural environment.

ENVIRONMENTAL CONCERN CORRELATION STUDIES

Research in the area of concern for the quality of the natural environment, typically, has initially developed a measure of concern for some aspect of the natural environment and then identified the measure's intra-personal (ideological) and social (demographic) correlates. From the use of this approach, and owing to different studies adopting different measures and indicators of environmental concern, two potentially confusing states have arisen. First, no consistent picture of the environmentally concerned person has been, or can be expected to be, identified. Second, no clear definition of attitudes pertaining to a concern for the quality of the natural environment has been made.

Attitudes about the protection of the natural environment have been defined as both issue specific and as an underlying general disposition. In both of these cases, this underlying attitude complex has been defined as concern for the quality of the natural environment, or simply as environmental concern.

MODELS OF ENVIRONMENTAL CONCERN

Many environmental concern correlation studies have assumed that the public's apparent concern about environmental quality is rooted in one or more abstract ideologies or philosophies. This ideology is seen to be unidimensional in nature and to underlie specific beliefs about isolated environmental issues (Pierce and Lovrich, 1980). The literature of mass-belief systems implies that environmental opinion is probably very crude, fragmented and narrowly focused upon mundane, personal irritants (Converse, 1964; Natchez, 1985). As a consequence of the shortcomings that have been noted of environmental concern correlation studies, research has recently attempted to produce more complex models of environmental concern. The development of these more elaborate models is a trend evident in the relevant contemporary literature. Van Liere and Dunlap (1981) reviewed environmental concern literature and, on the basis of this, developed a multivariate model founded upon two sources of variation in the results of the studies the authors reviewed. These were variations in the definitions used of environmental concern, and variation in the ways in which environmental concern had been measured. The model they proposed found little support for any equivalence in different measures of the same environmental issue. Neither did they discover there to be equality when different environmental concern issues were measured by the same research instrument. They thus concluded that concern for the quality of the natural environment was not a simple unidimensional attitude, and could not be assessed by the use of unidimensional designs and analyses.

Other researchers have developed models that have considered attitudes towards environmental conservation and concern for the natural environment as components of a broader attitude complex (e.g., Cotgrove, 1982; Buss and Craik, 1984). These models of 'contemporary worldviews' embody a set of dispositions not only towards environmental quality, but also towards expert decision making, bureaucracy, the risks associated with various industrial and technological processes, etc. In these research projects, environmental concern has been investigated as it exists as a component within a broader attitude complex, relating measures of environmental concern, or subdivisions of this concern, to other attitudes pertaining to modern sociopolitical issues.

The investigation of environmental concern has increasingly used multivariate techniques and approaches. A similar trend may be witnessed in contemporary studies in other areas of human experience which impinge upon, or may in some ways be seen to be related to, environmental concern: for example, experiences of places. In this research, facet theory and facet analysis techniques (Canter, 1985a; Shye, 1978a) have been used. In employing a facet approach, comparable research design and consistent results within a research area have been produced.

Studies of place experience typically have addressed the built environment (e.g., Canter and Kenny, 1981; Donald, 1985; Hackett, 1985). In these and other studies, a general model for place evaluation research has emerged, has been developed and refined within several different built environments (e.g., offices, hospitals and airports). This leads to the conclusion that a consistency exists in human-place experiences within built settings. To date, the model has only been used to design a pilot study to measure human experience within natural environments (Hackett, 1986). However, other research that has not employed a facet approach has discovered experience of the natural environment to be multidimensional (Ullrich and Ullrich, 1976).

THE DIMENSIONALITY OF MODELS OF ENVIRONMENTAL CONCERN

The dimensionality of human preferences for natural environment landscape features has been questioned for many years (Pierce and

Lovrich, 1980; Ullrich and Ullrich, 1976; de Haven-Smith, 1988). In this text, physical elements of the natural environment will not be the centre of attention. Rather, attitudes towards the conservation of natural environments will be studied, and attempts will be made to identify the dimensionality of these attitudes and social values, whilst perceptions of, or responses to, features of the natural environment (e.g., place experience) will be ignored. The commonly shared social value that emphasises the importance of concern for the natural environment and supports the need for environmental conservation will be the focus of attention.

SOCIAL VALUES

Within social psychological literature, social values have been defined in a variety of ways. In the present research the definition offered by Levy (1986) and Levy and Guttman (1974b) will be adopted. Levy defined a social value as a special case of an attitude. The specification of attitude she is using here is the one developed by Guttman (1973). This states an attitude to be an evaluation that ranges from positive to negative towards a specified event. A social value fulfils this criterion but also stresses the 'importance' of a certain event. Thus, evaluations indicative of a social value range from very important to not at all important, towards a specified objective. Furthermore, a value item may address an end state (how important a given instance is or isn't) or a goal (the importance of means or actions in attaining a desired end state). It is clear that by these definitions, concern for the conservation of the natural environment is both a social value and an attitude; environmental conservation issues and actions may be ascribed to a position along a scale ranging from positive to negative, and also along a scale that ranges from very important to not at all important. It is also possible to address environmental concern in terms of its goals or in terms of the means by which these goals are to be attained. In the former instance, the researchers would direct their enquiries at the means of attaining the aims of environmental conservation. In the latter case, concern for the quality of the natural environment itself would be the focus.

THEORETICAL DEVELOPMENTS

As has been commented upon above, environmental concern has been investigated by several researchers, each of whom has employed one of a variety of different measures. The investigations which will be conducted during this research will attempt to resolve uncertainty in regard to the dimensionality of environmental concern: whether a unidimensional or a multidimensional model for these attitudes is the most appropriate. It is hoped that in clarifying understanding of environmental concern in this way, less ambiguous measures of concern for the quality of the natural environment may be developed. Consequently, this research will offer a definition of environmental concern as it is experienced by the studies' samples: a 'personal', multivariate model will be developed.

In using a facet theory approach, a common definitional framework or taxonomy is developed. This classification system is explicitly stated as a taxonomy of items or variables within a mapping sentence. Facet research produces findings that are cumulative because a common taxonomy (design) is employed. Development of knowledge is achieved by using the same classification system for choosing variables and by observing these in different contexts. Knowledge is also assembled through modifying the facet design to suit context. By following both of the procedures, variation in research findings is systematically observed and related to changes in the research population, research setting, or research items specified in the study's design. In the research that follows, a template for the understanding of the personal and social meaning of environmental concern will be developed. This will be in the format of a mapping sentence (Canter, 1985a). By the end of the book a mapping sentence will have been developed which systematically accounts for the variation amongst the correlation coefficients between items assessing expressions of concern for the quality of the natural environment. To achieve this, a series of nine studies and analyses will be undertaken. Each of these will be concerned with developing a mapping sentence design template for the research. Consequently, attention will not be upon establishing the absolute value of concern across respondent samples for two reasons. First, a large body of this sort of research already exists (see Jowell *et al.*, 1985, 1986, 1987, 1988). In these publications the British population's concern for the environment is yearly documented. The second and most important reason for not adopting this approach is that whilst much research assembles measures of environmental concern, no clear definition exists of the psychological process of 'being concerned for the environment'.

The research presented in the following monograph will therefore establish a clear and concise definition of the intra-personal and social process of experiencing concern for the quality of the natural environment. This definition will be in the form of a mapping sentence that will explicitly state the variables considered in the investigations undertaken. The explicitness of this approach is of great importance as it allows other research to adopt the same definition. Adopting the model will allow replication, and further support may be given to these findings. It also avails researchers the opportunity of extending, modifying or refuting the mapping sentences within the context of their own research.

The procedure of investigating a mapping sentence has been adopted in many areas of applied social research. An example of this has been in the area of place experience (which was briefly mentioned earlier in this chapter). In this research area a mapping sentence was first developed by Canter and his colleagues (Canter and Kenny, 1981; Kenny and Canter, 1981) to explain nurses' experience of ward design. Subsequent research viewed place experience within many different physical settings, including public housing (Canter and Rees, 1982), offices (Donald, 1983) and airports (Hackett, 1985). The same mapping sentence guided all of the above studies and has allowed comparisons to be made between the findings of each study. Adopting such an approach has resulted in research being precisely directed at pertinent aspects of a particular environmental setting in a clear, unambiguous and thorough manner. It has also resulted in direct comparisons being possible between place settings. Consequently, two states have arisen. A standard design for place experience investigations has been established and a common model for place experience has been developed.

Within the research area of social values, ambiguous definitions have been forwarded for human experience. Several studies have been undertaken using the facet theoretical approach and employing a mapping sentence (Levy, 1986; Levy and Guttman, 1974a, 1974b, 1976, 1981a, 1981b, 1981c, 1985). However, all of these studies have concerned themselves with the 'overall' structure of the concept of social values. Subsequently, this concept has then been investigated in several settings, with different populations and across age groups. The present research will extend the knowledge base that has been developed in the above studies through the investigation of the social value of environmental concern.

This research contributes to both the research area of environmental concern and to facet theory investigations of social values. A mapping sentence template is developed out of a series of repertory grid interviews, and questionnaires constructed based upon this. Results are then subjected to both facet and other analysis techniques. This will enable comments to be made about the relationships between facets and attitude measures. At this stage of this introductory chapter it will be helpful to the reader if the book structure is briefly outlined.

THE STRUCTURE OF THE BOOK

In the remainder of Chapter 1 there follows a summary of the aims of the research. Chapter 2 outlines the environmental issues that will form the context of the study area. This chapter will review environmental conservation activities and issues about which the public may hold an opinion. In order to facilitate understanding, this review will be broken down into sections that reflect environmental conservation issues and actions at a series of different physical scales. Chapter 3 will contain a review of environmental concern as a characteristic of the British public. This will include the presentation of the findings of several major studies of public opinion. Chapter 4 will comprise a review of environmental concern as it has been viewed by the social sciences. Research findings will be presented to illustrate the variety of different measures that have been used to indicate environmental concern. The various different environmental issues which this research has investigated will also be reviewed. Furthermore, there will be a brief review of environmental concern as it has been modelled as a component of contemporary social values. The chapter will conclude by noting the lack of a clear definition of environmental concern and the need for the formulation of such a definition. Chapter 5 will propose environmental concern to be a social value and attitude. The chapter will continue by reviewing how the facet theory approach to social research has been used to define personal meaning in several areas of life. Facet theory's contribution to psychological research into social values will be presented. The use of mapping sentences as templates for designing research will be considered as a theoretical guide for studying social values. There will also be a brief consideration of the facet approach as an exploratory research technique. This will prepare the reader for the next chapter in which this approach will be used to explore environmental concern values. Chapter 6 will present the design of, and findings from, two exploratory studies. These studies will form a series of repertory grid interviews conducted with employees in environmental conservation. Actions and issues in environmental conservation will be entered into grids. Similarity Structure Analysis will then be used to analyse resulting data sets. On the basis of this analysis a mapping sentence will be proposed. In Chapter 7 the development of two studies using the mapping sentence is detailed and details of the results of these studies are given. These two questionnaire surveys will address specific concerns about two environmental issues (the seriousness of environmental hazards and the urgency of selected environmental problems). These two studies will be constructed in order to enable analyses that will facilitate the investigation of the detailed structure of the elements of facets and the importance of these elements in structuring attitudes. In Chapter 8 a more comprehensive study of environmental concern will be reported. This third questionnaire will address more general concern about environmental quality. Respondents will assess, using four different evaluative criteria, a number of different conservation actions. The use of these different evaluation measures will allow comparison between cognitive and behavioural elements of environmental concern. For each of the studies, the initial mapping sentence will receive any necessary modification.

Chapter 9 will form a discussion of the results of all of the studies that have been undertaken. The findings will be related to environmental concern research and will also be related to the area of psychological enquiry into social values and facet theory research. Suggestions for future research will be made. Finally, conclusions will be drawn in Chapter 10 about the findings of the research.

SUMMARY AND CONCLUSION – SUMMARY OF RESEARCH AIMS

The need for the multidimensional investigation of environmental concern is based upon the assumption that attitudes towards the conservation of the natural environment are made up of multiple (more than one) components. This hypothesis is derived from three separate sources:

1 contemporary environmental concern research,
2 the multidimensional nature of place experience,
3 the multivariate nature of social values.

Environmental concern attitudes and attitudes towards environmental conservation are distinct attitudinal areas. In the case of the former, the psychological domain of interest is of the degree of concern an individual experiences in regard to a specified environmental state. In the latter case, attitudes within this domain are in respect of an action or series of actions that have arisen due to environmental concern. It is apparent, therefore, that the two domains, whilst being similar, are distinct. In the present research a similarity between the two areas will be assumed. However, empirical support for the assumption will be sought.

This book is concerned with attitudes regarding the conservation of the natural environment (environmental concern). Research viewing other social values has found multidimensional descriptions to best fit these phenomena. Therefore, the research aims to develop a multivariate, descriptive model of environmental concern. The overall aim of this research is to develop a multivariate description of environmental concern in the form of a mapping sentence. A second aim will be to resolve the conflicting hypotheses present in the literature of multidimensional and unidimensional descriptions of environmental concern attitudes. Having developed this, a third aim will be to investigate the ability of the mapping sentence to represent opinion within a series of different behavioural modes of expression of environmental concern: attitudes of urgency, seriousness, the social value, the effectiveness, and levels of involvement with environmental concern and actions associated with these. The mapping sentence will also be investigated within a series of environmental concern contexts: environmental hazards, environmental conservation activities, environmental problems and general environmental concern. In achieving the above, facet theory research and understanding of social values and attitudes will be extended into this new value area. Finally, previously published mapping sentences will be used in the generation of the research instruments. These will be adapted and modified to the context of the current research. This will allow the fulfilment of the final aim: providing support for the mapping sentences as multivariate descriptive instruments within their respective content areas.

2 Environmental issues and conservation

When this century began, neither human beings nor technology had the power radically to alter planetary systems. As the century draws to a close, not only do vastly increased human populations and their activities possess that power, but we are also faced with major unintended changes that are occurring in the atmosphere, in soil, in water, among plants and animals, and in the relationships between all of them.

(WCED, 1988: 32)

In the above quotation from Gro Harlem Brundtland, then Chairperson of the World Commission on Environment and Development (WCED), it is clear that the issues facing the environment are many and of great diversity. This complexity is also found when attempts are made to define clearly the human activities that constitute the conservation of the environment. However, as the research reported in this text is concerned with attitudes towards environmental conservation, a definition of the area is necessary and one is offered below.

Conservation is concerned with the utilization of resources – the rate, purpose and efficiency of use. . . . Conservation has received many definitions because it has many aspects. It concerns issues arising between groups, and involves private and public enterprise. Conservation receives impetus from the social conscience aware of an obligation to future generations and is viewed differently according to one's social and economic philosophy. To some extent the meaning of conservation changes with time and place. It is understood differently when approached from the natural sciences and technologies than when it is approached from the social sciences.

(Parker, 1980: 127)

Inspection of the above definition illustrates the fact that conservation is concerned not only with the saving of endangered species or places. It also shows that it is not solely concerned with the restriction of the occurrence of deleterious events. It is both of these, but it is also about sensible use and development: the breadth of conservation's activities is clear in Parker's definition. This enormity of scope is also true of the effects of conservation which may be social, economic, ecological, etc.

In this chapter, the diverse strands present within the environmental conservation movement will be briefly reviewed. In doing this, conservation will be broken down under the headings pollution, countryside change and the wider environment. These were not the only possible categories under which environmental conservation activities and issues could have been grouped. However, these have been chosen since pollution and countryside change are both issues that directly affect the British public. This being the case, it would be expected that the public would have relatively well-developed opinions upon these more immediate and personal environmental issues (de Haven-Smith, 1988). Therefore two sections are devoted to these issues. The third section thus forms a 'catch-all' category, which reviews global environmental issues and other issues upon which the public is likely to have an opinion and which do not readily fall into the pollution or countryside change groupings. In this section there will be a review of a variety of environmental issues chosen to represent the breadth of issues and actions within contemporary environmental conservation. However, in the limited space of this book, it is inevitable that this review will not cover all possible issues and action.

It should therefore be immediately clear to readers that the categories being used are not independent classifications. For instance, an issue which is being reviewed under the pollution category may well encompass changes in the countryside (and vice versa). As McCormick writes: 'Most environmental problems and their solutions are local or national. . . . But many of the most critical environmental problems go beyond national frontiers. . . . many problems have their cause in one country and their effects in others' (McCormick, 1985a: 67). However, for the purposes of this research the threefold grouping chosen will fulfil the objective of outlining the diversity of issues which underlies the composition of attitudes towards environmental and nature conservation.

ENVIRONMENTAL POLLUTION

Pollution was one of the earliest environmental issues to attract widespread public condemnation (McCormick, 1985b). 'Many of the environmental problems of the past arise as a result of the pollution of the land' (Royal Commission on Environmental Pollution, 1984: 7): these are the opening lines from the tenth in a continuing series of reports from the Royal Commission on Environmental Pollution. Amongst other things, the tenth report emphasises the seriousness of the effects of pollutants within the environment. This point is illustrated by the definition of pollution initially proposed by Holdgate (1979) and adopted by the tenth report. Pollution is thus defined as: 'The introduction by man into the environment of substances or energy liable to cause hazards to human health, harm to living resources and ecological systems, damage to structures or amenity, or interference with legitimate uses of the environment' (Royal Commission on Environmental Pollution, 1984: 7). Whilst the above definition is very broad in its coverage, it is of particular interest as it denotes humankind's actions to be the source of pollution. It also emphasises both the human and environmental consequences of these acts.

It is clear in the above quotation that pollution may affect all types of environment. Pollution may be of the ground and soil, of aquatic environments, or of the atmosphere. Regardless of the specific environment affected by the pollution, it is human waste which causes these effects (WHO, 1984). Waste may be directly hazardous (e.g., toxic) to both human beings and other living organisms. Wastes may also be less direct in their destructiveness but none the less restrictive to amenity and recreational usages and detract from environmental quality and/or life quality through visible, audible or odorous intrusion.

Thus, pollutants have a wide scale of environmental effect. To quote the Countryside Commission:

> There is growing evidence that atmosphere, freshwater and marine pollution directly affect the environmental health of the country-side and coast – be it the suspected impact of acid rain on tree health, the quality of water in our rivers and lakes, or contamination of beaches by sewage and flotsam.
>
> (Countryside Commission, 1989a: 1)

All of the above types of waste can occur at any point during a wide variety of human activities. As far as their polluting effects are concerned, all forms of waste possess the common characteristic of not being required by their owner or producer. These are thus consigned to the environment, possessing no, little or negative economic value for the person generating it. These characteristics remove many of the incentives for the careful treatment of wastes, and thus waste is often introduced into the environment in a manner that will cause it to be a pollutant by the definition of pollution offered above. The introduction, or the prevention of the introduction, of wastes into the environment in a manner which would cause pollution, is then a solely human activity (Bradby, 1990). Furthermore, these actions are intimately linked to other areas of human action, such as manufacturing and wealth generation and with recreational amenity. Pollution may be the result of many forms of human activity, the consequences of this may then affect all of us. It is hardly surprising therefore that a considerable public concern regarding the environmental effects of pollution exists.

COUNTRYSIDE CHANGE

Another issue encompassed within environmental concern is change in the countryside or natural environment. Since the last war many rural areas have been transformed by the carrying out of major public works and private development. The construction of the post-war new towns presaged many of the issues that now attach to the building of motorways, airports, power stations, the Channel Tunnel and by the increasing number of people living or finding recreation in the countryside. Blunden and Curry (1985a) provide a detailed review of these changes, which are illustrated in a contemporary document which reviews the many changes that have occurred or are occurring in the social history of one particular Shropshire village. The sentiments expressed in this book exemplify reactions to the changes that are facing much of the British countryside. 'Change is a necessary adjunct to the survival of a settlement whether it is in the form of gradual development contained within the needs of the community or of sudden onslaught where the operative motive is now usually profit' (Davis, 1989: 3).

Blunden and Curry (1988) have commented upon changes in countryside and other rural land usage issues, claiming that the countryside in Britain is undergoing a radical transformation, a claim supported by other authors (e.g., Gaisford, 1992). Food surpluses in agriculture are being tackled in a number of different ways. These range from the imposition of quotas and taxes on production to taking land out of production and putting it to some other use. They note how: 'With possibly as much as one quarter of our existing farmland surplus to requirements, there are now unprecedented pressures to diversify the rural economy, free up planning controls and expand forestry and recreational opportunities' (Blunden and Curry, 1988: 23).

If their predictions are correct, these new uses for rural land will be at the centre of an extremely important environmental debate during the next few years. Countryside changes are all the more important as they come on top of equally important long-term, social change. Since the war there has been a gradual movement of unemployed farmworkers to the towns, whilst commuters, second homeowners and the retired have increasingly moved into the countryside. Bringing with them, it may be claimed, substantially different expectations and requirements of and from rural life. Their presence is having a significant impact on rural services and amenities, and on the infrastructure of village life. Potentially damaging changes to the countryside have been written upon for many years (see e.g., Williams-Ellis, 1928, 1937). These and many other documents have expressed concern about the use of countryside areas as a recreational amenity for the increasingly affluent and mobile urban dweller.

Countryside amenity

The growth in car ownership from the 1950s to the present day, has allowed an increasing number of urban residents to visit the countryside for recreational purposes. This factor, coupled with a booming economy, has enabled many city workers of the early 1990s to live rurally. In 1968 the Countryside Commission was formed with a mandate to manage countryside areas designated for amenity usage. The role taken by the Commission in fulfilling their duties is detailed by many of their recent publications (see below). Within these reports are described the changing patterns of the recreational use of rural land. It has been found that visits to the British countryside are undertaken for a variety of activities and purposes. In 1984, when asked why they visited the countryside, some eighteen different reasons were offered by respondents (Countryside Commission, 1984). Among these reasons were: visiting historic buildings, stately homes, museums, gardens, country parks or parks in the countryside, zoos, safari parks, or nature reserves, in order to, walk, hike or ramble, birdwatch/study nature, fish, hunt; or to take an active part in or to watch other organised sport; to visit friends or relatives; or to 'pick your own' fruit and vegetables or undertake conservation work. It was also discovered, in this research, that many more people visited these regions on a Sunday than at other times and, perhaps somewhat surprisingly, that there were only minor variations in visiting patterns over the seasons of the year. The survey questioned respondents about the frequency of their countryside visits in order to reveal the proportion of people visiting the countryside during a four-week period in the winter, spring and summer. It was found that in winter a little over half of interviewees had visited the countryside at least once. This proportion rose to 60 per cent in spring and 70 per cent in the summer. Those respondents who made frequent trips to the countryside (e.g., five or more trips in a four-week period) varied from 20 per cent of the visitors in the winter to 28 per cent in spring and 38 per cent in summer. As the number of total trips increases through the seasons so the proportion of frequent visitors also increases: the proportion of casual, infrequent visitors remains the same whilst the proportion of non-visitors declines (Countryside Commission, 1984). The Countryside Commission also investigated (for those who visit) the relative importance of a wide variety of recreational activities and venues. Whilst urban leisure activities are of great importance to people seeking recreational activities, overall it is the countryside which is the most important venue for recreational visits. Moreover, people show a strong preference for visiting the wider countryside. They favoured countryside that is not managed as a tourism asset, rather than areas set aside and managed as a recreational facility (Countryside Commission, 1984). This study discovered that the majority of recreational activities take place informally, without outside organisation and without specialised equipment or high-profile management. Furthermore, in their survey they found users tended to be general countryside visitors rather than specialists, concerning themselves with just one or two different activities.

Changes in the frequency of visits to the countryside over the last few years have also been noted. In 1984 the Countryside Commission conducted a survey that repeated a series of questions regarding the regularity of visits. The studies were initially carried out in 1977 and 1980. The results of this study showed that the number of trips per person during four weeks in a summer period fell from 2.5 in 1977 to 1.6 in 1980. By 1984, however, there had been a significant increase to 4.1 trips per person. This growth can be largely attributed to a decrease in the number of people who did not visit the countryside at all, coupled with an increase in the frequency of visits amongst those who were already very frequent visitors (Countryside Commission, 1984).

When enquiries were made about who visits the countryside, it was found that there was a small group of people (17 per cent of the sample) who visited the countryside regularly and who account for 68 per cent of all trips made. Conversely, a large section (40 per cent) of the population did not visit these areas at all during a specified four-week period. However, it is important to note that 84 per cent of people visit the countryside at least once a year (Countryside Commission, 1984). Furthermore, the visitor can be typified as possessing certain socio-economic traits. In the same report it was stated that 46 per cent of visitors had the use of a car of their own, 63 per cent were managerial, clerical and skilled manual workers, and 59 per cent were from affluent suburban areas living in intermediate and higher-quality family housing.

It is of great interest to the present research to note that membership of countryside protection and amenity-related organisations (e.g., National Trust, Royal Society for the Protection of Birds, Ramblers' Association, Youth Hostel Association) is significantly positively related to countryside visits. The Countryside Commission report (Countryside Commission, 1984) showed that members of countryside-related organisations use the countryside at almost twice as much as those who are not members of such organisations (67 per cent members to 37 per cent non-members). The report hypothesised that the distance that people lived from the countryside was not related to membership of these organisations. This suggests that membership is a reflection of interest in the countryside and countryside affairs rather than the ability to access countryside areas.

From all of the data presented above, it can be clearly seen that there has been growing interest and participation in countryside usage. This is summarised by the Countryside Commission: 'The level of countryside recreation has grown significantly, if irregularly, over the last eight years (1977–1985) and has attracted a broader span of the population' (Countryside Commission, 1984: 16).

However, the Commission noted a year later that whilst the 1984 National Countryside Recreation Study had confirmed the greater levels of countryside usage, this increase in itself was not the major feature noted about the alterations in countryside usage. Instead: ' it is the changing patterns of participation that are likely to be of increasing significance' (Countryside Commission, 1984: 15). These changing patterns of usage will not be dealt with any further in this research: the changing character of the rural visitor and dweller having already been noted. The relationship between environmental concern and visiting the countryside has also been documented. The interested reader wishing to further explore these features further is guided to the above-cited publications by the Countryside Commission and to other reports from the same body (e.g., Countryside Commission, 1988).

Farming practices and countryside change

Another area of change in the British countryside has been in farming practices. When asked about the causes of countryside change, 62 per cent of respondents agreed that modern farming practices damaged the countryside (Jowell *et al.*, 1987). Several recent reports have reviewed modern farming practices in Britain. Changes in these practices have included the increased use of chemicals to reduce pests and to increase yield (e.g., House of Commons Select Committee, in press; Jollans, 1985) and changes that have altered the appearance and ecology of countryside regions, such as hedgerow removal (e.g., Westmacott and Worthington, 1984). In their report of the following year Jowell *et al.*, (1988) found that most people perceived the countryside to have recently changed. As well as changes in the British environment, alterations are also perceived to be occurring in the international environment.

CHANGES IN THE GLOBAL ENVIRONMENT

In a brief review of environmental issues and environmental changes, such as that contained in this chapter, it is not possible to cover all such issues. This section entitled 'Changes in the global environment' will be made up of a selection of environmental issues not covered already in earlier sections of this chapter. The issues covered have been chosen to be illustrative of the problems and hazards facing the environment at a wider physical scale than solely Britain: rather than attempting to review all of the global environmental conservation scene, issues have been chosen which are examples of their type. A more thorough review is provided by McCormick (1985a, 1985b, 1985c.) and by the World Resources Institute (1990), whilst the area of environmental risks and disasters is considered by Smith (1992).

Environmental issues that are global or international in nature are many and extremely varied. Several of the issues already raised under the pollution or countryside change headings may be seen to be linked, to a lesser or a greater extent, to conservation issues at the global scale. For this reason, much of what has already been written in this chapter is also applicable to the global environment. For instance, public concern about pollution of the seas and rivers (Clark, 1991) may be understood by respondents to relate to both the British and to the wider environment.

CHANGES IN THE INTERNATIONAL ENVIRONMENT

Within this chapter we have already considered the conservation of the environment at the national and local scales. It is readily apparent that conservation may be practised at much larger scales. However, at these larger scales the definition of the boundaries of what constitutes an environmental conservation action or issue become less clear as, it may be argued, breadth of morals as well as breadth of physical scale increases. At these larger scales, green philosophies and considera-tion of ecological principles become increasingly pertinent (e.g., Borman and Kellert, 1991).

In the 1969 Reith lecture, Fraser Darling (1969) commented upon the global nature of environmental changes. The same theme was extended with greater detail in the 1989 Richard Dimbleby lecture given by HRH the Prince Philip (1989). A quotation from the latter of these two lectures serves to illustrate the complex and interacting nature of global, ecological changes in the natural environment:

> All life depends upon the interaction between the inorganic elements of sunshine, climate, fire, water, altitude and soil chemistry. The relative absence of any one element, such as fresh water for instance results in desert conditions. . . . In addition, the living world also affects the climate and atmospheric conditions around it. The carbon dioxide and ozone layers were created by living organisms and they are now being affected by human activities.
>
> (HRH the Prince Philip, 1989: 4)

Within the interacting system described above, it is of little surprise that problems that occur at this scale are complex. The following definition illustrates the range of issues and problems at this scale. Bunyard and Grenville-Morgan state that the earth now faces a new and different scale of environmental threat: 'the difference lies in the scale of the threat to the planet itself, through environmental destruction. This threat is largely created by man himself, whose enormous capacity for destroying already weakened systems is the factor which makes the position so grave' (Bunyard and Grenville-Morgan, 1987: ix). With such a wide-scale threat to the environment, the same authors state that human beings must respond with a broad, all-encompassing level of environmental concern: 'It means . . . concern for life on earth. Not just concern for one's own family or friends, for community, or the whole human race, but concern for the process of life itself and everything that nurtures and sustains that process' (Bunyard and Grenville-Morgan, 1987: x).

Many of the most crucial environmental problems go beyond national boundaries. Some, such as soil erosion, deforestation (Whitmore and Sayer, 1992) and over-fishing (Carson, 1971) are universal. The demand for more land for agricultural usage is causing further destruction of natural forests. As a consequence, this in turn causes soil erosion, the siltation of rivers and climatic changes (Goldsmith and Hildyard, 1989). Many problems may originate in one country whilst the effects are primarily experienced in another. This is the case with pollution, where prevailing winds can blow contaminates across continents, and sea currents can wash contamination from one shore to another (Hinrichsen, 1989). The output of carbon dioxide from the burning of fossil fuels and rain forests, and the methane gas which is a by-product of much agricultural production, is already greater than can be absorbed by natural processes. The use of chlorofluorocarbons (CFCs) in refrigerator coolants, aerosol propellants and foams is damaging the ozone layer (Lovelock, 1989).

As in the previous two sections (Pollution and Countryside change), over-usage, over-consumption and waste disposal lie at the roots of most international environmental problems. The difficulties associated with solving these problems are increased at this scale of operations as one country may exploit another for its resources, or to deposit its wastes. Attempts to resolve these environmental problems must therefore deal with a large number of complex human activities and interests. The fundamental issue that underpins environmental problems is the world's growing human population and the problem of waste disposal, caused by the sheer number of human inhabitants and their consumption of resources (Timberlake, 1989).

Much research has been conducted that has viewed the state of the international environment, leading to a large information base upon these issues. An important publication within this field of research is that of the DocTer Institute (1987). The publication does not take the global environment as its area of concern, instead it thoroughly reviews the state of the environment in Europe. The document subdivides environmental issues, problems and actions. In doing this it is able to consider the state of the European environment in considerable detail. Furthermore, through maintaining constant the categories into which environmental issues and actions are divided from country to country, inter-country comparisons are made possible. The DocTer Institute shows how it is therefore possible to approach the subject from either of two directions. First, it is possible to view the localised causes and effects of an environmental problem. Second, problems that affect the global system may be viewed, in terms of social, economic or ecological causes and effects, at a local scale: the employment that is created in a specified geographical area by forest clearance, and the alternative employment that would be needed if these practices were curtailed; the local effects upon the flora and fauna and habitat loss. A global perspective would be concerned with the same issues but at a far greater geographical scale.

The literature on change in the international environment has looked at the changes presently occurring there. The research has also extrapolated from the information on present effects to produce projections of (the research often claims these to be probable or certain) future environmental scenarios on the basis of this. Some of these international environmental issues will now be briefly outlined. References will be provided for each of these sets of issues.

THE LAND

Desertification

This is the process of desert conditions spreading to what was previously fertile land. Human pressure, specifically overcultivation, overgrazing, the clearance of trees and plant cover and careless irrigation, have all removed protective vegetative cover from the land. This has caused desertification to be occurring in more than 100 of the world's countries. Land so affected loses its fertility and economic value (Grainger, 1982). Desertification is continuing apace. Each year, 6.2 million hectares of land are lost in this way. The United Nations considered this issue and drew up an action plan for stopping the process. However, by 1984 the United Nations programme concluded that their hopes for halting this process were unlikely to be met (Tolba, 1984).

Forests

Forests perform many functions. They provide timber for paper, fuel and other products. They also support animal and plant life, soak up rain water (preventing flooding), bind the soil (preventing erosion), recycle oxygen and nitrogen and absorb carbon dioxide. Forests have taken millions of years to develop into areas that contain the richest concentrations of flora and fauna on the earth. However, these amenities are being lost at a considerable rate (Whitmore and Sayer, 1992). Forests are being burned and cut down to make way for farmland (Myers, 1979), roads and towns (FAO, 1982), and for hardwood timber (Pringle, 1976; Westoby, 1983; Myers, 1980). The rate of destruction is very rapid. In 1955 forests covered more than one-quarter of the earth's land surface, by 1977 they covered only one-fifth. By 1984 there were 4.9 billion hectares of forest globally. The annual loss of this is estimated to be 11.3 million hectares (Global 2000 Report to the President, 1982). Not all countries are losing forests at the same rate. Some Far Eastern countries have increased their amount of forest cover, whilst Asian, African and Latin American tropical moist forests are being lost at the rate of 7 million hectares a year (Caulfield, 1982).

In Britain, as in the rest of Europe, deforestation is not occurring at this scale. The problem in Britain is that since the war, nearly one-third of remaining ancient woodlands has been replaced with conifers (Rose, 1984). Acid rain (Tyson, 1992) is also a problem for the European forests. In 1983, nearly one-third of West Germany's forests were found to be suffering from acid rain damage, and damage has also been reported in Poland, Czecho-slovakia, Sweden and other European countries (Svensson, 1984). Hinrichsen (1989) provides details that show that much of the world is now subjected to the damaging effects of acid rain. He also claims that 67 per cent of British forests are acid rain damaged – this being the highest proportion of forests affected in Europe.

Erosion

This is the removal of soil due to the action of the wind and rain. This is, under natural (normal) conditions, an extremely slow process. However, owing to the results of deforestation, overgrassing and other inappropriate agricultural practices, the erosion of top soil is now occurring apace. Erosion is a world-wide phenomenon in the late twentieth century. However, the most serious effects of erosion are in tropical areas where good quality top soils are an especially rare and valuable resource (Parrington, 1983; Global 2000, 1982).

Erosion has been documented to be having a serious effect in many regions of the earth. The scale of this effect is demonstrated in the following Figures. For example, India (6,000 million tonnes of top soil lost annually); Ethiopia (1,600 million tonnes of top soil lost per year); USSR (2,500 million tonnes lost annually, 10 per cent of agricultural land affected); USA (one-third of crop land seriously affected, 4,000 million tonnes of top soil lost annually) (Goldsmith and Hildyard, 1989).

Agriculture

Many changes have occurred in the patterns of the world's agriculture over the last four decades (Carson, 1971; Conway and Pretty, 1991; Earthscan, 1984). These will not be commented upon in detail in this section as the main topics associated with agricultural effects upon the environment are reviewed elsewhere in this chapter. An example of this is the need for agricultural land. As a consequence of this need, forests are cleared in tropical regions. This leads to not only forest loss, but also extinctions and to damaging gases being introduced to the atmosphere through burning the felled trees.

Agricultural problems are often associated with the use of chemicals to improve yields. These chemicals then find their way into food chains. Once within the chain, they may have a directly toxic effect upon other organisms within the chain. A second way in which these substances may affect the environment is through causing alterations in growth patterns. This is illustrated in the process of eutrophication. In this process, a lake or a stream becomes richer and richer in plant nutrients until plants overgrow the water area. The decomposing remains of these plants causes the deoxygenation of the water, which then becomes foul-smelling and virtually lifeless. Eutrophication results as nitrate fertilisers and nutrients from animal wastes drain from fields to these wet areas.

THE ATMOSPHERE

Ozone

The ozone layer is being disturbed by long-living pollutants, which are a result of human activity (Gribbin, 1988). The responsible pollutants are: chlorofluorocarbons (CFCs) and nitrogen oxides, which deplete the ozone layer, and methane which increases ozone levels. Nitrogen oxides and methane are by-products of both agricultural and industrial activities; as such, they are difficult to control. However, CFCs are mainly produced from foam products, aerosol propellants, refrigerants, sterilants and solvents, and it is somewhat easier to reduce their emission into the atmosphere. The introduction of these chemicals to the atmosphere has lead to 'ozone holes' appearing in the atmosphere over the polar caps, and growing at an increasing pace.

Greenhouse effect

The atmospheric levels of all greenhouse gases (carbon dioxide, methane and chlorofluorocarbons) is increasing. These are atmospheric gases that warm the atmosphere by trapping heat around the earth's surface subsequent to its having been radiated into the atmosphere (Krause *et al.*, 1990; Leggett, 1990).

Many of the industrial processes associated with modern society produce carbon dioxide as a by-product. Half of this carbon dioxide is absorbed by natural carbon dioxide absorbing 'sinks' such as forests, oceans and the process of limestone deposition. The remaining half of the carbon dioxide emitted collects in the atmosphere. Since the beginning of the Industrial Revolution, carbon dioxide levels have been increasing and the rate of increase is at present increasing. This could lead to a doubling of the 1850 level by the middle of the twenty-first century.

It is estimated that by the year 2050 the atmospheric temperature could have risen by as much as 2 degrees centigrade (although such figures are disputed). The warming, however, would not be evenly globally distributed with increases of perhaps less than 2 degrees at the equator, to as much as 6 degrees at higher latitudes (Lovelock, 1989).

Acid rain

This environmental topic has already been commented upon in the section of this chapter concerned with forests. However, a more thorough review is given below. Acid rain, and the acidification of aquatic and terrestrial rain ecosystems, is one of the most major of the world's industrial problems (Hinrichsen, 1989).

The term 'acid rain' is used to describe the fall-out of industrial pollutants. These fall-outs sometimes occur as acidified rain water, and in other circumstances as dry depositions. Most of these pollutants are caused through the burning of fossil fuels (for instance in industrial processes and in power generation (*Scientific America*, 1991)). However, some acid depositions are the results of vehicle exhausts.

The effects of acid rain are many and varied. However, their impact is to a large extent biological (Wellburn, 1988). The extent of damage is illustrated by Goldsmith and Hildyard: 'Acid rain damages forests, plants and crops; acidifies lakes, rivers and ground water; and corrodes building materials. In Europe it has been falling for more than 100 years; and its effects are cumulative' (Goldsmith and Hildyard, 1989: 92).

THE OCEANS

Marine pollution

Dredged spoils, sewage and industrial wastes are dumped directly from ships in large quantities. The Atlantic Ocean and the North Sea are the main areas where it occurs as dumping has been banned in most regional seas. Many of the areas used for dumping wastes are now severely contaminated with high levels of pollutants being discovered on the sea beds and within fish (Eckholm, 1982).

There is now much legislation that governs the dumping of wastes at sea. Even so, heavy metals and carcinogenic wastes are still dumped legally under this legislation, which allows for trace quantities of banned substances to be present in wastes. Furthermore, whilst there has been a moratorium on the dumping of nuclear wastes at sea since 1983, before this date many drums of this form of waste were disposed of at sea (Gullard, 1975; Gwynn, 1987; Salvat, 1979). The effect of this pollution has been severe upon fish and other aquatic creatures (FAO, 1979) and has even reached the polar regions (Mitchell and Tinker, 1980; Cook, 1990).

POPULATION

Many of the world's environmental problems are rooted in a continuing growth in world population (Ehrlich, 1968; Eckholm, 1982; ICIDI, 1980) or in localised populations (Gupta, 1988; Conroy and Litvinoff, 1988).

A growing population requires more food to feed it, more land to live on and more organic resources for fuel, construction, etc. The rising rate of world population levels and the scale of this problem is made apparent in the report of the World Commission on Environment and Development (1988).

The world's human population may be expected to stabilise during the next century, depending upon when replacement level fertility rates are reached. If this rate is reached in 2010 the world population will stabilise at 7.7 billion by 2060; but if it is not reached until 2065, the population will stabilise at 14.2 billion in 2100.

(WCED, 1988: 109)

The rapid rise of world population levels is also shown in the speed with which the global population doubles. In 1800 the global population was one billion. This doubled in the next 135 years. The next doubling took just over fifty years, and it is projected that the next doubling will occur in twenty years (HRH the Prince Philip, 1989). The shortening of the doubling time of the world's population has been documented for many years. Continued growth is dependent upon improvements in agricultural yield, etc. to enable this size of world population to be fed. To these ends, technologies now manipulate natural systems to ensure regular food supplies: these technologies having been developed into highly efficient techniques for exploiting both the natural and mineral resources of the planet. Furthermore, humankind has learnt to control many of the previously lethal diseases. The extent to which these advanced technologies, future modifications and new discoveries will enable a growing world population to be supported is a matter of debate (e.g., Meadows, *et al.*, 1974).

WILDLIFE

Threats to the earth's wildlife exist as a result of many of the environmental problems commented upon in the preceding paragraphs. For instance, acid rain will affect the acidity of fresh water. In severe cases, this will result in the destruction of the life in lakes, rivers, etc.

The process and some of the consequences of extinction (Allen, 1980; Ehrlich, 1981; Halliday, 1980) are commented upon below. This is a process which is by no means a recent phenomenon, neither has it always been human-made. Species have become extinct because they were unable to survive or adapt to natural environmental changes, or they have evolved into different life forms. Extinction is now occurring at a rapid pace due to humankind's actions, which destroy habitats and consequently indigenous species (Worster, 1989). The loss of the world's tropical rain forests is an example of habitat loss on a massive scale. The loss of these regions alone could account for the extinction of one-third of the world's species. Other major habitats under threat include coral reefs and wetlands. With such a wide-scale threat, species are being lost at a faster rate than ever before (400 times faster than at any other recent geological time (Goldsmith and Hildyard, 1989)). These authors conclude by stating: 'The long-term outcome of today's extinctions cannot be predicted with precision: but the loss of species cannot continue with impunity forever. Sooner or later, the Earth's support systems will simply be overwhelmed' (Goldsmith and Hildyard, 1989: 144).

As well as research covering the above-mentioned issues, there has also been a steady stream of environmental literature which is of a more general nature. These publications have commented upon the state of the global system and have forwarded recommendations or recipes to enable environmental survival at this ecosystem level (ICIDI, 1980; Global 2000, 1982; IUCN, UNEP and WWF, 1988; Brown, 1991; Meadows *et al.*, 1974, 1992; Blueprint for Survival, 1972; UNEP, 1990; Ward and Dubos, 1980; McCormick, 1985a; Barr, 1971; Allen, 1980; Holdgate *et al.*, 1982; etc.).

CONCLUSION

The above environmental issues illustrate the vast range of problems the contemporary environment faces. Owing to this breadth, it also demonstrates the possible complexity of the attitudes about environmental issues which the public may hold. Whilst this chapter has broken down environmental issues under a series of subheadings, the interrelated nature of these problems is at all times obvious to the reader. Environmental problems do not stand as separate issues but rather are intertwined not only with each other but also with other areas of contemporary life such as economic decision making (e.g., Turner and Jones, 1990; Pearce, 1989, 1991). Together, the issues relate to human beings' relationship and interactions with their environment.

Whilst this chapter has briefly outlined the content area of environmental issues, the next chapter will consider the extent of support for groups, organisations and legislation aiming to ameliorate some of Britain's environmental problems. The degree of concern present in the British public about these problems, as it has been revealed through social surveys, will also be considered.

3 Environmental concern and nature conservation in Britain

> The environmental movement in the second half of the 1980s is very much at a watershed. It would seem to be going through one of its periodic peaks, where the issues in which its protagonists are involved coincide with people's everyday concerns to force politicians and 'decision makers' into a more open and responsible pattern of activity.
>
> (Porritt, 1986: 340)

In this chapter the British public's concern for the quality of the natural environment will be considered. There are several indicators of public concern for the natural environment, two of which are: (a) the number of voluntary groups actively concerned with environmentally related issues, and the size of the membership of these groups; and (b) the type and extent of legislative protection offered through the statutory designation of natural landscape features as protected areas. Both of these indicators of public concern may be used to gauge public support for the conservation of the natural environment through inference, e.g., by assessing activities present within society that are designed to achieve the aims of conservation, and inferring social support for environmental conservation to underlie the existence of these.

Another approach which may be adopted in attempting to assess public opinion is that of the mass social survey. Fortunately, for the present research, one such social survey conducted annually in Britain has, in recent years, contained a section specifically addressing environmental concern. The survey is that of the 'British Social Attitudes Survey' (Jowell et al., 1984, 1985, 1986, 1987, 1988). In the following chapter all of the above indicators of the British public's environmental concern will be reviewed, commencing with a brief overview of the growth of environmental groups in

Britain. It will continue by considering some of the ways in which land in Britain receives either statutory or voluntary protection. Finally, public opinion surveys will be considered.

ENVIRONMENTAL GROUPS

The emergence of environmental groups can be traced back to the late nineteenth century. In Britain the National Trust was founded in 1895 and the Royal Society for the Protection of Birds in 1889. Subsequently many more organisations emerged. As well as there being a significant increase in the number of environmental organisations, the membership of these groups has grown enormously. The National Trust now has over 1.6 million members (National Trust, 1989), whilst the Royal Society for the Protection of Birds has 540,000 members including 100,000 junior members (under sixteen years) (RSPB, 1988). By 1980 it was claimed that support in Britain for environmental groups had probably risen to 2,500,000–3,000,000 members (Lowe and Goyder, 1983). This represents approximately one in ten of the adult population. For a detailed review of the emergence of environmental groups the reader is guided to Sheil (1983) and Sinclaire (1973).

The early conservation groups were traditionally interested in the preservation of both the built and natural heritage of the nation. However, several authors have noted that in the 1960s, a new, more politically radical form of environmental organisation emerged (Lowe and Goyder, 1983). Over the last three decades new environmental groups have emerged that are not directly concerned with the protection of the national heritage through the purchase or management of countryside areas (McCormick, 1985b); rather, these groups have become more overtly politically active. Such groups include Friends of the Earth, Greenpeace, and others that are effective through being political pressure groups (Lowe and Goyder, 1983).

This new breed of groups has led to the voluntary sector of the environmental movement embracing an ever-more diverse range of issues. Stephen Cotgrove illustrates this point:

Environmental groups embrace a very wide diversity of interests and approaches, from the preservation of wildlife and the natural heritage of buildings, to the enjoyment of the countryside through rambling, hostelling and caravaning. Such a broad based movement attracting so much support is undoubtedly of importance. But the groups formed in the late 1960s and early 1970s took on a new and distinctive direction.

(Cotgrove, 1982: 2–3)

Many of the politically active environmental protection groups that emerged during this time are still operating. The activities of these organisations are now geared to the raising of awareness both in the general public (see Porritt, 1987) and in political parties (through attempting to bring the pressure, of what they claim is popular opinion, to bear upon government (see WWF *et al.*, 1988)).

Whilst the 1960s and 1970s saw the origination of the more politically radical environmental groups, the late 1970s and the 1980s have seen the emergence of two further types of group within the environmental movement. The first of these is the green movement (Porritt, 1984; Porritt and Warner, 1988). Green groups or parties are politico-environmental parties. These groups arose simultaneously throughout the world (Capra, 1982; Spretnak and Capra, 1984). They provide a coherent political approach to environmental issues. They also offer an environmentally sensitive approach to many socio-political issues and debates (e.g., Kelly, 1985; Spretnak, 1986) on which these groups and individuals have stood for parliamentary election in their respective countries of origin.

The second of the new strands of the environmental movement is the urban conservation groups (Smyth, 1987; Davidson, 1988). These groups are distinct from the traditional rural protection lobby both in terms of their area of concern and their activities. Property developers' reluctance to redevelop derelict urban land sites, and the amenity loss that this implies for the local communities, are important issues for the urban conservationist (Powell, 1986). Rather than purchasing natural sites of established wildlife or scenic value, the urban conservation or wildlife groups, through the reclamation of decaying urban areas, have been actively involved in the introduction of green spaces to cities. In so doing these groups have attempted to educate the public about the need for conservation through experience and to improve the life quality of urban dwellers.

The philosophy that lies central to the urban conservation approach is that of community involvement. Community involvement in nature conservation and environmental issues is a growing trend within the environment movement. Indeed, several professional conservationists have written texts calling for a greater level of community involvement in conservation projects (e.g., Wilson, 1984b, 1986). These publications also provide practical information for the individual, action group or community wishing to take direct action (King and Clifford, 1985; Tait *et al.*, 1988).

Throughout the whole of this period there has been another branch of environmental activity: the committees and research groups. These groups are not open to public membership; rather, they are groups of highly specialised experts. Examples of such groups are numerous, and the reports and publications they produce often have far-reaching effects in conservation practice. For example, there have been many extremely influential reports issued by committees working for a variety of official bodies: Stockholm (1970); Council on Environmental Quality (1970,1971); UKWCS (1983); ICIDI (1980); Global 2000 Report to the President (1982); 'Blueprint for Survival' (1972); IUCN, UNEP and WWF (1988); 'The limits to growth' (Meadows *et al.*, 1974); 'Our common future' (Brandt, Commission Report, 1987). These are just a few of the research publications that could have been cited. All of these (and many of those uncited) have been responsible, to some extent, for the shaping of contemporary environmental concern and modern conservation practice.

As well as these official reports, research has been carried out by individuals and groups which has also been influential in shaping modern environmentalism. Such publications are often more far reaching and perhaps more speculative than are the committee reports noted above. Many of these reports exist, and below are listed a few which will illustrate the breadth of environmental issues about which authors have found concern, for example: Shoad (1980); Carson (1971); Eckholm (1982); Brown (1982); Ward and Dubos (1980); Holdgate *et al.*, (1982).

COUNTRYSIDE PROTECTION IN BRITAIN

A second indicator of the extent of concern for the quality of the natural environment in Britain is the extent of protection offered to geographical areas that are of special interest or are particularly sensitive in terms of their indigenous wildlife or habitats.

The National Trust was the first organisation to own and designate land that was to be reserved for nature. By 1910 the Trust had thirteen sites. The then new concept of setting land aside and reserving it for nature was further expanded in 1912 by the establishment of the Society for the Promotion of Nature Reserves. The growth in the number of, and the increase in the amount of land covered by, nature reserves has continued to the present day. In 1987 non-statutory bodies owned a significant area of the land set aside as non-statutory protected areas (Royal Society for the Protection of Birds had 121 reserves totalling 574 sq km; Field Studies Council had 2 reserves totalling 14 sq km; Royal Society for Nature Conservation and the Local Nature Conservation Trusts had between them 1,665 reserves totalling 551 sq km; Woodland Trust, 247 reserves totalling 32 sq km; Wildfowl Trust, 8 reserves totalling 19 sq km (source, Department of the Environment, 1987).

Land that is to be set aside for nature may be designated under a series of different headings. The primary purpose of the UK system of designating areas is to identify and protect the finest landscape and the most important scientific sites throughout the country. Each of these land classifications offers a different form of protection and encourages or permits different specified uses for the land under its jurisdiction. In addition to the land owned or administered by voluntary organisations as nature reserves, several statutory bodies also own and manage reserve areas.

The ten National Parks in England and Wales were designated in the 1950s by the National Parks Commission (now the Countryside Commission). These were to safeguard and secure public access to the most beautiful wilderness areas. They are exceptionally fine stretches of relatively wild countryside, such as the larger unspoilt areas of mountain, moor, heath and some coastal areas. The National Parks cover 9 per cent of the total area of England and Wales and are mostly in private ownership. Each National Park has a committee or board that controls planning policies within the park. The Norfolk Broads and New Forest are not National Parks. However, owing to their unique landscapes, both of these areas receive protection.

As well as the ten National Parks, the Countryside Commission (or National Parks Commission) has designated thirty-six Areas of Outstanding Natural Beauty (AONBs) in England and Wales. These areas contain outstanding landscapes that are generally more intensively farmed than National Parks and are therefore less suitable to large numbers of visitors. AONBs at present cover 11 per cent of the area of England and Wales.

In 1987 five Environmentally Sensitive Areas (or ESAs) were established in England. In January 1992 the Minister responsible for these areas stated that there were to be a further twelve designated in England, representing a threefold increase in land covered by 1993. This brings the total of British ESAs to thirty-six. Furthermore, it was announced that there was to be an increase in budget, an expansion to existing boundaries and new prescriptions to give more encouragement for conservation. It was also announced that the Countryside Stewardship Scheme (whereby within ESAs farmers are paid to carry on with potentially less productive practices to encourage conservation) had been severely oversubscribed (Steel, 1992).

The Department of the Environment also announced in 1992 that the farmed landscape would receive greater protection through its 'Action in the Countryside' package, including protection for hedgerows and the Wildlife Enhancement Scheme which encourages positive management on Sites of Special Scientific Interest (RSPB, 1992). There are thirty-nine lengths of unspoilt coastline which have been designated as Heritage Coasts, in England and Wales. These are designated by local authorities and the Countryside Commission and cover 31 per cent of the total English and Welsh coastline. The majority of the land so covered is in private ownership, although the National Trust owns a substantial proportion.

As well as these designated areas, which have been established to reflect broader environmental aims, there are other categories of statutory protected areas. These have been established for the protection of natural features and fall into the categories of: National Nature Reserves with 269 reserves totalling 1,645 sq km; Local Nature Reserves with 141 reserves totalling 158 sq km; Sites of Special Scientific Interest, 4,724 reserves totalling 15,175 sq km; Other Special Protected Areas, 75 reserves totalling 5,522 sq km (source: Department of the Environment, 1987).

National Nature Reserves are established to protect, through appropriate control and management, the most important areas of natural or semi-natural vegetation with characteristic flora, fauna and environmental conditions such as notable geological and physiographic features. These areas are owned or managed by the Nature Conservancy Council.

Local authorities have powers to establish Local Nature Reserves, after consultation with the Nature Conservancy Council. The Local Nature Reserves include several Sites of Special Scientific Interest (SSSIs). Planning authorities are required to consult with the Nature Conservancy Council before permission may be granted for development on SSSIs.

The remaining categories of protected areas are the result of the UK's involvement with international conservation initiatives and include: Special Protected Areas, Biosphere Reserves, 'Ramsar' Wetland Sites and Environmentally Sensitive Areas. The above is a brief illustration of the breadth of contemporary concern for the environment together with some examples of conservation activity.

The remainder of this chapter will consider public attitudes with regard to different forms of conservation issues and actions, *viz.* environmental pollution; concern for the countryside; and concern for international and global environmental issues. In order to allow comparisons, these are the same categories used in Chapter 2 when consideration was given to contemporary environmental issues.

CONCERN FOR THE ENVIRONMENT IN BRITAIN

The British public's concern for the quality of the natural environment has been the subject of many reports and other publications over the last three decades, originating from a wide variety of government, statutory, private and academic bodies. These illustrate the extent of concern over the destruction of, and support for the protection of, the natural environment in Britain.

The fact that concern about the environment exists amongst the British public is indisputable. This is evident in the findings of a survey which asked respondents to say in their own words what were the most important problems facing the country today. Some 8 per cent of the sample included environmental problems amongst the most important problems the government should be dealing with (Department of the Environment, 1987).

Concern about environmental pollution

In 1984 the Royal Commission on Environmental Pollution published the results of a poll conducted by Jowell *et al.*, (1984) showing responses by a representative sample of the British public to questions regarding the 'seriousness' of the effects on the environment caused by six sources of pollution. In 1987 Jowell *et al.* again ran the questionnaire on a similar sample. The problems included industrial, power generation and transport-related wastes. This showed that whilst the ordering of the perceived seriousness of environmental hazard issues has remained constant, the degree of perceived seriousness has increased in all cases.

Perhaps not surprisingly, for both the survey years aircraft noise pollution was seen as the least serious of pollutants with 30 per cent of respondents rating this to be very or quite serious in 1983 and 42 per cent in 1986. The five remaining forms of pollution were seen to be much more serious in terms of their effects upon the environment. For these pollutants, between 66 per cent and 91 per cent of the sample in 1983 rated these as very serious or quite serious, whilst by

1986 this number had risen to 73–94 per cent. Overall, in 1983, 72.6 per cent of those completing the questionnaire thought these sources of pollution had a very or quite serious environmental effect (this rose to 81.6 per cent if aircraft noise pollution was excluded). Whilst by 1986, 78.8 per cent of the sample reported all hazards to be serious to some extent, with this number rising to 86.2 per cent if aircraft noise was again removed from the calculations. This also shows that there has been no large shift in attitudes over this three-year period. However, there is a general increase in the willingness of respondents to rate any of these environmental hazards as being problems to some extent.

In their 1986 report, Jowell and colleagues also enquired about what was the most serious threat posed to the British countryside. In this study industrial pollution was indicated to be the most serious threat to the countryside by 47 per cent of the sample. The two next most destructive practices were identified as other forms of pollution: the use of chemicals or pesticides in farming (43 per cent), and litter (26 per cent). This illustrates the point that pollution is seen as the single greatest threat to the British environment.

The present research is concerned with environmental concern in Britain. However, it is of interest to note that concern over pollution is international. Kessel (1984) made an international comparison of assessments of the 'urgency' of a series of environmental issues including pollution. His study was conducted in England, West Germany and the United States of America. In this study it was found that all issues were rated above the halfway point on a scale which ranged from 1 = not urgent, to 7 = very urgent. Toxic wastes were consistently seen as the most urgent of environmental problems. Furthermore, Germans reported there to be more overall urgency than did English respondents, who achieved an average rating for all problems of 5.5 on the above scale. This result shows the English public to perceive environmental problems (especially pollution) as an urgent problem to be tackled. The American sample expressed the least amount of perceived urgency.

Having considered the effects of pollution upon the countryside, the next section of this chapter will examine in greater detail public opinion regarding changes occurring in the countryside.

Concern over countryside change

The previous chapter viewed changes that have occurred in the British countryside over the past few decades. It is true to state that over this time period, 'the degree of concern about the countryside has increased markedly' (Jowell *et al.*, 1987: 329). In their report of the following year, Jowell *et al.* (1988) found that when asked whether the countryside had changed, 22 per cent said it had not, 21 per cent said that it had changed a little, and 55 per cent that it had changed a lot (3 per cent didn't know). Moreover, 56 per cent of respondents thought that changes in the British countryside had been for the worse, whilst 60 per cent thought that the countryside should be protected in some way. They further found that 44 per cent of respondents were very concerned about countryside changes, 33 per cent a little concerned, whilst 22 per cent were unconcerned. Pollution from industry was found to be rated as the greatest threat to the countryside.

In this survey, industrial processes were identified as being major sources of destruction to the environment, whilst farming was seen as somewhat of a lesser problem. However, modern farming methods are seen by the public to be damaging to the environment. It was also found that the public is increasingly wanting to see the natural environment in Britain receiving adequate protection. Trust in farmers' ability to look after the land is however present, as they are still seen as doing a good job in protecting the countryside.

In the 1988 survey Jowell and colleagues also asked what should be done with farmland that is no longer wanted or needed for conventional farming activity and which is to be taken out of agricultural production. The single largest category of responses to this question suggested that the land should be used to create wildlife areas; while 64 per cent of respondents replied that the best or the next best thing to do with this category of land was to set it aside or to use it for a conservational purpose. In the following section of this chapter a broader view will be adopted in order to illustrate concern for the natural environment at a larger physical scale.

CONCERN ABOUT THE ENVIRONMENT IN GENERAL

Many of the findings from the surveys listed above could also be applied to concern about the environment in general. MORI (1987) provides a review of public concern for these issues. Environmental issues and activities which are 'British' may also often exist at a larger scale. It is possible that what are local (British) activities cause environmental problems at a larger scale. Examples of this would include effluent and gaseous discharges from power stations and industry. Alternatively, the British environment may be the recipient of damage from extra-national sources: oil-slick pollution and damage would be an example of this.

The Department of the Environment has published Figures that illustrate the British public are concerned with these larger-scale environmental issues (DOE, 1987). For instance, when asked which environmental problems they were most worried about, the four issues to surface were all 'international' in character: chemicals in the rivers and seas (1), nuclear waste (2), wildlife destruction (3), and beaches and seas (4). Two more international issues were also included in the top ten issues, namely acid rain (8) and oil slicks (10). It is interesting to note that between 86 per cent (issue one) and 64 per cent (issue ten) of respondents reported being concerned about these environmental problems (DOE, 1987). In the same survey, respondents were asked to state how much they thought could be done about each of the specified environmental issues. Generally, the relationship between assessed seriousness and the ability to remedy the problems was positive. Furthermore, the sample reported a belief that a great deal could be done to relieve the problems: 84 per cent of respondents reported that a lot could be done to relieve the problem assessed to be the most serious environmental problem (chemicals in the seas); 61 per cent stated that a lot could be done about the tenth most worrying problem (oil slicks). These results serve to illustrate the point that the British public are concerned about problems at a scale larger than their own country. Furthermore, it shows them to believe that there are solutions to the most serious of these issues.

CONCLUSION

The data that have been presented have illustrated the presence of a considerable level of environmental concern within the British population. This has been achieved through noting the growth of environmental groups and their growing membership. It has been further shown by the extent of legislative protection afforded to parts of the British countryside, both voluntary and statutory. Finally, the results of opinion polls regarding concern about nature and the environment have been presented, which have shown concern to exist about the British countryside and Britain's environment in general. This has illustrated how concern exists about many different forms of environmental issue; countryside changes and pollution being two main categories of concern. Public concern over environmental issues which have a larger scale of effect have also been documented.

Environmental concern will again be the subject matter of the following chapter. However, this will consider research that has been undertaken by psychologists and social scientists.

4 The psychology of environmental concern

A large body of social research literature exists which takes environmental concern as its subject matter. In this chapter this literature, as it is pertinent to the present study, will be reviewed. A now somewhat dated review of research viewing public concern for the quality of the natural environment is presented by Dunlap and Van Liere (1978a). The same authors later noted that: 'In the past decade social scientists have shown a great deal of interest in public attitudes toward environmental problems and issues, as reflected by the large number of studies of public concern with environmental quality' (Van Liere and Dunlap, 1980: 181).

Research into environmental concern was initially solely interested in documenting the widespread existence of such concern. Much of this early research also provided information about the social basis of environmental concern (Dunlap and Van Liere, 1978a). In doing this, such studies viewed environmental concern as a general environmental attitude (e.g., Allen, 1972; Arbuthnot, 1977; Braithwaite, 1977; Craik and McKechnie, 1977; Dunlap, 1975b; Hay, 1977; Iwata, 1977; O'Riordan, 1971; Ray, 1974, 1975). Research has also viewed many different types of specific environmental concerns (e.g., Schahn and Holzer, 1990). For example, studies have viewed attitudes towards air pollution (Sharma et al., 1975; Wall, 1973; 1974, 1975); water pollution (Ditton and Goodale, 1974; Watkins, 1974); noise pollution (Camerson, 1972; Goodman and Clary, 1976); population issues (Albrecht et al., 1975; McCatcheon, 1974; Mindick, 1977; Stokols, 1973; Watkins, 1975); animals and wildlife (Bart, 1972; Erickson, 1971); science and technology (Bruvold, 1974; Goldman et al., 1973).

In conducting research into environmental concern, social scientists have attempted to answer the question 'What types of

people are most concerned about the environment?' or 'What typifies
the environmentally concerned person?' Investigations have therefore
viewed the extent to which environmentally concerned individuals
share patterns of ideological and demographic characteristics
(Cotgrove, 1982). Research has addressed the question of whether
environmental concern is a characteristic of a specific social group, or
whether this concern is present across various social subpopulations.
It was hypothesised that if the latter instance were the case, then the
degree of concern about particular environmental issues would be
unrelated to personal attributes such as political ideology, age,
education, income, etc. Conversely, if environmental concern were
found to be more of a sectarian phenomenon, these variables might
define the salient attributes of the environmentally concerned
individual (de Haven-Smith, 1988; Tognacci, *et al.*, 1972). As a
consequence of adopting such a line of enquiry, this research has
most commonly embodied a line of investigation that measures
features of environmental concern such as the knowledge, beliefs,
emotions and behaviour that an individual holds or adopts towards
the environment. These were then related to a host of socio-
demographic variables such as age, gender, education level,
occupation, etc. (e.g., Arcury, *et al.*, 1987; Braun, 1983). In these
studies a series of different measures and indicators of environmental
concern has been used (e.g., Amelang, *et al.*, 1977). The measures
used have included reported levels of support for environmental
protection actions (de Haven-Smith, 1988), concern for the quality of
the natural environment (Maloney *et al.*, 1975), support for and
participation in environmental protection actions (Kronus and Van
Es, 1976), membership of and active participation in environmental
groups (Manzo and Weinstein, 1987), etc.

   The results from these studies are reviewed below, and this is
followed by a review of some of the instruments and techniques that
have been used as indicators of environmental concern. When Van
Liere and Dunlap (1981) presented a review of environmental
concern research, they subdivided studies in terms of the substantive
issues addressed and the measure of environmental concern used.
Their approach will be adopted in this chapter. Following on from
this, research that has attempted to produce more complex
(multidimensional) models of environmental concern, or to depict
environmental concern as a component of a wider attitude system,
will also be presented. Preceding this, however, a brief overview is
provided of psychological research that has attempted to offer
solutions to ameliorate environmental problems.

PSYCHOLOGICAL STUDIES OF ENVIRONMENTAL PROBLEMS AND ENVIRONMENTAL CONCERN

Environmental psychology represents a distinct strand of psychological research. Stokols (1978) has differentiated environmental psychology from other areas of psychology on the basis of three major dimensions:

1 an ecological perspective,
2 an emphasis on scientific strategies for solving community/ environment problems, and,
3 an interdisciplinary approach.

Stokols went on to identify environmental psychology within eight topic areas. The most applicable of these to the present research he defined as 'the experimental analysis of ecologically relevant behaviour'. In the research presented in this book, the perspective of environmental psychology will be adopted: an ecological perspective will be assumed and a scientific strategy will be employed.

Over the past few years, psychologists have considered environmental problems within their research and discovered the application of a behavioural approach to be of some use. Cone and Hayes (1984) evaluated existing environmental problems research which has fallen within the behavioural school. In doing this they provide a guide to behavioural procedures aimed specifically at altering public behaviours that are damaging the environment. They suggest that environmental problems may be tackled and ameliorated through behavioural interventions. The environmental problems that they have viewed include: littering and pollution (e.g., Cone et al., 1972; Clark et al., 1972), community transport (e.g., Everett et al., 1974), transport (e.g., Everett et al., 1974; Hake and Fox, 1978) and energy conservation (e.g., Kohlenberg et al., 1976; Zarling and Lloyd, 1978). Within each of these areas of environmental issues, behavioural principles have been found to be effective in providing solutions to the problem. However, whilst accepting the usefulness of the approach, behavioural research does not attempt to understand the personal meaning attached to environmental-concern-related behaviours, for the individuals committing the behaviours. An alternative approach, which some psychologists have adopted when viewing environmental issues, has ignored the environmentally destructive behaviour and has focused upon attitudes that underlie environmental protection behaviours and the way in which persons conceptualise and comprehend their everyday physical environments (e.g., Craik 1969, 1970; McKechnie, 1974, 1978).

ENVIRONMENTAL CONCERN RESEARCH

Since 1970 'the environment' has been an important public issue and a considerable upsurge in public receptivity to these issues has occurred (Tognacci *et al.*, (1972). This has resulted in a growth in the number of studies of public attitude towards environmental issues by the social and psychological sciences. This growth has been accompanied by increasing attention to the measurement of public concern for environmental quality (Dunlap and Van Liere, 1978a. Kley and Fietkau, 1979; Weigel and Weigel, 1978). A central theme may be identified running through environmental concern research, namely an attempt to categorise the environmentally concerned person (Manzo and Weinstein, 1987). Most of these attempts have proceeded by correlating a wide variety of measures of environmental concern with other characteristics (variables) of the environmentally concerned individual (Milbrath, 1984; Dunlap and Van Liere, 1985).

SOCIO-DEMOGRAPHIC CORRELATES OF ENVIRONMENTAL CONCERN

There have been several important studies that have taken various measures of environmental concern and investigated the socio-demographic correlates of these measures (e.g., de Groot, 1967; Van Liere and Dunlap, 1980; Weigel, 1977; Millbrath 1984). The existence of a large body of literature (see Dunlap and Van Liere, 1978a) that attempts to identify these correlates is due to two facts. Much research has been concerned with the identification of the social basis of environmental concern, for theoretical reasons (Hornback, 1974) and because of potential policy implications (Dillman and Christenson, 1972). However, relatively little research in this area has attempted to document changing levels of environmental concern among the public (e.g., Buttel and Flinn, 1974; Grossman and Potter, 1977b).

In reviewing environmental concern/socio-demographic correlation studies, eight selected variables will be considered as they were considered by Van Liere and Dunlap (1980). The selection of these variables is due to the fact that the largest body of data exists for these social and demographic variables, which are routinely included when employing sample survey techniques. The variables are age, gender, income, education, occupational prestige, residence, political party and political ideology; and these are presented in terms of their associations with various indicators of environmental concern. Other demographic measures such as race and religion could also have been included. However, as relatively few studies have examined environmental concern's relationship with these variables, they will be omitted. Furthermore, in this review only bivariate associations will be presented. Studies that have employed multivariate analysis will be considered in a later section.

A review of the socio-demographic correlates of environmental concern suggests that age, education and political ideology show moderate but consistent relationships with environmental concern. Thus, Van Liere and Dunlap state that: 'we have confidence in concluding that younger, well-educated, and politically liberal persons tend to be more concerned about environmental quality than their older, less educated, and politically conservative counterparts' (Van Liere and Dunlap, 1980: 192).

The evidence for the relationship between environmental concern and the other socio-demographic variables reviewed by Van Liere and Dunlap is less conclusive. A link between urban residence and environmental concern is suggested, and is supported when environmental concern is limited to environmental problems at a local level (Tremblay and Dunlap, 1978). When environmental concern has been correlated with occupation, a series of occupational categories not related to occupational prestige categories, have been found to be negatively related to environmental concern, for instance, business occupations (Buttel and Johnson, 1977; Constantini and Hanf, 1972), technologically dependent occupations (Malkis and Grasmick, 1977) and nature exploitative occupations (Harry, 1977). However, gender and income do not appear to be systematically related to these measures of environmental concern.

From the above results of correlational research, Cotgrove (1982) found it possible to draw two conclusions, namely that it is: 'important to differentiate between different components of environmental concern, and secondly, that cognitive variables are just as important as socio-demographic variables in predicting environmental concern in the general public' (Cotgrove, 1982: 132).

The foregoing findings indicate that researchers have had limited success in explaining the social basis of environmental concern. This is owing to the relatively low correlations found to exist in bivariate analyses between a variety of measures of environmental concern and other characteristics of the environmentally concerned individual. In order to examine the explanatory power of socio-demographic variables when they are viewed in combination, some researchers have chosen to employ multivariate analysis techniques. As well as viewing the cumulative effects of several variables upon environmental concern, through multivariate analyses, the researcher is also able to answer questions in regard to the relative statistical importance of each of these variables in relationship with variables indicative of environmental concern.

Multivariate research into environmental concern

In conducting a multivariate investigation of the area of environmental concern, two approaches have been adopted. The first of these has attempted to depict environmental concern as part of an attitude complex. This attitude set is taken to include a variety of other attitudes to contemporary social issues. The second approach depicts attitudes towards environmental issues within a multi-dimensional context. The two approaches have been used in a non-exclusive manner. In these situations, the models produced, in multivariate analysis of environmental concern, are related to a more general multidimensional representation of social dispositions. Moreover, the elements of environmental concern models are also correlated with socio-demographic characteristics of the environmentally concerned individual. The study presented below is representative of such research.

Environmental concern as a multivariate attitude

An example of multivariate research into environmental concern is given in Cotgrove (1982). He investigated the relationship between three measures of environmental concern (damage, shortage, nature), four measures of socio-demographic variables (age, politics, income, market) and four measures of cognitive variables associated with contemporary worldviews (anti-industry, anti-science, post-materialism, anti-economy). The sample for the study was taken from the British public. The precise meaning of each of the eleven variables is of little importance to the present research; rather the relationship between environmental concern variables and socio-demographic and cognitive variables is of interest. For a full explanation of these eleven variables the reader is guided to Cotgrove's (1982) text. The relationships (intercorrelations) between these variables shows several interesting features. First, he discovered that several of the correlations were negative. Furthermore, these negative relationships are often of quite large magnitudes. Guttman (1982) and other researchers concerned with the theoretical study of attitudes (e.g., Levy, 1985) commented upon the presence of negative relationships in a correlation matrix of attitude items. The presence of these relationships is indicative of the heterogeneity of the items. More importantly, it is indicative of the heterogeneity of the semantic area addressed by the research instrument. Having stated this, it should be noted that the negative correlations involve three of the eleven variables (which he labelled X1, X2, X3). Variable X3 is income and may perhaps be expected to be negatively related to other measures of this largely charity-related area. Indeed, the majority of relationships between this and other variables is negative or low positive. The other two variables with negative correlations are age and politics. These correlations are neither consistently negative or positive and are of varying magnitude. As such, these variables can be seen to play a minor role in the systematic structure of the relationship between the attitudes contained within the matrix.

Some of the highest positions and most consistent relationships are present between variables X9, X10 and X11. These variables represent three measures of environmental concern. From these coefficients it may be claimed that a common attitude (which may be called concern for the environment) is being assessed by each of the measures employed. However, due to the 'relatively' small magnitude of the relationship of variable X10 with variables X9 and X11 it may be suggested that this variable (X10) is measuring a slightly different section of the environmental concern attitude complex (this is, however, purely speculative). Inspection of variable X10 shows it to be measuring shortages. Variables X9 and X11 are, however, measuring activities that are damaging to the environment. Shortages may be the consequences of environmentally damaging practices and therefore a difference in respondents' understanding of, and responses to, these two types of environmental concern may be explained.

The purpose of this exposition of Cotgrove's (1982) matrix has been for three reasons. It has been undertaken in order to illustrate that environmental concern attitudes may be both positively and negatively related to cognitive and socio-demographic variables. As a result of this, environmental concern may be correctly identified as a component part of an attitude set which may be labelled 'contemporary worldviews'. Second, the three measures of environmental concern are positively related, therefore enabling the hypothesis of a distinct subset of environmental concern attitudes within contemporary worldviews to be made. Finally, the environmental concern attitudes were all positively interrelated and consequently form a homogeneous subset of attitudes. However, differences in the relative sizes of these interrelationships enabled the attitudes to be divided into components of environmental concern. These relationships provide further justification for the multivariate investigation of environmental concern attitudes and values.

These relationships also show that cognitive measures (X5–X8) consistently correlate more highly with the three environmental concern subscales than do socio-demographic measures (X2–X3). Multiple regression analysis of this data was performed. Cotgrove found that on the basis of these analyses, it is possible to conclude that environmental concern is more a product of an individual's particular set of social values and attitudes than a reflection of social group membership (although group membership may influence an individual's social values, attitudes, etc.).

When inspecting Cotgrove's data, it can be further noted that there were different personal variables associated with his three types of environmental concern measure. When viewing awareness of environmental damage, high scorers on this scale were typically politically left wing, of lower income, older than average, and holding anti-economic and anti-industry values. When viewing the environmental shortages scale, anti-economic and anti-science values were found to be the best predictors. By contrast, age, politics and income have only a weak direct effect. Finally, concern about nature is very similar to awareness of environmental damage, except that anti-industry and post-material values have larger direct effects relative to the socio-demographic variables.

It can be seen from this analysis that both cognitive and socio-demographic variables have substantial direct effects relative to environmental concern. Cognitive variables are also found to be the most consistent predictors of environmental concern measures, due to the large differences that exist in the patterns of associations between the three measures of environmental concern and socio-demographic variables.

Cotgrove's research raises the important points that:

Awareness of damage and concern for nature are very similar, but the constituency for awareness of shortages is very different. This implies the need to analyse different types of environmental concern separately, and not to conflate them. . . . The general conclusions to emerge from this analysis is that there is no single

constituency for environmental concern [and] there is little
evidence to suggest that environmental concern is the exclusive
preserve of a particular social group.

(Cotgrove, 1982: 133)

Different variables are correlates of environmental concern
dependent upon which dimension of environmental concern is being
viewed. Studies have shown that concern tends to be somewhat
higher among people who are younger, female, more educated and
more liberal (Millbrath, 1984). However, as Van Liere and Dunlap
(1980) noted, and others have subsequently claimed: 'these
associations tend to be weak and are somewhat inconsistent from
study to study' (Manzo and Weinstein, 1987: 676).

There are also differences in which variables are correlates of
environmental concern dependent upon the manner in which this
concern is expressed (i.e., dependent upon how environmental
concern is being measured (Buttel and Flinn, 1976a)). In short, the
above correlation studies may be criticised for their lack of a
standardised variable or criterion that establishes or is indicative of
environmental concern (Van Liere and Dunlap, 1978).

Many of the studies mentioned so far in this chapter have gathered
together diverse measures of environmental concern (such as, air and
water pollution, population issues, animal and wildlife issues) to form
a global measure of environmental concern. It is unclear from the
research literature as to whether persons concerned with one of these
issues will be equally concerned with others. Indeed, from the
analysis of Cotgrove's (1982) data matrix it appears that they may not
be. Although one study has documented a relatively high degree of
consistency between attitudes towards different environmental
problems and policies (Tognacci *et al.*, 1972), many other studies
have concluded that environmental attitudes are issue-specific
(Simon, 1972; Lounsbury and Tornatsky, 1977; Van Liere and
Dunlap, 1981; Webber, 1982; Connerly, 1986), whilst Cotgrove
(1982) proposed three dimensions around which environmental
concern attitudes varied. In the section that follows, the measurement of environmental concern will be further considered, and
criticisms in regard to the measurement of environmental concern
will also be reviewed in greater detail.

THE MEASUREMENT OF ENVIRONMENTAL CONCERN

Past studies of environmental concern have measured the concept in
many ways. Attitude scales have been developed to measure

environmental concern (e.g., Albrecht *et al.*, 1982; Dunlap and Van Liere, 1978a; Langeheine and Lehmann, 1986; Maloney and Ward, 1973; Maloney *et al.*, 1975; McKechnie, 1974, 1978; Weigel and Weigel, 1978). It is often assumed that different types of measure are equivalent. In order to produce improved measures of environmental concern, researchers have generally adopted two strategies. First, multiple rather than single-item indicators have been used to improve reliability and to allow for the use of more powerful analytic techniques (such as regression analysis as opposed to tabular analysis). Second, standardised measures have begun to be used in attempts to allow comparisons among studies (e.g., Maloney *et al.*, 1975; Dispoto, 1977; Borden and Francis, 1978). This second point has started to lead to the production of a cumulation of results and generalisations about environmental concern (Van Liere and Dunlap, 1980). Comparability among measures is important because, as has been pointed out: 'The variety of indicators . . . [of environmental concern] is quite vast, and there is virtually no replication of early studies with comparable measures of ' "environmental concern" ' ' (Buttel and Johnson, 1977: 49).

Despite improvements in the measurement of environmental concern, problems remain. One measurement issue that has received little attention is the degree to which different measures serve equally well as indicators of the same underlying construct. This construct is conceptualised in the literature as 'concern for environmental quality' or simply as 'environmental concern'. Do the various measures of environmental concern constitute parallel tests, or are they measuring different underlying concepts? Other research has questioned the assumption that all of the different measures of environmental concern are in fact equivalent and measuring the same underlying concept. As one researcher suggested: 'attitudes towards over-population, growth management, pollution and nuclear power appear to be, at most, only loosely related. Additionally, different substantive dimensions of environmental concern have different demographic and ideological correlates' (de Haven-Smith, 1988: 278). This proposition has led to environmental concern measures being systematically differentiated in terms of two sources of intermeasure variation. First, measures differ in terms of the substantive issues they address (the issues reflected in measurement scale items) and second, the theoretical conceptualisations used in developing the items (the measurement scale used) (Van Liere and Dunlap, 1981).

What is meant by variation in the substantive issues addressed by measures is the extent to which they incorporate different environmental issues such as pollution, population, natural resources, wildlife and wilderness, etc. For example, some researchers have measured attitudes towards each of the above areas (e.g., pollution, population, etc.) as distinct dimensions of environmental concern (e.g., Tognacci, *et al.*, 1972; Lounsbury and Tornatsky, 1977). A more common practice has been to combine items dealing with these differing substantive issues into a single environmental concern measure (e.g., Buttel and Flinn, 1976a, 1976b; Dunlap *et al.*, 1973; Maloney *et al.*, 1975; Weigel and Weigel, 1978). However, it is unclear in the research whether attitudes towards these different substantive issues reflect to an equal extent a broader 'common' concept of concern with environmental quality. Analysis of the data from Cotgrove's 1982 study questions such an hypothesis. The supposition that support for all environmental issues taps a single underlying attitude is further questioned by the finding that different social subgroups have different environmental concerns (Horvat and Voekler, 1976).

The second source of variation in measures of environmental concern is that due to the different theoretical conceptualisations used to develop the research instruments. What is meant by this are the different implicit or explicit assumptions regarding what constitutes the respondent samples' expression of environmental concern. Furthermore, it questions the scale along which environmental concern should be measured. As an example of this, studies have examined the perceived seriousness of environmental problems (e.g., Buttel and Flinn, 1976a, 1976b; Kronus and Van Es, 1976); support for environmental protection (Dillman and Christenson, 1972; Marsh and Christenson, 1977); knowledge of environmental problems and issues (Arbuthnot and Lingg, 1975; Maloney *et al.*, 1975); support for environmental reforms designed to protect environmental quality (Buttel and Flinn, 1976a, 1976b; Buttel and Johnson, 1977); and actual involvement in pro-environmental behaviours (Dunlap *et al.*, 1981; Heberlein and Black, 1976; Weigel, 1977). Each of these represents a different theoretical approach to the conceptualisation of environmental concern.

There are many different substantive issues that fall within the area of environmental concern. The same is true of the possible ways in which these may be measured. This has resulted in numerous combinations of substantive issues and theoretical conceptualisations being made to produce many different measures. As a direct result of the different measures that have been used to indicate environmental concern, and the lack of comparable replication studies, three difficulties have arisen. It has been difficult to (a) establish the meaning environmental concern possesses for individuals, (b) compare the results of different studies of environmental concern and (c) establish empirical generalisations about the relationships between environmental concern and other variables (Lowenthal, 1972; Buttel and Johnson, 1977). At the same time there has been very little research examining the degree to which the different measures of environmental concern produce consistent results; rather, it is generally assumed that all measures tap concern for environmental quality equally well. This assumption is accompanied by the supposition that environmental concern is a single, well-defined attitude or attitude complex.

Van Liere and Dunlap (1981) examined empirically these assumptions by incorporating them into a model and testing hypotheses based upon this. Their model illustrated the relationships between specified socio-demographic characteristics and environmental concern. Conceptually, the model shows a socio-demographic variable to be measured once and environmental concern to be measured more than once. Socio-demographic variables may be age, gender, income level, etc., whilst environmental concern measures could be based on different substantive issues (e.g., pollution, population, etc.) or on different theoretical conceptions (e.g., attitude scales, frequency of behaviour scales, etc.). The model also explicates the assumption that all environmental measures are influenced by the single underlying construct of environmental concern.

Van Liere and Dunlap (1981) conducted a study to test their model. If the model was correct and the environmental measures were tapping the same construct of 'environmental concern', they predicted that two types of consistency should be found amongst the correlations between the variables of a study based upon the model. They hypothesised that the correlations between the environmental concern measures and any specified socio-demographic variable would be of similar magnitude and direction.

Van Liere and Dunlap (1981) constructed scales that differed only in terms of their substantive issues. To do this they included issues on three environmental problem areas and constructed three scales: Population Scale, Pollution Scale, Natural Resources Scale. They also constructed three scales with measures that focused upon pollution and natural resource issues but differed in terms of their range of responses; these three measures formed: the Environmental

Regulation Scale (measuring attitudes towards government regulation to protect the environment), the Environmental Spending Scale (measuring the level of government spending on environmental protection favoured by respondents) and the Environmental Behaviour Scale (respondents reported frequency of engaging in environmental protection behaviours). The scales constructed were deemed, by the authors, to have adequate internal consistency. The results revealed that whilst all coefficients are positive, there is considerable variation in the size of correlation between the scales. These ranged from 0.10 to 0.64, refuting the hypothesised consistency of the size of correlation implicit in their model. Furthermore, when the average correlation of each scale with all other scales was considered, it was the Population and Environmental Behaviour Scales which were primarily responsible for the low correlations between items (with their coefficients being considerably lower than the other four scales' average correlations). With the Population and Environmental Behaviour Scales omitted, Van Liere and Dunlap conclude that the remaining correlations are both substantial and consistent and, consequently, the pattern of overall correlations does not support the model. However, if the measures of environmental concern are restricted to those concerned more with 'ecological' than with 'human' issues, support is found for the hypothesis.

The second form of consistency predicted by their model is a consistency between measures of environmental concern and socio-demographic variables. If the predicted relationships were correct, then the correlations within any row of their matrix should be approximately equal. Their results did not support this hypothesis. They found that for four out of the five socio-demographic variables, the correlation coefficients are significantly different from one another. In only one case (residence) are there no significant differences between the two correlations in the fifteen pairs. However, if the Population Scale and the Environmental Behaviour Scales are ignored, there is much greater consistency. With these two scales removed, only in the case of age were the correlations in any of the pairs significantly different from one another.

A further important issue may be raised from inspection of the correlation matrix. The correlations between all variables reveals there to be positive associations. However, the correlations between the Environmental Behaviour Scale and other measures are relatively low. This is perhaps indicative of the differences in the types of assessments involved in each of the six scales. In the Environmental Behaviour Scale, subjects were asked to assess the frequency with which they engaged in a variety of pro-environmental behaviours. In the five other scales the assessments made by respondents were purely cognitive. This raises the important point that whilst different attitude measures may have the same substantive content area, they may differ in terms of their assessment criteria. Cognitive involvement is different from behavioural involvement. Inclusion of a 'mixed range' of responses (cognitive and behavioural) may facilitate understanding, for the researcher, of how these behavioural modalities are related to the research content area. However, if the modality of response is ignored by the researcher, variation may be present in a data set which is not accounted for by a corresponding variation in the substantive focus of the attitudes being investigated. The modality of behavioural expression is of great importance to environmental concern research. This issue is one that will be comprehensively addressed in the present research.

Van Liere and Dunlap (1981) concluded that when scales are limited to cognitive measures of pollution and/or natural resources, considerable consistency is found between correlations. Furthermore, this consistency is present in the correlations between environmental concern measures and in the correlations of socio-demographic variables.

From the above findings it is possible to form the conclusion that Van Liere and Dunlap found little support for their proposed model. This model embodies the implicit assumption that all measures of environmental concern are equal. The results suggest, however, that different types of environmental concern measures may be more distinct than previously assumed. In the same report these authors found that in terms of consistency among different substantive issues, concern about population issues appeared to be rather distinct from concern about natural resources and pollution, whilst these latter two measures were highly correlated. Furthermore, if the substantive issues were restricted to pollution and natural resources, all attitudinal measures were highly correlated, whilst the behavioural measures appeared less so. This lends further support to the hypothesis that environmental concern possesses more than one dimension to its substantive content area. Furthermore, it suggests that behavioural and cognitive evaluations form distinct modalities of assessment in relation to the content area.

Other research supports this claim as it has found a similar division of the relationships between environmental concern measures to be present in the environmental concern literature. These studies report that population and behavioural items tend to load on separate dimensions, distinct from other kinds of environmental issues (Horvat and Voekler, 1976; Lounsbury and Tornatsky, 1977). Consequently, it would appear that environmental concern may be a fairly broad concept. It would also appear to possess at least two separate dimensions, one which is best represented by the ecological items of concern about pollution and natural resources, and one which is better characterised by the more human population and behavioural items. Van Liere and Dunlap (1981) also found support for a multivariate model of environmental concern when the relationship between differing measures of environmental concern and socio-demographic variables were viewed. Overall these authors concluded that different types of environmental concern measures were differentially related to socio-demographic variables. More specifically, however, this variation was found to be mainly due to the Population Scale and Environmental Behaviour Scale. The correlations between the other four (ecological) scales and socio-demographic variables were found to be much more consistent. The authors thus conclude that concern about population issues and behavioural involvement (more human issues) are tapping dimensions of environmental concern which are understood somewhat differently by the public than concern about pollution and natural resources (more ecological issues).

CONCLUSION

From the research evidence presented in this chapter it would seem appropriate to state that somewhat more attention should be paid by researchers to the measurement of environmental concern. In particular, the combination of a range of broad-based issues into a single research tool may produce internally inconsistent results: 'a composite scale including diverse dimensions of environmental concern might "mask" the true relationships between the dimensions and, for example, selected demographic variables' (Van Liere and Dunlap, 1981: 669). In general, over the past few years there has been an increase in the theoretical and methodological sophistication of studies of environmental concern, although there is still room for much improvement (Dunlap and Van Liere, 1978a). 'In short, further research is needed to establish clearly the "boundaries" of the concept of environmental concern' (Van Liere and Dunlap, 1981: 670). It is apparent from the evidence presented in this chapter that the boundaries of environmental concern have not yet been clearly established. It is also evident that different types of environmental concern measures may be more distinct than was initially assumed.

An approach to social research that has been used successfully to help delineate a content area is the facet theoretical approach. This orientation has been applied to several content areas of social experience. In the next chapter, studies that have employed a facet theory approach in their research design and data analysis will be outlined as they are applicable to the study of attitudes and social values.

5 Facet theory studies of attitudes and social values

In the preceding chapters support for environmental conservation, both generally and within Britain, has been reviewed. The relevant psychological literature on environmental concern has also been presented. This has led to three conclusions:

1 that environmental concern is a pertinent social value in Britain in the early 1990s;
2 that no commonly accepted definition or reference criterion has developed which may be used to establish the existence of environmental concern amongst a sample of respondents;
3 that due to points (1) and (2), some anomalies and discrepancies are present in the environmental concern literature (these have been detailed in Chapter 4).

The lack of a clear definitional framework has been noted to be present in other areas of psychological study (Levy and Guttman, 1985). Facet theory (Borg and Shye, in press; Shye and Elizur, in press; Canter, 1985a) has been used in a wide variety of research areas to provide a framework in the format of a definitional taxonomy. In this chapter the facet approach to social research (Canter, 1985a) will be reviewed. This review will be of facet research in the applied areas of, and as it relates to, the study of attitudes (Guttman, 1982) and social values (Levy and Guttman, 1985).

A brief introduction to facet theory will now be given. For the interested reader, a more comprehensive description of the facet theoretical approach to social science research, along with some further details of facet analysis procedures, are given in Canter (1985b), Shye (1978a) and Borg, (1981) and a comprehensive review provided in Donald (1987).

FACET THEORY

Facet theory is a coherent meta theoretical approach to the design of research projects, measuring instruments and data analysis (Shye, 1978a). It also provides guidelines for the manner in which research should be conducted and a rationale for why it should be done in that manner (Runkel and McGrath, 1972). The approach has been applied to many aspects of scientific endeavour. However, facet theory has found its major applications and has achieved its principal impact within the social sciences. As the social sciences have developed over the past few decades, their subject matter of human behaviour and experience has become theoretically and empirically more complex. As a consequence of this increase in complexity of the subject matter of the social sciences, the questions asked of the social scientist have become more sophisticated (Canter, 1982b). As this has happened, the need for a means of specifying the conceptual content of a variety of research areas in a systematic and precise way becomes more urgent. As Roskam states:

> Psychology seeks answers to the questions how and why people think, feel and behave in the way they do. . . . Progress of [psychological] science depends on adequate definitions of its concepts. . . . Psychology must define its empirical concepts of behavior by means of an objective definitional system.
>
> (Roskam, 1981: 198–199)

Facet theory provides a way of meeting such needs. Facet theory research has proved most useful in social science investigations that have been concerned with complex behavioural systems. Facet theory has been used as an exploratory technique for the investigation of new content areas (Hackett, 1989). It has also been used as a technique for the broadening of knowledge within previously researched or analogous research areas (e.g., Donald, 1987; Hackett, 1985; Hackett *et al.*, 1989; Morrison *et al.*, 1991). Hackett *et al.*, (1989) provides an example of both these orientations in the use of a facet approach within a single research context.

As Canter (1983) states, the approach grew out of the work of Louis Guttman (1954) and his colleagues (e.g., Foa, 1958; Borg, 1978; Shye, 1978a), who were mainly based at the Israel Institute for Applied Social Research. Canter claims that facet theory:

> utilizes three major constituents of scientific activity: 1) formal definition of the variables being studied, 2) hypothesis of some specified relationships between the definition and an aspect of

empirical observations, and 3) a rationale for the correspondence between one and two.

(Canter, 1982b: 144)

In undertaking the above activities, it proposes a definitional framework in the form of facets.

Since the development of facet theory in the 1950s, the approach has been applied to many areas of concern to the social scientist. Indeed, several authors have commented upon the wide range of its application (e.g., Borg, 1979; Shye, 1978a). Illustrations of the theoretical and applied topics of this research are numerous and include: social values (Levy, 1986; Levy and Guttman, 1976; Levy and Meyer-Schweizer, 1989; Hackett and Florence, 1991); job satisfaction (Payne *et al.*, 1976); well-being (Levy, 1976a; Levy and Guttman, 1975); involvement (Levy, 1979); attitudes towards work and technological change (Elizur and Guttman, 1976); energy conservation (Miles and Canter, 1976); place evaluation (Donald, 1985); intelligence (Schlesinger and Guttman, 1969); social attitudes (Harrelson *et al.*, 1972) and many others. At present, facet theory is being used to, amongst other things, illustrate several professional, occupational and applied areas of interest to the social scientist. For instance: organisational perception (Donald, 1987); dental treatment (Hackett *et al.*, 1989); perceptual development within the architectural profession (Wilson, 1989); and the facet evaluation of offices (Donald, 1989).

Facet theory recognises the fact that human beings and human characteristics may frequently be defined in terms of several relevant dimensions 'at the same time' (McGrath, 1967). Such conceptual dimensions are referred to as facets. The constituent parts of these facets are called elements and make up the values on that dimension. Let us consider a definitional framework developed by J. Brown as an illustration of the facet approach. She stated that:

> people may be classified in terms of the facet 'marital status', whose elements would be defined as single, married, divorced, separated, widowed. At the same time they can be categorised by the facet 'number of children', whose elements might be none, two, three, or more.

(Brown, 1985: 21)

This definition illustrates well that the researcher may propose any number of related although mutually exclusive facets in an attempt to develop a classification system of their research area. However, facet research goes beyond this speculative enterprise through the gathering of empirical data and analysing this in order to support the hypothesised dimensions (facets). At an even later stage of a facet research project, the relationships between the elements of facets within a study may be analysed.

The paragraphs above are intended to provide the reader with some idea of the scope and nature of facet research. It is not the intention within this book to review in detail the approach. However, from the aforementioned it is immediately apparent that the approach is applicable to the investigation of environmental concern. The many ways in which the facet approach to social research have been utilised has included the investigation of social values and attitudes, acts of protest and socio-political involvement. This research is of direct relevance to the present studies and will now be reviewed.

DEFINITION OF SOCIAL VALUES

The earlier sections of this book have demonstrated that support for environmental conservation is widespread (Lowe and Goyder, 1983). Therefore, environmental concern is similar to many other social belief systems or social values. Inspection of the social science literature concerning social values reveals, however, that considerable disagreement exists over the definition of social values. Furthermore, while such discord exists, it is not possible to identify a single clear framework within which a study of a social value may be undertaken. In the section that follows, this lack of clarity will be considered.

The concept of social values has been defined in a variety of different ways. Many of these definitions are vague in specifying the concept they are attempting to define. These definitions have also been criticised as being too 'complex and unclear' (Levy, 1986). These claims are illustrated in the following definition: 'The term "values" may refer to interests, pleasures, likes, preferences, duties, moral obligations, desires, wants, needs, aversions and attractions, and many other modalities of selective orientation' (Williams, 1968: 363).

This definition encompasses many modalities of human behaviour and typifies these by defining them as types of selective behaviour. Selection is identified as being important in distinguishing values from other human activities. However, the criterion of selective orientation (for assigning the presence of 'value' to a selective instance) is not specified. A further example of a complex and unclear definition of values is given by Scott and Scott: 'A value is a hypothetical construct assigned to that class of hypothetical constructs known as an individual's phenomenology, the way one views the world and himself in relation to it' (Scott and Scott, 1965: 97).

By categorising values as hypothetical constructs, in this imprecise manner, the definition of value within a specified context is left unclear. However, Scott's definition offers some further criteria which may be used to identify values: 'Value is an individual's concept of an ideal relationship (or state of affairs), which he uses to assess the "goodness" or "badness", the "rightness" or "wrongness", of actual relationships that he observes or contemplates' (Scott and Scott, 1965: 99). The greatest shortcoming in all of the above definitions is lack of clarity. The social researcher who adopts one of the above definitions in the investigation of social values (as an area of human behaviour) would encounter considerable difficulty in delimiting an area for study. The same is true of research viewing a specific area of human activity in terms of its social value. This point is illustrated by Levy when she states: 'Any review of the research literature on "values" immediately reveals that the concept has been rather vague. . . . definitions are complex and unclear, and almost invariably include external aspects that are but empirically related to the concept values (are but correlates)' (Levy, 1986: 2).

Scott and Scott's (1965) definition allows a hypothesised construct to be identified as a value if its selective orientation involves choice along a positive to negative dimension. However, many positive to negative orientations occur which may not involve the ascription of value (Levy, 1985). Thus, it is necessary to define this dimension more clearly by stating the form that such a positiveness may take. In 1974, Levy and Guttman (1974a, 1974b) developed their own definition of the concept of values. The facet theory approach has used a mapping sentence to define social values, as shown in Figure 5.1.

This definition avoids many of the criticisms that have been made of other definitions of the concept 'values'. For instance, the definition is precise and not vague. It does not simply specify correlates of values. It allows for both change in values and the measurement of such changes. The definition's clarity arises from the precise specification of the component parts of the concept. It also states that the 'value' of a phenomenon is indicated by its importance: something that is valued is perceived to be important. Therefore, a positive to negative dimension running from important to not-

'An item belongs to the universe of value items if and only if its domain asks for a (cognitive) assessment of the importance of a –

A	**B**
(goal)	(cognitive)
(behaviour)	in a (affective)
(instrumental)	

C
(itself as a)
modality in life area (y) for (a more primary)
purpose in life (z), and the range is ordered

(very important that it should)
from   TO
(very important that it should not)

exist for that purpose.'

Figure 5.1 General mapping sentence for social values
Source: Levy and Guttman, 1976: 68

important is defined as indicating choices (selective orientation) which ascribe value within their selection process.

According to the above definition, the concept of 'values' has three component parts. First, facet A distinguishes between goal and behaviour. For example, it is possible to assess the importance of a goal (e.g., happiness) or the importance of a behaviour (e.g., helping others). Second, if goals are considered, in facet B it is specified that these may be of an affective modality (e.g., happiness), of a cognitive modality (e.g., equality), or of an instrumental modality (e.g., wealth). Behaviours may also be of these three modalities. They may be of an affective modality (e.g., to love), of a cognitive modality (e.g., to learn), or of an instrumental modality (e.g., to make money). Finally, it is possible to assess the importance of the goal or behaviour in itself, or as a means for attaining a more primary goal or behaviour (facet C). For example, it is possible to assess the importance of learning to drive as a goal or end in itself or as a means of attaining a more primary goal (e.g., attaining a job). Therefore, the question must be asked: 'important for what purpose?' This is necessary as the meaning of the assessed importance depends on the goal. Also, the assessment of a goal or behaviour may change in accordance with purpose (Levy and Guttman, 1981c).

It has therefore been possible to assemble a definition of social values through the use of the facet theory approach. The value of employing this approach to research is that it forms both a starting point and a conclusion (providing hypotheses for investigation and the format for, and results of, an investigation). Having developed a taxonomy of elements of the concept of social values, research has applied this definition to specific social value contexts. This procedure has found empirical support for the theoretical classification system and allowed understanding to be developed of the social values that have been investigated within a real-life setting. The results that have been obtained from the facet theory investigation of social values will now be reviewed.

Faceted investigation of social values

Several studies exist within the facet theory literature which have attempted to develop an understanding of the personal and social values of a variety of issues within a given social population (Levy, 1986; Levy and Guttman, 1974a, 1974b, 1976, 1981a, 1981b, 1981c, 1985). The populations that have been studied have been from different countries (Levy and Guttman 1981c). This research has found it possible to distinguish between values that exist in different areas of their respondents' lives. For example, religious, economic, leisure, work and family are all life areas that have been researched.

These life areas have all been separately identified as components of respondents' value systems. This has been possible as these value areas all possess an internal consistency amongst social value items which relate specifically to them (Levy, 1986). To illustrate this, Levy discovered that when questions about value in specific life areas (such as religion) were inter-correlated, these relationships were nearly always positive or zero. However, when values from different life areas were mixed, this positive direction in the relationship was not always present: religious and some other social values were found to be consistently negatively correlated. For instance, they discovered that the religious values 'to be religious' and 'to believe in God' were negatively related to the value of 'to be rich' (Levy, 1986).

When social value items are correlated, it has been found that the size of the coefficients between any two items in a values set is dependent upon three facets. These are: the life area to which the social value refers, the expression modality of a value (internal expression or external expression), and the mode of the value (for itself or for some more superordinate goal).

In all of the studies that have used a facet theory approach in the investigation of social values, a common structure of life area categories (elements) has emerged. Levy (1986) provides a discussion of the life area facets and elements involved in social value judgements. The common structure that has been observed has been circular: a structure known within facet literature as a circumplex (Runkel and McGrath, 1972: 357). Within such a structure, elements or items within an analysis are qualitatively different. This ordering amongst elements possesses neither a beginning nor an end (Lorr and McNair, 1963). The precise elements have been found to vary, dependent upon the precise values within the study.

Owing to the similarity present within the results from the research cited above, it has been possible to develop a general model of social values. Using this approach, findings are stated in the form of a mapping sentence (Levy, 1976b). This has already been carried out for social values (Figure 5.1 lists the general mapping sentence for social values).

The specific context of values research

In any facet-designed study of social values, the general mapping sentence definition of social values must be adapted to the specific context of the research: 'To the general definition of values (and attitudes) each research must add those facets that are specific to it and classify concrete types of values' (Levy, 1986: 7). Adapting a mapping sentence to the research context is achieved through adding facets and facet elements to the general mapping sentence as they are necessary to allow classification of the social values within the area of interest. This results in the modification and refinement of the original mapping sentence. This adapted mapping sentence then provides a conceptual framework which helps the researcher precisely to investigate the concept under consideration. This is achieved as the modified mapping sentence offers a detailed definition of the content of a social enquiry. It also allows the development of specific research items and provides hypotheses about the empirical structure of the relationships between the items included.

There is a growing body of facet theory analytic research into social values. Each of these studies has commenced by taking the Levy and Guttman (1974b) mapping sentence (the general mapping sentence) and adapting this template to the specific value context. Published examples of this process are reviewed below. These have been included in order to illustrate:

1 how each of these mapping sentences is related to the general mapping sentence;
2 how each of these mapping sentences has been adapted to the specific research context;
3 the possibility of adapting the general mapping sentence to the investigation of environmental concern.

FACET ANALYTIC RESEARCH INTO SOCIAL VALUES

Levy and Guttman first applied the facet theory approach to the study of social values (Levy and Guttman, 1974a, 1974b, 1976). In these studies the general mapping sentence for social values was developed (Figure 5.1). Since these publications, the mapping sentence has been applied to a variety of social value research problems. The general mapping sentence for social values has been used in both the design and interpretation of findings in social value studies. These studies, and the facets that they have included in their mapping sentences in order to make them pertinent to context, are now reviewed. The studies are presented so as the reader may observe the cumulative nature of the research findings produced.

Fundamental problem values

Levy and Guttman (1985) provide a mapping sentence for the investigation of fundamental values in society. Their study examined responses to a questionnaire that was generated from this mapping sentence. Questions were devised, each of which could be categorised by systematically selecting and combining elements from each of the two content facets.

Their mapping sentence has three facets. The first of these is defined as S and represents the research population. Facets A and B together constitute the domain of the research. The third facet type is designated R and symbolises the range of responses to be collected. Of the domain facets, facet A specifies the direction to which the value is oriented (personal, interpersonal, impersonal). Facet B specifies the modality of the value-related behaviour (cognitive, instrumental, affective). The study employed a cross-cultural sample from Israel and Switzerland. It was possible, through the use of Similarity Structure Analysis, clearly to identify both the common structure of social values for the two groups and intercultural differences in these values. From their results Levy and Guttman concluded that: 'The faceted common definition framework enabled development and testing of a cross-cultural theory of values,' (Levy and Guttman, 1985: 218). The faceted definition employed by Guttman and Levy in their mapping sentence enabled the development and testing of a cross-cultural theory of the stability of the structure of social values. Similarity Structure Analysis (Borg and Lingoes, 1987) of results suggested that two more facets were present in responses. Therefore the authors modified their mapping sentence to incorporate these. Similarity Structure Analysis is the more recently used name for the multidimensional analysis technique known as Smallest Space Analysis or SSA. In SSA the correlation coefficient between any pair of items in an analysis is represented as space between these items in a series of two-dimensional plots. In such plots, multiple items are included and the space between item pairings is representative of their level of association, so that the more highly their correlatedness, the closer to each other they are placed. Further details of this technique will be found later in this book, and the approach will be used in the present analysis.

In the revised mapping sentence the orientation and modality facets, which were formerly labelled A and B, are stated now in somewhat greater detail (A = respect, help, feel for; B = self, others, non-human natural phenomena, transcendental being). This expansion of detailed elements allows the construction of more (and more representative) questionnaire items. The order of these two facets is reversed in the modified mapping sentence. The latter of these two facets now also includes specific sub-varieties of behaviour which may be studied as they are listed in the orientation facet. Levy and Guttman (1985) found this elaboration of these two facets to focus their research upon the main issue of interest to them. Elements were added to facets to allow a broader and more detailed study to be undertaken.

Facet D was added to the mapping specification. This lists the social institution components of a social value (life, property, principles/regulations, procedures). Facet C is specified so as to modify facet D in terms of the generality or specificity of the respective institution. The modified mapping sentence was produced initially to explain the data Levy and Guttman had gathered. However, the revisions were also made to enable future research to assemble more well-structured items when investigating fundamental problem values (Levy and Guttman, 1985).

Values as guiding principles

In another study conducted by Schlomitt Levy, social values were investigated as they perform in the role of guiding principles in life

(Levy, 1986). In this research, as in the research reviewed above, the general mapping sentence for social values was extended to bring more social values within its definition. This was then modified in accordance with context. The revised version was then employed in the construction of research items and hypotheses. The mapping sentence is considerably more complex than any of those reported in the previously detailed studies. Indeed, it includes nine content facets. The mapping sentence for observations on social values requires a respondent to assess the: (facet A) importance to/execution by/ attainment by himself of a: (facet B) social precept (situation/ behaviour) to a: (facet C) given reference group (himself/most people/his [sic] government/unspecified) by: (facet D) internal/ external behaviour in a: (facet E) series of modalities (cognitive/ affective/instrumental). The object is then specified as being (facet F) personal/interpersonal/impersonal in support of: (facet G) one's own well-being/the state's well-being/other precepts/the precept itself, which originates from: (facet H) general/specific aspects of: (facet I) institutional components (principles/procedures/manpower/property) in general with: (facet J) the areas of life (social acceptability/ religion/family/society/government and politics/leisure/work/econo- mics) in general. Respondents were then to answer in terms of their assessment of the social support the precept provided. As can be seen, such a mapping sentence is highly complex and is essentially a theoretical statement of the content area.

This mapping sentence was reduced in size to enable questionnaire items to be generated. The reduction of the size and complexity of a mapping sentence is often performed in order to address specific research problems. The Levy (1986) mapping sentence was used to develop a list of twenty-eight social values. Respondents were then asked to indicate the degree to which they considered each value important as a guiding principle in the lives of both themselves and others. Therefore, each question referred to the importance of the value objective in itself and not as a means of attaining other goals (this is shown in element one of facet A).

Facet J is a life area facet. It specifies the life areas of specific concern within each questionnaire item. This form of facet was not present in either of the previously discussed mapping sentences. The reason for this was that the aforementioned research was concerned with only one specific life area. This mapping sentence posits nine elements of life area (with further subregions). It further hypothesises that life area will be modified by the judgements contained in facet H. Through specifying more facets in this way it is possible to hypothesise more complex relationships. However, the facet researcher will often choose first to develop a complex mapping sentence for a research area. Having done this, the specific facets may then be isolated for more detailed forms of analysis.

Indeed, the mapping sentence that was used in Levy's research was an abbreviated form of a mapping sentence developed to observe social values as guiding principles in life (Levy, 1986). The difference between these two sentences is not in the number of facets present. Rather, in the case of facets A, C and G (in the revised sentence), only one element is included for each facet (these facets are held constant). Adopting this procedure enables the relationships both within and between the remaining facets to be hypothesised and tested.

In the first stage of testing the hypotheses of a mapping sentence, correlation (monotonicity) coefficients are calculated between each pairing of items in a study. These coefficients for the Levy study showed that some of the relationships between variables are negative (with values up to −0.17). These negative relationships are unusual in facet research. This is because (as already noted in previous chapters) observations are designed in order to address a single content area and, as such, it would be expected that all of these homogeneous items were positively correlated. Levy explains the negative correlations in her data by stating that:

> although all these values share the common concept of 'guiding principle', 'the extent of importance' does not refer to that general concept, but rather to the value itself as a guiding principle. There may be contradictions between various values as guiding principles, especially if they are not recognised as such in society. Thus, one cannot assume that all correlations among the values will be positive or zero.
>
> (Levy, 1986: 12)

Closer inspection of the coefficients between value pairings reveals that negative relationships are systematically and logically between specific variables. For example, as was noted earlier, religious values are negatively related to leisure values. To understand the overall structure of correlations between items, Levy performed Similarity Structure Analysis (SSA). This geometric analysis method presents each value item in two-dimensional plots of multidimensional space such that the greater the distance between two items, the lower the non-linear coefficient for the pairing. This relationship is held constant between all combinations of item pairings. A facet is a meaningful component of respondents' experience of the area under investigation. These facets structure responses and are identifiable in SSA. The individual items in a series of two-dimensional plots together form geometric shapes which, if present in SSA, can support the existence of a facet in an analysis. A mapping sentence for a study lists hypothesised structure (expected facets) which may be disconfirmed in later SSA through their non-presence. Further details of SSA, along with examples from the results of the present research, are given in the next chapter. Levy's analysis revealed that a three-dimensional cylindrical-shaped space best represented relationships between value items. In this space each value item occupied a point within the cylinder.

Such cylindrically shaped space in facet theory is called a cylindrex. This form of partitioning of space has been found in several research studies from a variety of research domains (Levy, 1985). The two-dimensional SSA plots together form the three-dimensional cylindrex of Levy's data. The two projections are orthogonally related in the combined form of a cylinder.

Levy's analysis revealed partitioning in a circular order corresponding to the elements of facet J (life area). A circular arranged 'polarising' facet has been found in a large number of facet studies to be the best representation of the qualitative role played by a life area facet. The modality and mode facets (facets D and E) were also present in this plot. The two-dimensional interpositioning of the two facets show that evaluations present in facet J are modified by those inherent in facets D and E. Thus, life area judgements are seen to be 'modified' by whether they are internally or externally expressed behaviours.

The third facet of this analysis demarcated values in accordance with each value item referring to a value situation or behaviour (facet B), which combined orthogonally with facets J and D/E to form a $(3 \times 2) \times 2$ classification for values as guiding principles in life.

The value of social control

Levy and Guttman (1981c) provide an example of an extension in the use of the general mapping sentence for social values (Figure 5.1). In doing this they use the mapping sentence to guide their research through the design of questionnaire items. Levy and Guttman found that as all the questionnaire items addressed a common value object, all were monotonically interrelated.

The values in this study were all concerned with social control. The authors hypothesised three elements to be present in a life area social control facet. The facet and facet elements of this study embodied the positive to negative attitudes of respondents towards the: result, application, approach (facet A) of social control by the country's government in life area: political, economics, religion, general (facet B).

This shows that the observations are to be made of the positiveness of respondents' attitude to the three forms of social control within the four life areas. Consequently, it is attitudes which are being assessed. However, as these attitudes are towards the value of social control for respondents, the study is of social values.

The mapping sentence hypothesises two orthogonal facets of control type and life area, with three and four elements respectively. SSA of the study's data found support for these facets. The life area took the structural form of a circumplex with the facet polarising assessments (life area facets are discussed in Levy, 1981c). The control type facets were found to be quantifiably differentiable. The two facets contained independent judgements and were therefore orthogonal: for each evaluation of a questionnaire item made in terms of the life area it addressed an independent assessment of control type.

A similar structure was obtained for both the Israeli and Swiss samples in the study. However, Levy and Guttman (1981c) made the important point that: 'Having established a similarity in the general structure of values . . . it is worth examining the difference in extent of positiveness on each value separately.' (Levy and Guttman, 1981c: 57). The same authors continued their study by analysing the average values attained on each of the questionnaire items. They went on to stress that: 'Similarity in structure of correlations does not necessarily imply similarity in level [averages] . . . there are differences among the various countries in the extent of positiveness with regard to different topics, despite similarity in the structure' (Levy and Guttman, 1981c: 56).

Continuation of social value research

At a recent international conference, it was reported that facet research employing the mapping sentence for social values was continuing. However, the populations now being studied had been broadened to include subjects from countries not previously sampled (Levy and Meyer-Schweizer, 1989). The findings of facet research that has employed the mapping sentence are summarised below.

Specific content area

The specific content area of social values may be defined by the addition/deletion of facets/facet elements from the general mapping sentence for social values.

Relationships between values

These may be expected to be non-negative only if the values observed are oriented towards a single general principle and this principle is clearly recognised by respondents.

Life area of value

These may be specified and investigated as a constant within a mapping sentence. Alternatively, they may be specified by multiple facet elements. Within social values research, life area facets are usually found to be arranged as a circumplex.

Behaviour modality facet

'The behaviour modality facet can play different roles under different circumstances, depending on the notions of order of the other content facets of design. This simple looking facet can require very complex consideration' (Levy, 1985: 89).

Value range

The range facet specifies the responses that the researcher will observe and gather during a study. Attitudes are cognitive dispositions which are arranged along a positive to negative dimension. Social values are ordered from positive to negative towards an object. These therefore fulfil the criteria to enable their classification as attitudes. However, values are specific in that positiveness is related to the importance of existence, attainment or maintenance of the object of value. The actual behaviour which is measured may be cognitive, affective or instrumental towards the value item.

It is possible to assess environmental concern in terms of its perceived importance to a social group. In such an assessment, environmental concern is being investigated as a social value. The general mapping sentence that has been developed in the research reviewed above forms a template which may be used in value investigations. The adaptation and modification of the general mapping sentence to investigate the social value of environmental concern will be undertaken in the present research. However, the first stage in achieving this contextualisation of the mapping will be a series of exploratory studies. The hypotheses implicit in the mapping sentence will then be subjected to investigation.

In the next chapter, details are given of the design of a series of exploratory studies. These will directly address the content (life) area of environmental conservation activities. The sample for this investigation will be environmental conservation employees. Restricting the sample to this 'knowledgeable' group is intentional: interviewees will be asked to identify actions and activities within environmental conservation and subsequently to assess the similarities between activities. Facet analysis will be used as a multidimensional geometric technique for the exploratory analysis of this data. This will enable a taxonomy representative of the respondent sample's dimensions of evaluation of the similarities and dissimilarities between environmental conservation activities to be assembled. Content facets (and their elements) for the environmental conservation life area will be identified and a mapping sentence produced.

The mapping sentence produced at this stage will be reflective of individual values. In order to achieve the aims of this research and to investigate environmental concern as a social value, this mapping sentence will lead to the development of a series of questionnaire studies. To facilitate the development of these studies, the individual values mapping sentence will be combined with the Levy and Guttman (1985) general mapping sentence for social values (Figure 5.1). Questionnaires will be designed to enable examination of both specific environmental concerns and more general environmental concern.

SURVEY DESIGN

In the present research both the life area and mode facets will be present. The external mode element alone will be used, as the only environmental-concern-related value reported in the literature, 'to protect flora and fauna', was found by Levy (1986) to be an external modality social value. The situation and behaviour elements of the second mode facet will both be included.

From inspection of the texts on facet theory (e.g., Canter, 1985a;

Shye, 1978a), it is clear that it has been used in many different areas of social research. The studies briefly reviewed above are directly applicable to the present area of research: environmental concern. As has been noted from the literature, facet research has provided a template which may be used to aid in the design and interpretation of research viewing social values. However, the area of environmental concern values has not been studied by facet researchers, and as a consequence no precise statement in regard to the structure of this attitudinal area exists. Therefore, the initial survey that will be undertaken will be exploratory in its nature and will aim to provide a template of the semantic structure of environmental concern in the form of a mapping sentence. Canter (1985b) comments in some detail upon the procedure of developing facet research projects. He cites the development of an initial mapping sentence as the first objective of this form of research. However, he also notes the diverse ways in which a mapping sentence may be developed.

> The initial mapping sentence may be developed from any of a mixture of sources. If the area of research has already been thoroughly studied within a facet framework, . . . then already established mapping sentences will exist which can be raided from the particular purpose that the researcher has in mind.
>
> (Canter, 1985b: 266)

Details of the design of this study are presented in the following chapter.

6 Exploratory studies: design, samples, procedures and results

The design of the research instruments to be used in the exploratory studies are outlined in this chapter, including the logistics for the research design. The samples for each of the studies will also be discussed. This will be followed by information in regard to the procedure adopted in each study. Later in the chapter, data analysis of results will be presented. The studies will be presented in the order in which the surveys were conducted.

EXPLORATORY STUDY 1: REPERTORY GRID INTERVIEW STUDY OF ENVIRONMENTAL CONSERVATION EMPLOYEES' ATTITUDES TOWARDS THEIR PROFESSION'S ACTIVITIES

In the previous chapters it has been found that no single definition or classification of environmental concern is present within the social science literature. In order to remedy this omission it was decided to conduct a series of repertory grid interviews with employees from the environmental conservation profession. These studies were designed to assess respondents' personal understanding of environmental conservation. In doing this a detailed classification system will be developed for environmental conservation actions and issues as these are understood by respondents from the sample. After this classification system has been assembled, it will be used as a template to develop research instruments that reflect environmental concern in a way that is meaningful to respondents. In order to enable the exploration of the personal meaning of environmental concern, two repertory grid studies were designed; the first of these is reported below, after a brief description of the repertory grid approach.

Repertory grid technique

The repertory grid technique was developed as a means of collecting data within the framework of personal construct theory (Kelly, 1955; Fransella and Bannister, 1977). The repertory grid technique was designed by Kelly (1955) as a technique for measuring personality. More specifically, repertory grids measure cognitive assessments of the perceived similarities between a series of items (the procedure for achieving this is detailed below). Kelly (1955) labels these assessments, which the individual makes, as personal constructs. Through requiring respondents to differentiate between items that have been selected, or supplied, as being representative of a research domain, the psychologist develops a picture of a respondent's personal understanding of this domain.

The repertory grid is a means by which the researcher may bring some order to an attitudinal complex. Fransella and Bannister (1970) describe the repertory grid procedure as: 'a way of getting individuals to tell you, in mathematical terms, the coherent picture they have of say . . . [a specified object]' (Fransella and Bannister, 1970: 59). Kelly further emphasises the point that human beings possess clear understanding of the things they do in their lives. It is these cognitions that Kelly states as being of greatest importance in psychological investigations that attempt to produce understanding of human behaviour: 'the ultimate exploration of human behaviour lies in examining man's undertakings, the questions he asks, the lines of enquiry he initiates, and the strategies he employs' (Kelly, 1969: 16).

Many forms of repertory grids have been, and are being, used in psychological enquiry. However, all of the different grids have the same basic characteristics (Fransella and Bannister 1977). Grids are all attempts to:

1 elicit from a person, the relationship between a set of constructs;
2 develop understanding of the ways in which these dimensions of understanding (constructs) interrelate;
3 all grids are context-specific (they are designed to assess specified content domains);
4 they are all of a quantifiable format which allows statistical analysis.

The mathematical component of the repertory grid is extremely important in the present research. Kelly (1955: 277–291) developed a non-parametric technique for the mathematical analysis of repertory grids. In the present research a facet theory approach is being adopted, this too employs non-parametric analysis procedures.

Repertory grid technique has been applied to a large variety of research settings, including the study of socio-political issues (Slater, 1980). A review of the application of the techniques is provided by Beail (1985), whilst Phillips (1989) develops a critical review of the use and misuse of the approach in applied research and work settings. More specifically, Phillips notes how there are principles that the researcher must be aware of during the different stages of administering, analysing and interpreting a repertory grid. Throughout her paper, Phillips issues warnings about labelling any study that employs a 'repertory grid like approach' as personal construct research. These caveats have been noted but will not be further commented upon as the present research will employ a repertory grid approach but will not refer the results to construct psychology.

The sample

The sample in this study was of employees working in environmental conservation. Organisations concerned with a wide range of actions and issues within the environmental movement were selected. This was an attempt to include a variety of the many different environmental conservation activities and jobs within the research. Once the organisations had been selected they were approached and their assistance in conducting the research interviews was requested. On no occasion was any difficulty encountered in obtaining an organisation's permission for their employees to be approached. After an organisation had agreed to participate, individual employees within the organisation were approached and an interview requested with them.

The selection of individual respondents proceeded along the following lines. Individual employees were identified in terms of the operations they performed in their work. Individuals selected for possible inclusion in the sample on the basis of this categorisation. Attempts were made to include respondents from as many different types of work as possible. Individual employees were then asked if they were willing to be interviewed. All individuals and employing organisations approached agreed to participate; this resulted in a sample of sixteen respondents being assembled. However, before the interviews commenced, three potential respondents withdrew. This left thirteen subjects who, it was decided, formed an adequate sample for the study. Table 6.1 shows

Table 6.1   Respondents' gender, work area and work type (individual grids)

GENDER	
Males	5
Females	8
WORK AREA*	
Urban conservationists	6
Rural conservationists	3
Global conservationists	6
Single-issue conservationists	3
WORK TYPE	
Education	1
Administration	3
Information officer	1
Conservation planning	3
Landscape architect	2
Conservation research	2
Reserve warden	1

Note: This category represents the major areas of respondents' work; as such, some respondents fell into more than one of these categories

the thirteen respondents' employment categories and gender. Of the initial sixteen interviewees who agreed to participate in the study, the three potential respondents who withdrew before the interview stage were members of the following categories: 3 males, 2 urban conservation, 1 rural conservation, 2 educational conservation, 1 landscape architect. This resulted in the sample shown in Table 6.1.

No other variables were controlled for in the opportunity sampling of respondents. As this initial stage of the research took an exploratory format, no mapping sentence was specified or used to guide subsequent data analysis.

Procedure

Once the thirteen respondents had agreed to participate in the study, interviews with each of the respondents were arranged and conducted. Each interview was carried out at the interviewee's workplace, with only the interviewer and interviewee present.

In conducting a repertory grid study that took the conservation of the natural environment as its subject matter, no a priori rationale existed for the specification of features of environmental conservation as elements in a repertory grid study. This was owing to the many different scales used to assess environmental concern in the literature.

This was also true of grid constructs. It was therefore decided to elicit both elements and constructs from each respondent individually.

Each interview lasted between one and three hours and included the completion of a repertory grid. During the initial stages of each interview the respondent and interviewer informally discussed environmental conservation. The interviewee was then asked to identify all the categories of environmental conservation issues and actions that they were able to, and, by discussion, the categories were reduced to the minimum number of separately identifiable areas of conservation action. Between six and twelve separate areas were identified by any one respondent, and a total of ninety-one (non-exclusive) categories were obtained from the whole sample (these are listed in Appendix A.1). For each subject, their list of actions was then entered on a repertory grid as elements. Respondents were then required to differentiate between triads of elements and to report these differences and similarities. Differentiation was achieved by respondents replying to the question 'Look at these three areas of environmental conservation, can you tell me how two of these are similar to one another but are different from the third?' This is the procedure known as triadic sort technique (Fransella and Bannister, 1977). The distinctions obtained in this way were then entered onto repertory grids as emergent construct poles. The contrasting pole was identified by answering the question 'What would be the opposite or contrast of this (referring to an emergent pole) within environmental or nature conservation?' These answers were then also entered into the respondent's repertory grid. Triads of elements were repeatedly selected by the interviewer for subjects to differentiate between. This procedure was repeated until no new constructs were emerging. When the process of identifying elements and construct was finally complete, respondents were asked to identify the more favourable pole (emergent or contrast) for each construct. Elements were then rated in terms of the constructs. The element best described by, or containing the most of, a construct's favourable pole was given a score of 1 on this construct. The element best described by the less favoured pole was given the score of the total number of elements present for the respondent. All elements were then ranked without ties at a point between these two extremes.

In order to investigate environmental concern as a valued attitude, it was decided to produce a standardised repertory grid. The design of this study is reported in the section that follows.

EXPLORATORY STUDY 2: A STANDARD REPERTORY GRID STUDY OF ENVIRONMENTAL CONSERVATION EMPLOYEES' ATTITUDES TOWARDS THEIR PROFESSION'S ACTIVITIES

Sample

The population of respondents from which the sample for this investigation was to be drawn is the same population as was used in the individual repertory grid study: people working full-time in the environmental conservation profession.

In this study several environmental conservation groups were initially contacted. These organisations were asked to circulate test materials to their employees. All of the organisations approached agreed to do this. In order to obtain responses from as wide a cross-section of environmental conservation employees as possible, a variety of different organisations was selected. Each participating organisation was sent five repertory grids along with detailed instructions for their use and reply-paid envelopes for returning these. This resulted in thirty-five repertory grid packages being sent out. The organisations were asked to distribute the repertory grids to a varied selection of employees. Resulting from this procedure, thirteen completed and usable repertory grids were returned. A breakdown of respondents is given in Table 6.2.

Table 6.2 Respondents' gender, work area and work type (group grid)

GENDER	
Males	8
Females	5
WORK AREA*	
Urban conservationists	4
Rural conservationists	7
Global conservationists	3
WORK TYPE	
Education	3
Administration	5
Conservation planning	3
Conservation research	1
Reserve warden	1

*Note: This category represents the major areas of respondents' work; as such, some respondents fell into more than one of these categories

Repertory grid design and procedure

The repertory grid that was circulated to environmental conservation employees in this study had both elements and constructs supplied. These were derived by assembling all different elements and all different constructs which subjects had supplied in the initial repertory grid study. This resulted in a repertory grid being assembled which had nineteen elements and forty-nine constructs. Each grid had a detailed set of instructions attached to it which was designed to enable a respondent to complete the grid unaided. Both the grid and the instructions went through several iterations in development. The instructions were tested upon a group of undergraduate students and members of the general public before the final version was arrived at (see Appendix A.2 for an example of the standard repertory grid and instructions).

Each grid was accompanied by a reply-paid and addressed envelope. Each respondent was given a date by which they were required to return the completed grid. Eleven completed and usable grids were returned by this date. On this predetermined date all organisations were contacted and requested to contact their employees who had not returned the grid and request them to do so. This resulted in a further two grids being returned. Unfortunately, several further grids were returned a considerable time after the final return date. Consequently, these grids were not included in the analyses. The results from the above two studies are now presented.

RESULTS 1: ENVIRONMENTAL CONSERVATION EMPLOYEES' ATTITUDES TOWARDS THEIR PROFESSION'S ACTIVITIES: INDIVIDUAL ENVIRONMENTAL CONSERVATION REPERTORY GRIDS

Reported in this section are: (a) the result from a series of repertory grid interviews, and (b) the results from the administration of a standardised repertory grid based upon the results of the first-stage interviews. Similarity Structure Analysis, otherwise known as Smallest Space Analysis (SSA) (Borg and Lingoes, 1987), is employed to identify similarities present in the data of the repertory grids. Through the use of SSA as a graphical exploratory data analysis technique (du Toit, Steyn and Stumpf, 1986), the result is the production of a mapping sentence. Such a mapping sentence would then provide a framework through which the similarities which are present within and which structure a data set may be understood. The similarities are represented as regions (facets and facet elements) in arrays of spatial plots. The combination of these facets as they relate to the subject of investigation result in a research design instrument known as a mapping sentence (Canter, 1985b). This mapping sentence may then be used to guide future research design. Through this procedure, SSA may be used first to explore data structure and later to confirm such structure in allied contexts.

Initially, the facets that have emerged from the analysis of the repertory grid data are presented. Subsequently, the potential usefulness of these facets in designing research instruments for use in the next stage of this enquiry, into environmental concern, will be briefly discussed. It should be noted at this stage that the square boxes within which SSA plots are enclosed should not be interpreted as axes to the plot. Rather, it is more useful to think of these as simply being present to aid in the presentation. This is the case for all SSA plots in this book.

The results from the analysis of a series of repertory grid interviews with individual environmental conservation employees are presented in the section that follows.

Data analysis

The data that emerged from each repertory grid were analysed to reveal its smallest space partitioning using Similarity Structure Analysis (SSA). This was performed individually for all thirteen subjects in order to reveal semantic similarity between grid elements. It was only possible to analyse grid data individually owing to the individual nature of the grids; elements and constructs were different for each respondent and therefore it was not possible to collapse grids into a single grid representative of the whole sample. The analysed data therefore revealed facets of semantic similarity for each respondent.

The plots resulting from the SSA are summarised in this chapter. A schematic form of these results is produced through the combination of the results of all individual grids. The plots in Figures 6.1 and 6.2 are summaries of how the individual facets were found to combine for three of the thirteen respondents. Other individuals had sub-combinations of these three facets (in similar combinatorial structure).

SSA of the repertory grid interview data is schematically presented in the diagrams of the plots contained in Figures 6.1 and 6.2. This analysis revealed four facets which respondents possessed in a variety of complete and incomplete combinations. The facets were: environmental conservation life area, scale of environmental conservation action or issue, relevance to environmental conservation and personal relevance to the respondent. Guttman Lingoes coefficients of alienation were all at levels of 0.20 or below. These levels are usually taken as acceptable (Kenny, 1981). A four-dimensional explanation of environmental conservation experience for conservation employees is therefore proposed. Each of the four facets is now considered in some detail, and an overall facet model compiled from these individual plots is also proposed.

Environmental conservation life area

Figure 6.1 shows the life area referent facet in schematic form. This facet formed a circular structure distinguishing between life areas associated with environmental conservation. The plot of this facet shows clear partitioning existed in the following format. This reflected the 'socialness' or 'ecologicalness' of conservation actions. The elements of this facet were: ecological conservation (conservation primarily for the sake of the environment); educational conservation (conservation aimed primarily to educate or inform the public); social conservation (conservation primarily for the sake of human beings).

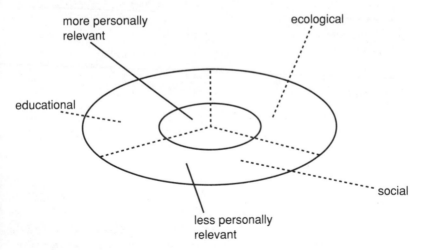

Figure 6.1 Individual repertory grid study. Schematic representation of life area facet and personal relevance facet

This facet makes it possible to state that the environmental conservation employees in the sample possess a facet of their assessment of environmental conservation actions and issues which assigns these to one of the above three life areas. The areas form a modulating continuum and are arranged: ecological, educational, social. As can be seen in Figure 6.1, a second facet was present in the same plot in multidimensional space. This second facet of assessment modified the judgements of the life area facet with assessments of personal relevance.

Personal relevance facet

The facet took the format of a modulating facet and modified the assessment criteria present in the referent facet A, of life area (Figure 6.1). The structure of the facet was as follows. It reflected the extent of personal experience or personal value attached to a given environmental conservation action or issue. The elements of this facet were: personally relevant/less personally relevant.

The repertory grid elements that were of greater personal relevance (issues and actions with which the individual had personal contact or to which they ascribed importance) were placed centrally in the plot. Those elements of less personal relevance, in the above terms, were found peripherally in this projection of multidimensional space. As this facet appears in the same plot as the life area facet, the two facets can be seen to interact. What this means in practice is that assessments of the social, educational or ecological content of an issue or action will be modified by the criteria of the personal relevance of the issue or action under consideration.

Physical scale facet

A second circularly arranged facet was discovered during the analysis of repertory grid data for this respondent sample (Figure 6.2). This facet made reference to the physical scale addressed by an action or issue.

This facet reflected the scale of an action or issue, in both its area of environmental concern, the scale of actions and operations associated with this, and in terms of the resources it consumed. The elements of this facet were: ethical conservation; global conservation; international conservation; national conservation; local conservation.

These elements are found to be circularly ordered (the facet is angular), similar to the life area facet. It performs a similar role in structuring assessments to the life area facet (Figure 6.1). As with the life area facet, the facet of conservation scale was also modified by a second facet. This is shown by the presence of a second facet in the same SSA projection and by the relative positioning of these two facets within the projection. The modifying facet in this case being a focus of conservation relevance.

Conservation relevance facet

This reflected the perceived relevance to environmental conservation of the specified action or issue. The elements of this facet were: more conservation relevance; less conservation relevance.

Figure 6.2 shows that the configuration of this facet is such that the facet elements considered to be of greater relevance to environmental conservation were placed centrally in the plot. Those items of lesser importance in these terms were found peripherally. The facet of conservation relevance was found in the same SSA plot as the referent of conservation scale with the facet modifying the judgements present in the facet of conservation scale. Therefore, for environmental conservation employees in our sample, the assessment of the physical scale of a conservation action or issue interacted with assessments of the action's or issue's perceived relevance to conservation and the environment.

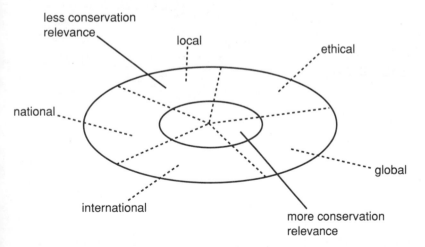

Figure 6.2 Individual repertory grid study. Schematic representation of scale facet and environmental relevance facet

Individual facets of assessment

The facet model proposed above reflects the ways in which environmental conservation is understood and assessed by the sample of respondents in the study. The specified facets are separately identifiable, interrelated areas of the sample of environmental conservation employees' understanding of actions and issues within the environmental conservation movement. It must be noted, however, that not all four facets were necessarily present for each respondent. Table 6.3 shows a breakdown of the four facets as they appeared for each respondent. It is important to note that when any of the specified facets did appear, they were present in the format shown in Figures 6.1 and 6.2 on all occasions. This being the case, the following may be concluded: whilst the judgements embodied in the facet model were not present in their complete, combined form for all subjects, due to similar structure of the facets in all instances of their occurrence, the model may be seen as depicting the 'complete' experience and evaluations for the sample investigated.

No statement in regard to the facets as they relate to any background characteristics of respondents can be made. This is owing to the relatively small number of respondents and also because no a priori rationale exists for the specification of such relationships. Similarly,

Table 6.3 Breakdown of facets by respondents

	FACETS			
	Life area	*Personal relevance*	*Environmental relevance*	*Physical scale*
Respondent				
1	*	*	*	
2	*	*	*	*
3	*	*	*	*
4	*	*		*
5	*	*	*	
6	*	*	*	
7	*	*	*	
8	*	*	*	
9	*			
10		*		*
11	*	*	*	
12	*	*	*	*
13	*		*	

* indicates the presence of the specified factor for the respondent

it is not possible to make statements in regard to the presence or absence of facets in relation to background characteristics. It should be noted that a circularly arranged (qualitative) facet (scale and/or life area) was present in all analyses.

Combined model of facets of assessment

The four facets listed above and shown schematically in Figures 6.1 and 6.2 compose two forms of assessment, each modified by separate and different facets of relevance. The two radex configurations so formed occupy an interacting position in four-dimensional space. The two radexes illustrate the manner in which individual respondents utilised two angular (circularly arranged) and two radial (linear) facets in evaluating environmental conservation.

Each of the radial assessments was modified by a different modifying judgement: an area of environmental conservation was ascribed to one of the life areas of social, educational or ecological, and was conjointly assigned to being of more or less relevance to the respondent. Simultaneously, the same area of environmental conservation was allocated to one of the five physical scales: ethical, global, international, national and local. At the same time it was deemed to be of more or less relevance in terms of environmental conservation. Having discovered these four facets of respondents' experience, a convenient manner in which the facets may be stated is through the specification of a mapping sentence.

Mapping sentence for environmental conservation

Mapping sentences are statements that arise through the specification of all the variables (facets and elements) within the area of enquiry, along with any relevant background features (population or observational characteristics). Connective words are used between facets to suggest their interrelatedness and a 'range' into which data may be classified is specified.

From the results of the present study it is possible to formulate the following mapping sentence for environmental conservation (Figure 6.3). The mapping sentence represents a framework within which the attitudes of environmental conservation employees may be understood.

Person (x) being an environmental conservation employee, assesses the specified –

Facet A
(social conversation)
(educational conservation)
(ecological conservation)

action or issue, which is of

Facet B
(more personal relevance)
(less personal relevance)

being a

Facet C
(ethical)
(global)
(international)
(national)
(local)

action or issue, which is of

Facet D
(more conservation relevance)
(less conservation relevance)

to be,

Range
More – to – less

of the specified construct.

Figure 6.3 Environmental conservation mapping sentence (individual evaluations)

Conclusions (exploratory study 1)

The study reported above has investigated the personal understanding of environmental conservation for a sample of employees in this area of work. The results from this investigation clearly show a common structure to these evaluations. However, owing to the idiosyncratic nature of the study (the individual nature of the repertory grids completed), few (if any) comments may be made in regard to the topic of major interest to this present research, namely the structure of environmental concern as it exists as a social value.

In order to investigate environmental concern as a social value for the same population as completed the repertory grids reported above, it was decided to produce a standardised repertory grid.

RESULTS 2: ENVIRONMENTAL CONSERVATION REPERTORY GRID GROUP STUDY

The results will now be presented for the standard repertory grid study administered to a sample of environmental conservation employees.

Data analysis

Data analysis was again performed using SSA on elements in the repertory grid (this was similar to the procedure adopted in the previous exploratory study). However, due to the common nature of the grids, all data were analysed together. This produced a series of plots for this group of environmental employees.

Through SSA of the data, three facets were revealed with a Guttman Lingoes coefficient of alienation at the acceptable level of 0.15. The facets were: (a) life area, (b) relevance to environmental conservation, and (c) action purpose. A three-facet structure to conservation employees' group attitudes is therefore proposed. These results are now considered in some detail.

Life area facet

Figure 6.4 shows the plot of the life area facet. This facet was circular in structure which showed it to differentiate life areas associated

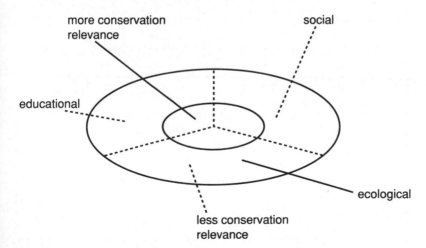

Figure 6.4 Group repertory grid study. Schematic representation of life area facet and conservation relevance facet

with environmental conservation. Partitioning reflected the 'socialness' or 'ecologicalness' of conservation actions. The elements of
this facet were: ecological conservation (conservation primarily for
the sake of the environment); ethical/educational conservation
(conservation concerned with education or environmental morals);
social conservation (conservation primarily for the sake of human
beings).

The facet elements form a radial continuum and are arranged:
ecological, ethical, educational, social. In Figure 6.4 a second facet is
present in the same plane of multidimensional space. This is the
second facet of assessment: the facet of environmental conservation
relevance.

Facet of environmental conservation relevance

This facet, which is also shown in Figure 6.4, was a modular facet,
modifying the assessment present in the facet of life area. The facet
reflected the extent of conservational value attached to a given
environmental conservation action or issue. The elements of this facet
were: of greater conservational relevance; of lesser conservational
relevance.

Items from the element of greater conservational relevance were

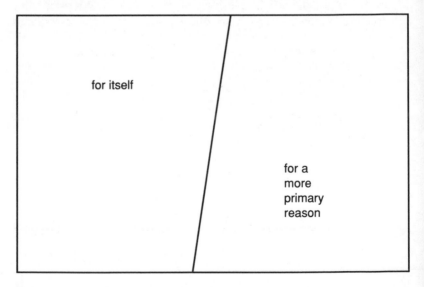

Figure 6.5 Group repertory grid study. Schematic representation of action
purpose facet

placed centrally in the plot. Those items from the element of less conservational relevance were found to be located more peripherally. As this facet appears in the same plot as the life area facet, the two facets interact.

Action purpose facet

This third facet is found in a separate plot and can be seen in Figure 6.5. The division of the facet is in two parallel halves. The two sections divided conservation actions and issues in terms of their purpose. The structure of this facet was an action or issue undertaken in order to have an effect – for itself – for a more primary aim within conservation.

Conclusions (exploratory study 2)

This study has investigated the understanding of environmental conservation for a group of respondents employed to work in this area. The large number of elements and constructs (19, 49) with the small number of respondents (13) was an essentially unstable data set.

Person (x) being an environmental conservation employee, assesses the specified –

Facet A
(social conservation)
(educational/ethical conservation)
(ecological conservation)

action or issue, which is of

Facet B
(conservation relevance)
(less conservation relevance)

Facet C
(for itself)
(for a more primary reason)

to be

Range
More – to – less

of the specified construct.

Figure 6.6 Environmental conservation mapping sentence (group evaluations)

However, the facets present in SSA suggest that the similarities in responses to the grid task were both generalisable and stable. The results of this group's standard repertory grid show that the structure of this analysis is represented by the three facets detailed in the mapping sentence in Figure 6.6.

The results clearly show that a common structure for the social evaluation of environmental conservation exists for this respondent sample, as shown in the mapping sentence above. Inspection of the two facet models (mapping sentences) produced in these two studies reveals these to differ significantly. However, these differences and their implications for further studies are discussed in a later section of this book.

The mapping sentence for the internal structure of environmental concern, developed above, will be used to develop a questionnaire. This will investigate environmental concern as a social value. Therefore, the mapping sentence will be used in conjunction with mapping sentences that have been developed in published facet theory research into social values. Attention will now be turned to these investigations.

7 The design, development and results of three studies to evaluate environmental concern

The exploratory studies reported in the previous chapter resulted in a mapping sentence being generated for the internal structure of the evaluation of environmental conservation. Following on from these exploratory investigations of environmental concern activities, the section below will report the design and development of three research investigations to study the social values, attitudes and personal involvement associated with environmental concern. It must be noted at this point that the repertory grid studies were designed to assess the sample of environmental conservation employees' understanding of their profession's activities – their personal understanding of environmental conservation and their personal environmental concern values. However, in the studies presented in this and the following chapters, it will be lay (public) concern for the natural environment that will be assessed. In order to evaluate the structure of environmental concern among this population, two questionnaires will be devised which view specific areas of environmental concern attitudes. A three-part questionnaire will also be developed which will allow the investigation of the entirety of the semantic area specified in the mapping sentence for environmental conservation.

The issues and actions addressed by all of these research instruments will be based upon the mapping sentence in the preceding chapter. The manner in which environmental concern issues are developed into questionnaires will, for each of the questionnaires, be facilitated through reference to the general mapping sentences for social values (Levy, 1986). In this chapter details will be given of the development of these questionnaires. Data arising from the three questionnaires will be analysed using facet analytic techniques. This will be followed by other statistical analyses of the final questionnaire as and where this is appropriate. The results of these analyses will be combined with the results from the earlier repertory grid studies. Together this information will form an answer to the questions that motivated this research.

GENERAL ISSUES IN QUESTIONNAIRE DESIGN

The mapping sentences developed out of the repertory grid studies were used as a template for the design of items to be included in the present questionnaire. The incorporation of facet elements into questions as defined by a mapping sentence can produce potentially complicated statements for respondents to digest. Shye (1979) has demonstrated that if the researcher clearly understands the precise meaning of the elements in the mapping sentence, questions can be developed that express the meaning of each of these elements without explicitly stating them (it is this explicit statement of facet elements which may make facet questionnaires turgid and difficult to understand).

The questionnaires in the present series of studies are derived from and understood through the mapping sentence in Figure 7.1. This mapping sentence is a result of combining the mapping sentences for the internal structure of environmental conservation (Figures 6.3, 6.6) with the Levy (1986) mapping sentence for social values (Figure 5.1). The mode (2) facet is included as it allows the comparison (and the broadening) of the analysis of environmental concern values to include the performance of value-related behaviours. Levy (1986) also adapted an existing social value mapping sentence in her research. In doing this she was able to examine the relationships between assessments of the importance of values, value-related actions and the attainment of value goals. The design of the questionnaires will now be presented separately. The mapping sentence in Figure 7.1 represents an idealised form for the structure of environmental concern attitudes. Furthermore, no specific range is given into which responses may be mapped. Inspection of the environmental concern literature shows immediately that little concern has been paid to the specific range of responses to environmental concern questions. As noted in Chapter 4, it is often the case that different measures of concern have been taken as being equivalent. In this research, different ranges will be used in the different questionnaires in order to permit the direct comparison of these ranges. Thus, environmental concern will be investigated in terms of its perceived value to respondents, the perceived effective-

The extent to which person (x) makes a cognitive assessment of the:

Scale	**Life Area**	**Type**
(local)	(social)	(action)
(national)	(educational)	(issue)
(international)	(ecological)	
(global)		
(ethical)		

issue, within environmental conservation for,

Mode (1)
(itself)
(a more primary purpose)

within environmental conservation, by

Mode (2)		**Range**
(cognitively)	expressing this to be	(very positive)
(behaviourally)		to
		(very negative)

in terms of their concern for the quality of the environment.

Figure 7.1 Mapping sentence for the definition of environmental concern

ness of conservation actions, and respondents' involvement with these actions.

THE DEVELOPMENT OF TWO QUESTIONNAIRES INVESTIGATING THE URGENCY OF ENVIRONMENTAL PROBLEMS AND THE SERIOUSNESS OF ENVIRONMENTAL HAZARDS

From the facets and the facet elements present in the mapping sentence in Figure 7.1 a matrix of facet elements may be produced. This would produce a set of all possible combinations of facet elements in a $1 \times 5 \times 3 \times 2 \times 2 \times 2$ combination, and would result in 120 possible elements. Questions could be then generated which were representative of all of these combinations (an illustration of an exhaustive combination of elements is given in Hackett, Shaw and Kenealy, 1993). However, such a lengthy instrument would be extremely time-consuming for respondents to complete. It may therefore be beneficial to conduct several studies, each of which is specific in terms of its context and in terms of the facet elements that will be included. Furthermore, in specific contexts it is often found that certain facet and facet element combinations are nonsensical.

The instruments developed will investigate attitudes regarding the perceived urgency of environmental problems and the seriousness of selected environmental hazards. The first two questionnaires to be developed will be based upon the division of environmental problems into two categories (such categories of environmental problems have previously been used to classify environmental concern in published research (e.g., Kessel, 1984; Royal Commission on Environmental Pollution, 1984)). Details are now presented of these instruments.

The seriousness of environmental hazards questionnaire

In choosing the specific environmental hazards that were to be included in the questionnaire, items were selected based upon the environmental hazards identified in the questionnaire used by the Royal Commission on Environmental Pollution (1984). It was found that these hazard areas could be represented by elements of the facets in the mapping sentence in Figure 7.1. A further facet of time scale was added to this mapping sentence. This was done as it was thought that when viewing the seriousness of environmental hazards, the time scale over which the seriousness of effect was perceived would be pertinent to respondents.

The revised mapping sentence is given in Figure 7.2. This mapping sentence resulted in $1 \times 3 \times 1 \times 2 \times 1 \times 2 \times 1 =$ twelve possible combinations. All of these twelve elements appeared at least once in the six questions that were selected for the final questionnaire. This small number of questions was chosen for the following two reasons. First, the questionnaire was to be given as a street questionnaire and it was felt that a lengthy instrument was inappropriate. Second, the aim of the study was to attempt to support or refute the environmental concern mapping sentence through direct reference to existing research in this area, and the research used as a model was made up of these elements.

Whilst it may be inappropriate to base conclusions upon facet models that have been derived from such a small number of items, it is not the intention of this research to do this. Rather, the findings from this questionnaire will be combined with the results from two further questionnaire studies. One of these will view another specific area of environmental concern, whilst the other instrument will take a much broader view. In combination, the results from these questionnaire studies will be used to develop further hypotheses about the structure of environmental concern attitudes.

The questionnaire developed to assess the perceived seriousness of

The extent to which person (x) makes a (cognitive) assessment of the:

Time Scale	**Scale**	**Life Area**	**Type**
(present)	(national)	(social)	(issue)
(future)		(ecological)	
(no effect)			

environmental hazard, being a problem in,

Level
(itself) (a direct problem)
(a more primary) (a less direct problem)

within the area of environmental concern, and,

Mode (2)		**Range**
(cognitively)	assesses this to be	(very serious)
		to
		(not very serious)

in terms of their concern for the quality of the environment.

Figure 7.2 Mapping sentence for the seriousness of selected environmental hazards

environmental hazards which resulted from the above procedure can be found in Appendix A.3. In the next section of this chapter the details are given of the construction of a questionnaire to investigate the perceived urgency of selected environmental issues.

The urgency of environmental problems

As with the environmental hazards questionnaire, items to be included in the questionnaire were derived from the results of a published study in the area (Kessel, 1984). The mapping sentence used in generating this questionnaire was again a modification of the mapping sentence in Figure 7.1. The revised mapping sentence is shown in Figure 7.3.

This mapping sentence resulted in $1 \times 1 \times 2 \times 1 \times 2 \times 2 \times 1 =$ eight possible combinations. Each of the eight elements appeared at least once in the ten questions selected for the final questionnaire. The rationale for the inclusion of ten questions in the questionnaire is the same as that given above in respect to item selection for the environmental hazards questionnaire. The questionnaire that was developed to assess the perceived urgency of selected environmental issues can be found in Appendix A.4.

The extent to which person (x) makes a (cognitive) assessment of the:

Scale   **Life Area**   **Type**
(national)   (social)   (issue)
                                   (ecological)

                              Level
being an urgent problem in, (itself)
                              (a more primary)

context within environmental conservation, and with which

                     Level
respondents have   (direct)   personal contact by,
                     (indirect)

Mode (2)   **Range**
(cognitively)   assessing this to be   (very urgent)
                                  to
                                  (not very urgent)

in terms of their concern for the quality of the environment.

Figure 7.3 Mapping sentence for the urgency of selected environmental issues

Samples

In the exploratory repertory grid studies, samples were drawn from a population of individuals working professionally in environmental conservation. This was to sample 'expert opinion' about environmental conservation action and issues. In the studies that follow, samples will be drawn from a 'lay' population.

It was decided to administer the environmental seriousness of pollution and the urgency of environmental issues questionnaires together to a single sample. The sample comprised 211 members of the general public. Respondents were opportunity-sampled in main streets in a British city centre. The survey was carried out at several times of the day and on all days from Monday to Saturday during a single week. Potential respondents were approached and asked if they would complete a short questionnaire. This was completed in the street with the help of the interviewer. Several respondents asked the interviewer questions about the study after completing the questionnaire, and questions were answered honestly and to the best of the interviewer's ability. The interviewer attempted to sample equal numbers of male and female respondents, and to ensure that a wide age range was represented in the sample.

THE DEVELOPMENT OF A QUESTIONNAIRE TO INVESTIGATE SOCIAL VALUES, ATTITUDES AND INVOLVEMENT ASSOCIATED WITH ENVIRONMENTAL CONCERN

Design

In the final and most comprehensive study undertaken, the mapping sentence in Figure 7.1 was used as a template for the design of questionnaire items. This resulted in $1 \times 5 \times 3 \times 2 \times 2 \times 2 = 120$ possible items for inclusion. It was decided, after several iterations of draft questionnaires, that the format to be adopted was the one that would be most easily understood by respondents. To this end, it was decided to develop questions that reflected the elements of the scale and life area facets.

This resulted in a total of twenty-five questions. The mode (2) facet reflecting the form of behaviour that was to be taken as indicative of environmental concern was further subdivided. In the format shown in the mapping sentence (Figure 7.1), this facet has two elements: behavioural and cognitive. It was decided that each of these elements should be represented by two subdivisions. This was in order to facilitate the later investigation of the relationship between different types of attitude towards (cognitive) and different levels of involvement with (behaviour) environmental concern.

In the previous two questionnaires the issue element of the type facet that specifies the modality of environmental concern to be either action or issue was employed in the design. In the present questionnaire it was decided to incorporate the alternate element of actions. This resulted in a $25 \times 4 = 100$ set of questions in the final questionnaire (the final questionnaire is included in Appendix A.5).

The precise wording of questions was finalised after a short pilot study in which fourteen subjects participated. In this study, data were not fully analysed using facet analytic techniques, but were instead analysed to ensure that a wide range of responses was being gathered. Subjects were also encouraged to make suggestions and comments about this. Respondents were also asked about the questionnaire's structure and to state how complicated they thought it would be to complete the questionnaire 'without the aid of the researcher'. In all cases it was felt that there were no problems with self-completion.

Sample and procedure

The questionnaire was given to two samples of undergraduate students. It was decided to use undergraduate students as the population for the study for a number of reasons. First, students were felt to be a relatively well-informed group and would therefore provide useful information when attempting to establish the internal structure of this attitude area. Second, undergraduate students were also a readily available respondent group. Furthermore, the study was attempting to view the internal structure of environmental concern attitudes and not attempting to make comments upon the social or personal correlates of environmental concern and it was therefore felt to be justified to use this group of respondents. Respondents were approached in halls of residence and in refectories and after lectures. These different locations were chosen in order to sample as wide a range of both campus and non-campus living students as was possible. Potential respondents were initially approached and their assistance requested. Those who agreed to participate were given the questionnaire along with instructions for its completion. The names and addresses were taken of residential students and a time was agreed when the completed questionnaires were to be collected.

Non-residential students were approached in a similar manner. However, they were asked to return the completed questionnaire through internal post at the university by an agreed date. In sum, 240 questionnaires were distributed in this manner. A total of 218 completed and usable questionnaires were returned. The results from each of the three questionnaire studies are now presented.

RESULTS 3: URGENCY OF ENVIRONMENTAL PROBLEMS AND SERIOUSNESS OF ENVIRONMENTAL HAZARDS

During this section the results from two attitude surveys will be presented. The first set of results will be from a questionnaire to assess public evaluations of the urgency of selected environmental problems. After this, the results will be detailed from the environmental hazards questionnaire given to the same sample. Similarity Structure Analysis (SSA) (Shye, 1978a, 1985c, 1986) will be performed upon both of these questionnaires. This will result in facets of assessments being established for each study. The environmental hazards questionnaire will also be analysed to reveal how assessments are structured by the facets and facet elements revealed in SSA. This questionnaire was chosen for this partial order format of analysis as the facets specified in its design were ordered making it ideal for this type of analysis. Partial Order Scalogram Analysis (POSA) (Shye, 1978a: Ch. 10; 1985b; 1985d; 1986) will be performed to illustrate the ways in which the facets and facet elements are meaningful divisions of environmental attitudes (to respondents): facets are not simply a researcher-imposed classification system.

The results from the questionnaire investigation into the perceived urgency of environmental problems are first analysed to reveal similarity structure.

Results 3a: the urgency of environmental problems

Responses were analysed using SSA. This revealed three facets of assessment at an acceptable level of stress: GL = 0.15. There now follows a discussion of these facets.

Life area facet

The SSA plot in Figure 7.4 shows the facet of life area. This facet partitioned into two main regions: environmental problems which were primarily 'social' or 'ecological'. In this projection of multidimensional space, the ecological element is placed to the top left of the diagram. The social element is to be seen to the bottom right of the plot. These two elements are divided by the solid line in the diagram. As well as these two regions, the ecological element further divided to reveal three sub-elements. These were environmental problems that addressed pollution issues, ecological waste issues, and resource depletion issues. The sub-elements of this facet were arranged in a manner that reflected primarily ecological or social effect. Ecological items, and elements which had more of a social effect, were located closer to the social region. The more ecological items were placed centrally in the ecological regions.

The structure of this life area facet may therefore be specified:

(a) Social problems
(b) Ecological problems – pollution
                        – waste
                        – resource depletion

The presence of these subregions showed this facet to be an angular facet (to be arranged in a circular order). The main elements of the facet were in the format specified in the mapping sentence. However, the subregions were not hypothesised. The presence of this facet and its structure implied that when evaluating the urgency of the selected environmental problems, respondents assigned each problem to one of the above listed categories.

It may be seen in the plot of the life area facet (Figure 7.4) that some items were located slightly towards the centre of this plot. Indeed, one item (2) was placed centrally, thus effectively removing it from the circular arrangement of the life area facet. This was owing to the influence of a second facet interacting with the facet of life area. The facet was a facet of personal relevance.

Personal relevance facet

The circular arrangement of the life area facet was modulated (modified) by the facet of personal relevance (Figure 7.4). However, only one item in the analysis was of central relevance to respondents

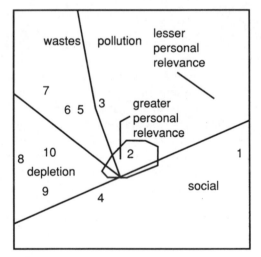

Item numbers
1 noise. 2 air pollution. 3 water polution. 4 over-population.
5 solid waste disposal. 6 toxic waste. 7 nuclear waste.
8 destruction of town/landscape.
9 depletion of natural resources. 10 energy.

Figure 7.4 Projection of the SSA of the urgency of environmental issues questionnaire showing partitioning of the life area facet and personal relevance facet (item 2). Therefore, the element of more personal relevance comprised one item. However, more peripheral environmental problem items approached central positions as they became more personally relevant in terms of their urgency. The elements of this facet were, an environmental problem of:

(a) greater personal relevance
(b) lesser personal relevance

Future research is needed to clarify the role of this facet in structuring evaluations through the inclusion of more items representative of the central element.

Environmental relevance facet

The third facet present in this assessment was a facet of environmental relevance (Figure 7.5). Within this facet were embodied judgements regarding the relevance in, environmental terms, of a specified environmental problem. The elements of the facet were:

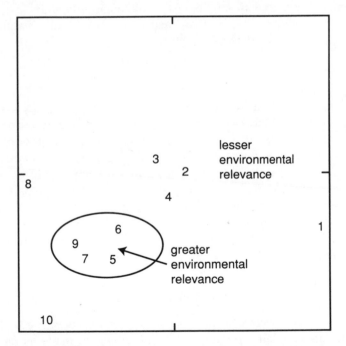

Figure 7.5 Projection of the SSA of the urgency of environmental problems questionnaire showing partitioning of the environmental relevance facet

(a) greater environmental relevance
(b) lesser environmental relevance

The structure of this facet was such that it caused some items to be placed centrally in relation to other items. This structure is characteristic of a modulating facet. This format of facet may cause the judgements carried in a separate facet to be modified. However, in this plot, no other facet was identifiable.

Summary of plots

From the plots presented above, three facets have been identified. The facets identified are: life area; personal relevance; environmental relevance. As well as simply stating the facets of the assessment, the relationships between facets are revealed. The facet of life area radially arranged problems. Respondents perceived the environmental issues to be problems of: pollutants, wastes, resources depletions, or in human terms. These judgements are modified by evaluations of personal relevance. Simultaneously, although relatively independently, judgements were also made by respondents about the environmental relevance of the problem.

Conclusion

To conclude this analysis, the results may be summarised by a series of questions in which each facet of the assessment is represented by a question. These are the questions an individual asks himself or herself each time an evaluation of the urgency of an environmental problem is undertaken. The questions posed regarding the urgency of environmental problems are: How urgent is the social/waste/pollution/resource depletion problem as it is relevant to me? How relevant is this problem in environmental terms? The answers formulated to these questions will effectively determine the evaluation of an environmental problem's urgency.

Results 3b: the seriousness of environmental hazards

Reported in this section of the chapter are the results of the analysis of the questionnaire produced to investigate evaluations of the seriousness of environmental hazards. SSA of data is performed to reveal the structure of attitudes. In the latter sections of this chapter, further analyses will be performed that will provide more details of the facets identified in the section below.

The structure of assessments of the seriousness of environmental hazards

This section reports the results of the analysis of the total data set collected from the administration of the questionnaire. The analysis investigated the mapping sentence in Figure 7.2 through SSA. This produced three facets of assessment at an acceptable level of stress – Guttman Lingoes Coefficient of Alienation (GL) = 0.11 (0.20 or below usually being accepted). The facets are presented in the section that follows.

Life area facet

Figure 7.6 shows the projection of the life area facet. The plot clearly partitioned into two regions, namely social conservation and ecological conservation. Items referring to the social or human consequences of pollution were located towards the upper left of the plot. The region towards the lower right was comprised of items addressing the ecological consequences of hazards. This facet divided issues in terms of the life area of the consequences of the specified environmental hazards. The facet was present in the format specified in the mapping sentence (Figure 7.1). From the structure of this facet it may be stated that the first facet in the assessment of the seriousness of one of the specified environmental hazards involved that its consequences be ascribed to either the human or the ecological areas of life. Due to the existence of only two facet elements, the facet took a dichotomous format. However, a similar life area facet appeared in the SSA of both the environmental urgency questionnaire and the repertory grid interviews. In these analyses the life area facet contained the above two elements. In addition a third element of education was present: the arrangement of this facet was circular. Closer inspection of this facet reveals a circular arrangement in the positioning of items rather than a dichotomy. Items were arranged in a circle as follows: less social, social, less social, less ecological, ecological, less ecological. . . . This arrangement leads to the conclusion that the circular order of a circumplex was present in the analysis.

It should be noted that in the present analysis the life area facet has been shown to consist of two elements. However, a circular order of items has also been identified. More precise understanding of the structure of the life area facet may be established by the development of a more extensive questionnaire. This research instrument would contain a greater number of questions representative of these and other possible facet elements.

The circumplex hypothesis was given extra support by the central placing (removing them from the circular order) of two items (items 2 and 5). These items represented hazards: that of lead from petrol and that of industrial air pollution. As the sample was drawn from the population of a large city, it may be proposed that these hazards were those with which respondents had the greatest degree of personal contact. The displacement of these items was due to the presence of a second facet in the same plot of the analysis. This second facet modified the judgements present in the life area facet (this can be seen in Figure 7.6).

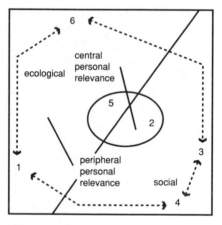

Item numbers
1 noise from aircraft
2 lead from petrol
3 industrial waste in rivers and seas
4 waste from nuclear power stations
5 industrial fumes in the air
6 noise and dirt from traffic

Figure 7.6 Projection of the SSA of the seriousness of environmental hazards questionnaire showing partitioning of the life area facet and personal relevance facet

Personal relevance facet

It was noted above that the facet of life area appeared to have a circular structure. This facet was modified (modulated) by a facet of personal relevance (Figure 7.6). Due to the small number of questions in the questionnaire, the partitioning of this facet resulted in one element of the facet being made up of two items. The two elements of the facet of the personal relevance were environmental hazards of:

(a) central personal relevance
(b) peripheral personal relevance

These two elements were in a configuration characteristic of a facet playing a modifying role upon a circumplex. The small number of items (6) in this analysis made the identification of structures more difficult. However, this is a matter for future research: the facets and facet elements identified by the present research still remain valid.

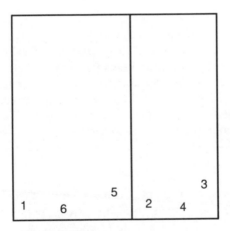

Item numbers
1 noise from aircraft
2 lead from petrol
3 industrial waste in rivers and seas
4 waste from nuclear power stations
5 industrial fumes in the air
6 noise and dirt from traffic

Figure 7.7 Projection of the SSA of the seriousness of environmental hazards questionnaire showing partitioning of the environmental relevance facet

Environmental relevance facet

A third facet, of environmental relevance, is shown in Figure 7.7. The facet referred to the level of environmental importance which was attributed to a given environmental hazard-related action or issue. The facet was arranged along a straight line (a simplex structure) structure with two elements:

(a)　greater environmental relevance
(b)　lesser environmental relevance

Time scale facet

This facet formed the fourth facet of assessment and may be seen in Figure 7.8. The facet had three identifiable elements (regions) in a linear (simplex) arrangement. These were:

(a)　no effect
(b)　future effect
(c)　present effect

　As with the facet of personal relevance, owing to the small number of questionnaire items, 'no effect' and 'present effect' facet elements were made up of single question items (see Figure 7.8). This does not represent a problem in the identification of facets or facet elements. However, future research should aim to assemble a greater number of questions representative of these facet elements. This facet also played an axial role in structuring assessments.

Summary

From the three plots presented above, four facets are clearly identified. These are facets of: life area; personal relevance; environmental relevance; time scale effect.

　Furthermore, it can be seen that the focus facet of personal relevance interacts with (is in the same plot as), and thus modifies, the life area facet. The level of conservation relevance and time scale of effect also appeared as facets of the appraisal of the seriousness of environmental pollution. Moreover, these latter two facets appeared as relatively independent facets of the appraisal; as axial facets. It should be noted that the elements of the life area and environmental relevance facets have identical items comprising them. It is the differences in the structure of these two facets which enables their differentiation. Evaluations of the seriousness of environmental

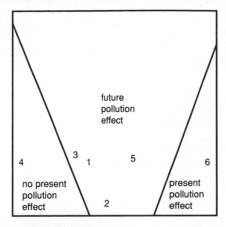

Item numbers
1 noise from aircraft
2 lead from petrol
3 industrial waste in rivers and seas
4 waste from nuclear power stations
5 industrial fumes in the air
6 noise and dirt from traffic

Figure 7.8 Projection of the SSA of the seriousness of environmental hazards questionnaire showing partitioning of the time scale of effect facet

pollution in terms of its effect upon either humankind or the planet's ecology were the life areas that respondents perceived to be affected by the specified hazards. However, personal relevance of these hazards modified these ascriptions.

Conclusion

In conclusion, it may be stated that an individual from the study's sample asks a series of questions to him/her self each time the seriousness of an environmental hazard is considered. These questions may be thought of as facets of a person's assessment. The questions that were posed took the following format: How serious is the environmental hazard's effect upon human or ecological areas of life and how relevant is this to me? Is this of central or peripheral environmental relevance? How serious is this at present, not at present, or in the future? The answers to the three sub-questions of this question will determine the overall assessment of seriousness an individual attaches to a given environmental hazard.

Individual responses to the environmental hazards are structured in terms of the facet elements. The qualitative and quantitative ways in which these facets affect assessments are the subject matter of the next section of this chapter. In this section a partially ordered structure will be presented.

Individual response profiles

The results have been presented of assessments of the seriousness of environmental hazards. A mapping sentence has been developed from the similarities in respondents' assessments. The next stage in this analysis is to consider the structure of these attitudes in more detail. It has already been possible to establish a new and important understanding about these evaluations; there remains, however, the question as to exactly what role each of the facets' elements play in shaping individual judgements. During the next section, analyses will be reported that examine the ways in which individuals' evaluations differ. The principal items differentiating between assessments will be identified and considered in greater detail.

Qualitative and quantitative differences in evaluations

It is possible to identify two basic ways in which individuals may differ in terms of a given evaluation they make. The first of these differences is purely quantitative. In this study this would be an individual's total score in their assessments of the seriousness of all specified environmental hazards.

The second way in which individual responses may differ is qualitative. At each quantitative level assessed of seriousness, qualitative differences may exist between respondents. What this means is that at each level of quantitative similarity in evaluations there is agreement amongst respondents in regard to the seriousness of all environmental hazards. However, these totals may differ in terms of the individual scores comprising them: these are the qualitative differences in evaluations. Both the qualitative and quantitative similarities and differences in the questionnaire data are now considered.

Partial Order Scalogram Analysis

Partial Order Scalogram Analysis (POSA) or Partial Order Scalogram Analysis with base Co-ordinates (POSAC) are analysis methods which have been used in a variety of research settings. They have proved both appropriate and useful when studying qualitative and quantitative dimensions of judgement (Brown, 1985). Detailed descriptions of POSA and POSAC are provided by several authors (e.g., Brown, 1985; Shye, 1985b; and 1985d; Dancer, 1989). The reader requiring further information about this procedure is guided to these texts and to Shye (1986), who thoroughly reviews the procedure of scaling. However, it is appropriate to note several points at this stage.

POSA and POSAC provide two types of information. First, total scores are provided for individuals' responses to a specified questionnaire item. Second, differentiation is made between responses that are similar in their totals but that differ in the items that compose them: their qualitative differences. This allows for the observation of differences in the composite scores and the identification of the basic qualitative dimensions' differentiation.

It is possible to subject a total raw data matrix to analysis through POSA. However, it is usual practice within facet research to reduce the matrix to a smaller set of variables. This reduction helps greatly in the interpretation of POSA (Donald, 1989). It should be noted that by collapsing the original data matrix into a matrix comprising variables representing the facet elements revealed in the previous semantic similarity analyses, several tasks are simultaneously performed.

1 It reduces the data matrix to a more easily interpretable format;
2 helps to provide further support for the facet elements identified in SSA;
3 facilitates an understanding of the roles played by these elements in structuring evaluations.

The above-mentioned advantages of collapsing the data matrix into variables representative of the SSA facet elements formed the rationale for the procedure adopted in the present POSA. Other techniques might have been employed to reduce the data matrix for subsequent analysis to reveal partial ordering. These techniques include the random selection of variables for inclusion or selecting variables deemed to be representative of the original matrix. However, none of these procedures has the above advantages of calculating average scores. A further problem associated with random or systematic selection of variables is that the specific area addressed by the chosen variables may confuse the more fundamental facets of evaluations. Including all variables in a collapsed format ameliorates these problems.

The procedure adopted in the present research for the calculation of subscales prior to their entry in POSA was developed by Donald (1983) and used by others (Canter and Donald, 1985; Zeibland, 1986). In this procedure, a mean score is calculated for all questionnaire items which comprise each facet element of a study's original mapping sentence. For example, in the present research, each questionnaire item that included a social element from the life area facet is summated and divided by the total number of such items, e.g.:

Social
Element = *Social/Present, Social/Future, Social/No effect*
Score   3

In selecting facet elements for inclusion in POSA, the modulating facet was not included. This was because the facet was not specified in the initial mapping sentence. This procedure of discarding unspecified modulating facets is in accordance with previous research (e.g., Donald, 1987).

It has already been noted that the elements of the life area facet and the elements of the environmental relevance facet were composed of the same questionnaire items. This being the case, only the life area facet was included for POSA. The element scores calculated were for the following environmental hazards: social/human; ecological; no present effect; present effect; future effect.

Element item composition

Following the procedure detailed above, five element item scores were calculated. The items comprising each of these were:

Element 1 Social effects: questions 1, 5, 6
Element 2 Ecological effects: questions 2, 3, 4
Element 3 No present effect: question 4
Element 4 Future pollution effect: question 6
Element 5 Present effects: questions 1, 2, 3, 5

A further point to note is that due to the small number of questionnaire items (6), only this number of items existed for combining to form element scales. This has resulted in some element scales having single representative items. However, this does not affect the role played by this item as a facet element; such items are simply deemed to play a perfect role in terms of the element scale they represent.

In POSA the option exists to dichotomise data. This procedure may be accomplished using a wide variety of techniques. However, this will not be done; rather, the full data set will be included so as to represent more accurately the variations in the data matrix.

Internal consistency of element scales

It is necessary to establish the internal consistency and reliability of each scale prior to conducting POSA. Therefore, alpha coefficients and standardised alpha coefficients were calculated for each element scale (see Table 7.1). In the context of the present research, all the above levels of alpha are within acceptable levels as described by Nunnally (1967).

It should be noted that items comprising an element scale contain the element as part of their definition. However, they also are made up of items from the other facet being investigated through POSA. As this is the case, element scales should display acceptably high alpha coefficients whilst displaying variance due to the presence of this second facet: items do not come from unidimensional scales (Guttman, 1954). Partial Order Scalogram Analysis with base Co-ordinates (POSAC) (Shye, 1978b) was used to reveal ordering present in the data. The results of this analysis are presented in the following section.

Element scales Partial Order Scalogram Analysis

Partial Order Scalogram Analysis has two axes. The first runs from the top right of the rectangular plot (such plots are known as space diagrams) to the bottom left. This is known as the joint axis, and is quantitative in its nature. It represents quantitative differences in the data. Individuals with the highest summated element profile scores will be located towards the top right-hand corner of the POSA plot. Along this line, individuals who have progressively smaller

Table 7.1 Alpha coefficients for element scales

Element	Alpha	Standardised alpha
Social	0.72	0.72
Ecological	0.73	0.74
No present	0.67	0.67
Future	0.62	0.63
Present	0.69	0.71

summated element scores will be found progressively closer to the bottom left location.

The second axis in a Partially Ordered Scalogram Analysis runs from the top left-hand corner to the bottom right-hand corner of the space diagram. This axis is termed the lateral axis. Along this line, or any other line running parallel to it, will be found individuals with the same scores on the joint axis. However, whilst summated profile scores may be similar, individuals may have very different scores on any one element item in their respective profiles. Differences in this essentially qualitative dimension are represented along the lateral axis. Individuals with the same scores on any specific profile element item are located in a similar position along the lateral dimension.

The location of individuals in a space diagram is thus derived from their full data profile. What may be termed the qualitative and the quantitative variations in the data are both taken into account in locating an individual profile. The distance apart of two profiles in a space diagram is dependent upon: (a) the summation of the profile and (b) an attempt to locate all similar scores for each profile item in adjacent two-dimensional space. The print-out from POSAC provides a space diagram of all individuals as they are located by the above rationale. A plot for each item (element scale) in the investigation is also provided. In the case of this particular study, there are five element scales and thus five item diagrams. In these plots, the locations of the profiles are the same as in the space diagram. However, the item score for the particular profile appears in the position that was previously occupied by the item number. This allows the boundaries of the item scores to be easily identified and thus greatly reduces the time required to interpret the roles played by elements in an analysis.

In order to facilitate interpretation of the plots, lines are drawn (which should be as straight as is possible) to partition regions. Each region contains a single score for an item. The direction of lines reveals how the items structure the POSA. The different shapes produced in partitioning regions enable the researcher to identify clearly the role played by that element in structuring the attitude, value, behaviour, etc. The partitioning lines reveal the role of elements in determining the qualitative (lateral) dimensions of evaluations. The joint (quantitative) axis is simply the sum of a profile score. If no qualitative differences existed between respondents, individuals would be found along the joint axis. This is rarely, if ever, the case. What is attempted through the use of POSAC is to identify the important features of a given content area which cause differentiation between items. The more that lines partitioning regions deviate from being straight, or the more element items that are excluded from a region by the fitting of straight lines, the less 'important' the element item in structuring evaluations. However, more minor roles may be identified. These take the polarising roles which produce an 'L' shape partitioning, and moderating roles causing an inverted 'L' shape partitioning. With a polarising element, high values on this are associated with extreme values upon the lateral axis. The second type, the moderator, tends to have high scores upon its axis associated with mid-value scores upon the lateral axis. The above description assumes that high scores are located at the top left of the space diagram. However, the psychological meaning of the scores may be reverse in a plot, so that 'psychologically greater' is located bottom right. If this is the case, the roles of items in partitioning space will be reversed in respect to the shape of partitioning. In the present research the criteria to enable the descriptions of partitioning are fulfilled. The partially ordered structure of the total data set arising out of the administration of the seriousness of environmental hazards questionnaire is now presented.

Partial Order Scalogram Analysis: results

Figures 7.9a to 7.9e show the plots for each of the five items (elements). The role played by each item in structuring the assessment of the seriousness of environmental hazards, along qualitative dimensions, is shown by the partitioning lines in these diagrams. Each plot will now be considered in turn.

Element 1: Social/human item plot (Figure 7.9a)

Vertical partitioning can be seen in this plot. This form of partitioning shows the human/social effects of hazards to be one of the elements that define the first qualitative pole which differentiates between respondents. The 'straightness' of the partitioning lines show this element to play an important role in the structuring of assessments.

Element 2: Ecological item plot (Figure 7.9b)

This element is shown to partition space into vertical regions. The partitioning is in a similar direction to the social/human element, this being the case, the element plays a similar role to this element. It forms the second component of the first qualitative pole.

From the common direction of the partitioning of the first two items, these items structure data in a similar manner. The first axis of qualitative differentiation between perceptions of the seriousness of environmental hazards is as follows:

High – social environmental hazard
High – ecological environmental hazard
TO
Low – social environmental hazard
Low – ecological environmental hazard

If we now consider the remaining item diagrams, the second qualitative axes of the partial ordering of responses may be identified.

Element 3: No present pollution effect (Figure 7.9c)

The partitioning lines for this item run in the opposite (horizontal) direction for items one and two. The lines partitioning the item diagram are relatively straight. The horizontal partitioning shows this item to be the first component of the second qualitative axis of differentiation. The straightness of partitioning lines shows this item to play an important role in structuring attitudes.

Element 4: Future pollution effect (Figure 7.9d)

The partitioning of this item is essentially horizontal, therefore, it forms part of the second pole of the qualitative axis. However, partitioning is not straight and the element has a relatively minor effect within the qualitative evaluations. From the partitioning of the above two item diagrams, it is possible to state that the second qualitative axis of assessment is as follows:

High – no present environmental hazard
(high – future environmental hazard)
TO
Low – no present environmental hazard element
(low – future environmental hazard)

(The future environmental hazard element is enclosed in parentheses to indicate the relatively minor influence of this element in structuring assessments).

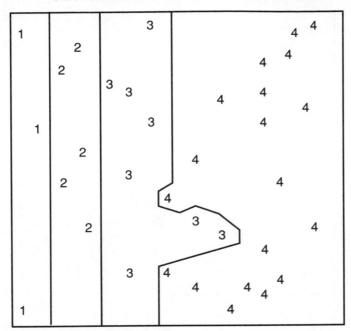

Figure 7.9a Item diagram of the social element of evaluations of the seriousness of environmental hazards

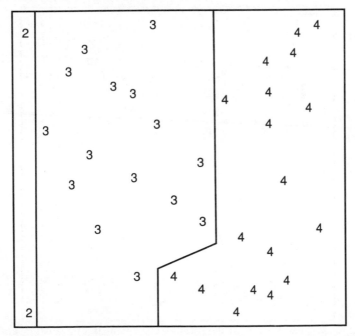

Figure 7.9b Item diagram of the ecological element of evaluations of the seriousness of environmental hazards

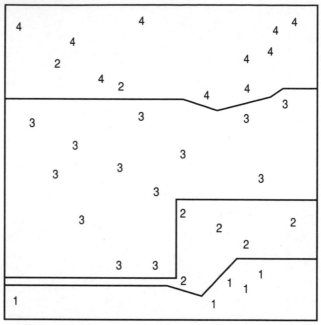

Figure 7.9c Item diagram of the no present hazard element of evaluations of the seriousness of environmental hazards

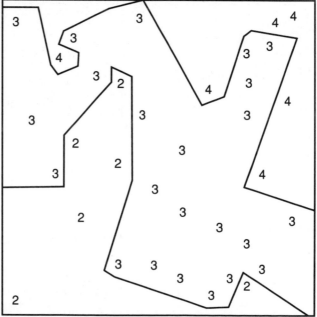

Figure 7.9d Item diagram of the future hazard element of evaluations of the seriousness of environmental hazards

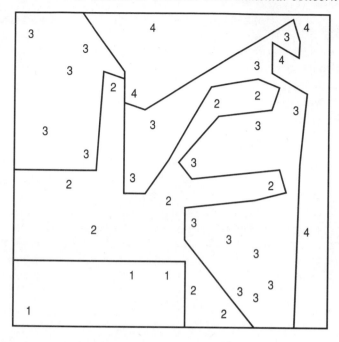

Figure 7.9e Item diagram of the present hazard element of evaluations of the seriousness of environmental hazards

Element 5: Present pollution effect (Figure 7.9e)

This item formed an inverted 'L' shape in partitioning the item diagram. Even though the shape of partitioning is far from forming a perfect 'L' shape, there is a definite trend. It can therefore be concluded that this item plays the role of a polariser. What this means in the area under investigation is that individuals with high scores on the present pollution element will tend to have extreme value scores on the lateral elements (human/social, ecological, future effect and no effect).

From the item diagrams a summary of the results may be provided. One way of simplifying the POSA results for presentation is the easily understandable format provided by the Hasse diagram. Figure 7.10 presents a schematic version of the Hasse diagram for the present analysis.

The Hasse diagram is a POSA plot which has been rotated clockwise through 45 degrees. The dimension running from A1 to A2 is the quantitative (joint) axis, which represents overall assessments of the seriousness of environmental hazards. The qualitative (lateral) axis runs from B1 to B2 and is composed of social, ecological, no present effect and future effect elements.

The joint axis (A1–A2) is quantitative in its nature. Respondents located at A1 perceive all specified environmental hazards as being more serious problems overall than respondents located towards A2. Those respondents located at B1 and B2 perceive the specified hazard issue as being moderately (and equally) serious in their effects: positioning upon the lateral axis (B1–B2) does not affect the overall assessment of the seriousness of a hazard.

Persons located at B2 evaluate hazards which have high social/ human and ecological effects as being extremely serious. Also located at this position are persons ascribing little seriousness to hazards which are assessed as 'low - no present effect' (i.e., they may have an effect at present) and a low - future effect. Persons located at position B1 are typified by the opposite set of evaluative criteria, low, human/social, ecological, high, no present, future effect. Respondents

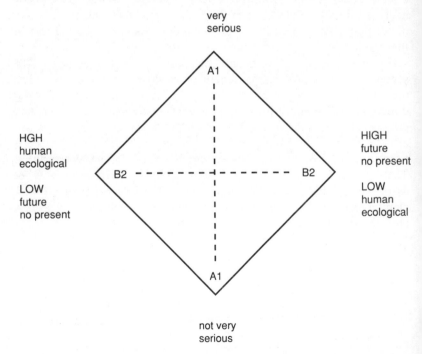

Figure 7.10 Schematic representation of the essential aspects of the POSA of the seriousness of environmental hazards

located at position (B2) are concerned with the present effects of environmental hazards upon both the human and ecological aspects of the environment. However, they are less concerned with the future effects of hazards.

To summarise, the target of the environmental hazard effect and the time scale over which the hazard will have its effect discriminate between ratings of the perceived seriousness of environmental hazards; these form the important qualitative differences in evaluations. Furthermore, the POSA provides further support for the facets (and their elements) discovered in SSA.

Summary

Above, the partially ordered structure of respondents' profile scores has been viewed. The raw scores of responses to all questions have been used to provide mean scores for the five facet elements of: social/human, ecological, no present pollution effect, future pollution effect, and present pollution effect. Element scores have been analysed through POSAC and their respective roles identified (two dimensions: one quantitative and the other qualitative). The former of these dimensions is representative of the total reported perceived seriousness of all environmental hazards within the enquiry. The second formed a qualitative dimension of differentiation. The items defining this qualitative dimension can be represented by two bipolar dimensions. The first of these comprised social and ecological hazard effects. The second consisted of no present hazard and future hazard effects. The role of the present effects of an environmental hazard is to moderate the roles of the above two qualitative lateral dimensions. That is, high scores on the present effects of hazards will be associated with the middle-value scores on other elements. In the chapter that follows, the results are presented of a study of general environmental concern.

8 A facet study of environmental concern

Contained in this chapter are the results from a questionnaire study investigating a wide range of environmental issues and actions (the questionnaire is listed in Appendix A.5). The design of the questionnaire used, along with details of the sample, have already been given. Similarity Structure Analysis (SSA) was again used to analyse the data from this questionnaire, which was designed to investigate the social value of environmental concern through a questionnaire comprising 100 questions. This included four subsections of twenty-five questions per section. Each of the sections addressed a different response, by subjects, to the environmental conservation actions and issues specified as social values in the mapping sentence in Figure 7.1. Therefore a subsection of questions was assembled which assessed the perceived importance and effectiveness of the actions, and the reported level of monetary and time contribution each respondent was willing to pledge to each of the environmental conservation activities. Analysis will first be presented for the questionnaire as a whole. Subsequently, each section of twenty-five questions will be analysed independently.

SIMILARITY STRUCTURE ANALYSIS OF THE ENVIRONMENTAL CONCERN QUESTIONNAIRE

Similarity coefficients

The first stage in the Similarity Structure Analysis of a data set is the calculation of similarity coefficients between each pairing of all variables in the set. This is done for two reasons. First, it provides the coefficients that will later be used to locate points in plots of smallest space. Second, it enables the investigation of the directionality of the correlation between each of the variables under investigation (copies of the matrix for the present study may be obtained from the author). The matrix produced in this manner for the data arising out of the 100 questions of the entire questionnaire reveals interesting relationships in the data. It shows there to be a significant number of negative relationships. Some of these negative correlations are of quite large magnitudes with several exceeding -0.20. The presence of a substantial number of negative correlations within a matrix is indicative of the fact that more than one semantic area is falling within the research area, i.e. the small scale is not unambiguously addressing a single content area. This is supported as all except one of the pairings of the importance variables (variables 1–25) are positive. The single negative association is almost zero (-0.02), which suggests the importance of environmental concern questions addressing a single area. The same positive relationships are present between correlations for each of the modes of expression of concern when each of these modes is analysed separately.

It would appear therefore that each of these modalities comprises a single area of meaning to respondents. However, when effectiveness variables are entered into the matrix, the relationships are frequently negative and often greater than -0.15. A similar though less consistent relationship is found when the variables of time and monetary pledges are correlated with the other two modalities. However, for all four response modes (importance, effectiveness, time pledge and monetary pledge), the internal relationships are relatively monotonic. The negative correlations that do occur are usually of relatively small magnitude.

However, the presence of the negative correlations between the 100 variables should be noted. Variables that are consistently negatively related to other variables will tend to be located towards the edges of SSA plots. The negative direction of their relationship will moreover tend to destroy or obscure any other relationships present in a data set. This was found in the case of variables 26–50 (effectiveness variables) when SSA was performed upon all 100 items. These variables are found consistently to the periphery of the plot in Figure 8.1. Furthermore, variable 35, for example, which is negatively related to a large number of other variables, is placed on the edge of the plot. With this caveat in regard to the large number of negative relationships noted, and with little expectation of finding support for the mapping sentence, it is possible to continue with the interpretation of the SSA plots.

Similarity Structure Analysis plots

Analysis to reveal similarity structure present in the 100-item data set was performed. This produced a single facet of evaluation, at an acceptable level of stress (Guttman–Lingoes coefficient of alienation = 0.14).

Mode of Expression Facet

Figure 8.1 shows partitioning for the mode facet as stated in the mapping sentence (Figure 7.1). Space in the plot was divided into two regions. These reflected cognitive and behavioural elements of the mode of expression facet. The cognitive element of the facet further divided into two separate areas. These regions were of importance and effectiveness; reflecting the wording of the questionnaire. However, the behaviour element did not divide to show the two types of behaviour (time and money) specified in the questionnaire. Consequently, the elements of this facet were:

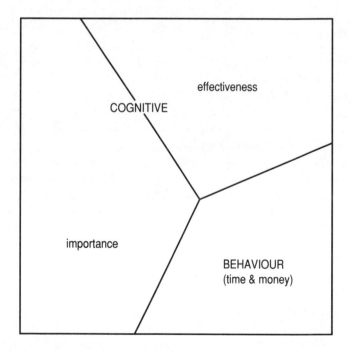

Figure 8.1 Projection of the SSA of the overall environmental concern questionnaire showing partitioning of the mode of expression facet

1 cognitive (1a importance)
            (1b effectiveness)
2 behavioural

This indicates that the assessment of importance and effectiveness are distinct modalities of evaluations. The time and monetary pledges, however, appeared to be assessed in terms of involvement.

It should be noted that the caveat issued earlier in regard to the negative correlation of effectiveness variables with other variables is important when interpreting these results: the other plots from the analysis failed to produce any other interpretable regions. The failure to find support for the other facets in the mapping sentence does not negate the mapping sentence used to produce the questionnaire, as the response range (mode) was not constant between studies. Consequently, Similarity Structure Analysis was performed upon the four modes of expression separately. These results are listed below.

The importance of environmental conservation

This analysis produced three facets with a coefficient of alienation of 0.17. The facets are now described.

Life area facet

In Figure 8.2 is shown the plot of the facet of life area. This facet was proposed in the mapping sentence (Figure 7.1). However, the facet structure discovered modified the format of this facet. It was hypothesised that the facet would take a polar form; this was in fact the case. The proposed structure was of three elements: social conservation (which has a primarily human effect or benefit); educational conservation; and ecological conservation (primarily to benefit/affect animals or the environment). In Figure 8.2 it can be seen that the elements of this facet were not as proposed. In terms of the importance of environmental concern the life area facet had elements of:

1 area/habitat conservation
2 species/animal conservation
3 moral issues in conservation

The circular arrangement of elements originating from a central point differentiated between environmental concern issues that addressed the different life areas. Furthermore, those items at the

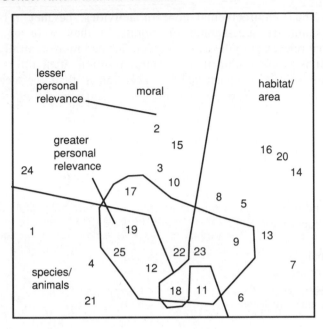

Figure 8.2 Projection of the SSA of the importance of environmental concern questionnaire showing partitioning of the life area facet and personal relevance facet

boundaries of the elements were described (to some extent) by both their own and their neighbouring element category. A second facet, of personal relevance, was also present in this plot.

Facet of personal relevance

In Figure 8.2 can be seen the second facet of this analysis present in the same plot as the life area facet. The facet embodied evaluations related to the personal relevance of a conservation issue or action and had a format that modified the assessments of the life area facet. The elements of this facet were:

1 greater personal relevance
2 lesser personal relevance

Actions of greater personal relevance were located more centrally in the plot.

The elements of this facet interact with the elements of the life area facet. Thus, environmental concern activities, be they related to species/animals, area/habitat or morals, if they were of greater personal relevance to the assessor, were located more centrally in the plot. It is worth noting that a central position often refers to the juncture of the elements of the facet rather than the geometric centre of the plot. The third facet of this analysis was a second polar facet.

Scale of action facet

The third facet present in SSA was a scale of action facet. This is shown in Figure 8.3. The format and structure of this facet was that proposed in the original mapping sentence (Figure 7.1). The elements of the facet were:

1 global
2 international
3 ethical
4 national and local

The relative positions of these facet elements show them to play a polar role in the structuring of attitudes with elements forming sectors around a common origin. This is so for all elements except the national conservation element. This was located in the same sector as the local conservation element. However, the element was separately identifiable as it occupied a more central area of the region. The explanation for this lies in the fact that the facet of personal relevance is also present in this projection. Therefore, this second facet modifies the scale facet. The reason for the positioning of the national concern element is therefore explained by the amount of personal relevance attached to this in comparison with concern at a local scale. It is therefore the case that national concerns were more central and therefore more personally relevant/important.

Together, these three facets structure respondents' assessments of the importance of the selected environmental concern actions and issues. In the next section the perceived effectiveness of environmental conservation in these areas of concern will be evaluated.

The effectiveness of environmental conservation

SSA produced a solution with three facets (Guttman–Lingoes coefficient of alienation = 0.16).

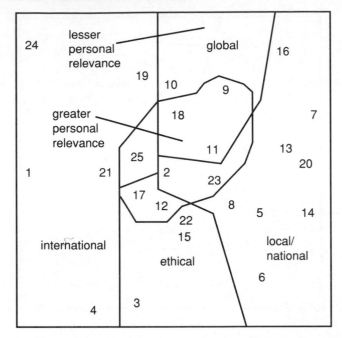

Figure 8.3 Projection of the SSA of the importance of environmental concern questionnaire showing partitioning of the scale of action facet and personal relevance facet

Life area facet

This facet (Figure 8.4) took an identical format to the life area facet identified in the analysis of the subsection of importance questions. The facet had three elements:

1 animal/species
2 area/habitat
3 moral

The elements were circularly arranged, showing a polar structure to assessments of the effectiveness of environmental conservation. A second facet was found to be present in the same plot. This facet reflected environmental relevance.

Environmental relevance facet

This facet was present in the same plot as the facet of life area (Figure 8.4). It therefore modifies the judgements implicit in the former facet. There were two elements in this facet:

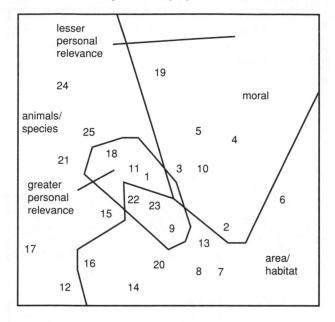

Figure 8.4 Projection of the SSA of the effectiveness of environmental concern questionnaire showing partitioning of the life area facet and personal relevance facet

1 greater environmental relevance
2 lesser environmental relevance

The facet structured assessments in a similar way to the relevance facet in evaluations of the importance of environmental concern. However, the items that comprised the elements of the two facets are different, allowing different processes to be attributed to each of the two facets. The third facet in effectiveness assessments was a second polar facet.

Facet of scale

A facet of physical scale was present in this analysis (Figure 8.5). The facet was circularly arranged, suggesting a radial arrangement to be present in respondents' judgements. This facet had elements of:

1 international
2 national

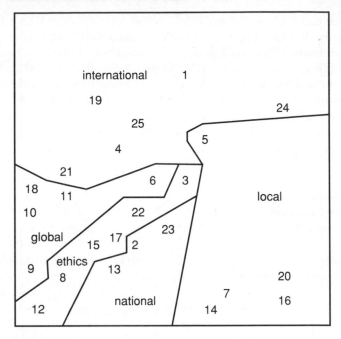

Figure 8.5 Projection of the SSA of the effectiveness of environmental concern questionnaire showing partitioning of the scale facet

3 local
4 ethical
5 global

Time pledged to environmental conservation

The data that originated from this section of the questionnaire was analysed to reveal similarity structure. This produced three facets with a coefficient of alienation of 0.13. These facets are described below.

Action type facet

In Figure 8.6 is the plot of the action type facet. This facet was not proposed in the research design (mapping sentence, Figure 7.1). A life area facet was expected which was similar to the facet present for evaluations of importance. It was hypothesised that a polar facet would be present; this was the case. The structure hypothesised was of three elements with these being: social (conservation which had a primarily human effect or benefit); educational; and ecological (conservation which has a primarily environmental effect or benefit).

In Figure 8.6 it can be seen that these regions are not present. What was revealed was a facet with a circular arrangement of its elements. The positioning of elements reflected the type of conservation action to which respondents were being asked to pledge time. The elements of the facet partitioned the plot into the environmental conservation types of:

1 saving and protecting species and the environment
2 regulating and controlling environmental hazards
3 promotion of actions supportive of, or which advanced,
   the aims of conservation

In the same plot was found a second facet of respondents' evaluations: an involvement/benefit facet.

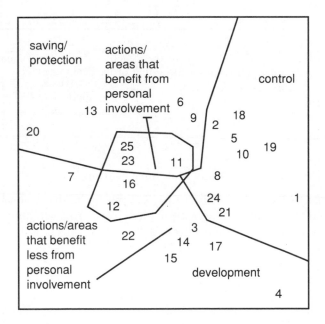

Figure 8.6 Projection of the SSA of the time pledged to environmental concern questionnaire showing partitioning of the action type facet and the involvement/benefit facet

Involvement/benefit facet

The second facet for which partitioning occurred was for a facet that modified the action type facet. This facet was therefore located in the same plot as the action type facet (Figure 8.6). Judgements involved in this facet were complex and initially difficult to label. The items that fell within the central region (element) of the facet were all actions that would benefit most from the 'personal', direct involvement of respondents. The items that fell within the peripheral region (element) were conservation actions that would benefit less from such involvement.

As with the facet of action type, this facet was specified in the initial mapping sentence (Figure 7.1) but with an extremely different element structure. This difference in structure is of little surprise as the structure of the action type facet, upon which this facet has a modifying effect, was also not in the structure specified a priori. The elements of the involvement/benefit facet were:

1 more benefit from personal involvement
2 less benefit from personal involvement

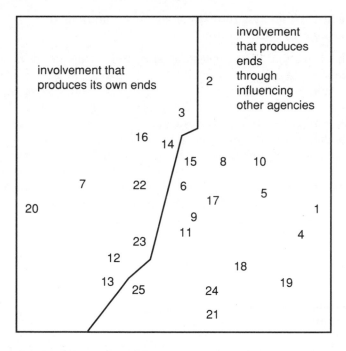

Figure 8.7 Projection of the SSA of the time pledged to environmental concern questionnaire showing partitioning of the action purpose facet

Action purpose facet

The third facet to emerge through SSA is shown in Figure 8.7. This was the action purpose facet as specified in the mapping sentence in Figure 7.1. The facet was found to have its precise nature modified by the context of the questionnaire. The elements of the facet were therefore:

1 involvement which attained results for conservation in their own right
2 involvement which produced results for conservation through influencing other agencies, policy, etc.

Together, the three facets that were found in SSA structure respondents' expressions of willingness to pledge time to various environmental conservation actions. Respondents were also questioned upon their expressed willingness to donate money to the same activities and issues associated with environmental concern. The results of this survey follow in the next section of this chapter.

Expressed willingness to make monetary donations to environmental conservation

The final section of the questionnaire dealt with the respondent sample's expressed willingness to donate money to environmental conservation. The intercorrelations between variables were mainly positive, showing this to be a relatively homogeneous area of the expression of environmental concern. The conservation areas that were addressed by the questionnaire were the same as for the previous three sections of this study. The questionnaire data were again subjected to SSA. This produced a solution with three facets at an acceptable level of stress (Guttman–Lingoes coefficient of alienation = 0.14). Details of this analysis now follow.

Action type facet

This facet (Figure 8.8) reflected the broad type of action involved. The elements of this facet were:

1 development actions
2 controlling actions
3 regulatory actions

The action type facet that emerged was similar, in the elements that composed it, to the action type facet of time pledged. These elements

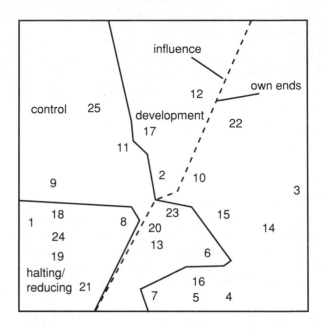

Figure 8.8 Projection of the SSA of the money pledged to environmental concern questionnaire, showing partitioning of the action type facet and action purpose facet

have been described in the preceding section and they will not be commented upon further in this section. However, a major difference existed between the structure of this action type facet and the one reported in the previous section of this chapter. The action type facet for time pledge was polar. The present facet, which emerged from the SSA of the expressed willingness to donate money, was axially differentiated.

Elements of the facet formed three parallel regions in the plot. Elements were ordered:

1 halting actions
2 control actions
3 development actions

The mean scores for these elements show that respondents were most willing to donate money to (in descending order): halting actions (1.2), controlling actions (0.8), development actions (0.5). A second facet was present in the same plot of SSA, reflecting the purpose of the conservation action.

Action Purpose Facet

Present in the same plot of SSA as the action type facet was found a second facet (Figure 8.8). This facet reflected the purpose of the conservation action. The facet took the format of the facet specified in the mapping sentence in Figure 7.1. The elements of the facet were:

1 actions that attained results for conservation in their own right
2 actions that produced results for conservation through influencing other agencies, policy, etc.

The facet was obliquely related to the action type facet. Together, these facets formed a 3 × 2 division of the space in the plot. It should be noted that the plot was actually divided into (3 × 2) −1 regions. This was owing to no item being present in the analysis which was a member of one of the elements of the possible combinations.

Physical scale facet

A physical scale facet emerged in this analysis (Figure 8.9). The physical scale of environmental conservation actions was specified in the mapping sentence in Figure 7.1 as having five distinct elements. However, in the context of donating money to environmental conservation, the facet was found to divide into two distinct regions. The facet elements were therefore:

1 local and British conservation
2 conservation at a larger scale

The data from the general environmental concern questionnaire will now be analysed to produce mean scores for the elements of the facets which have been revealed due to their semantic similarity. This form of analysis will enable the identification of the relationships between the modality of expression of environmental concern and other components of its social value.

FURTHER ANALYSES

SSA of the questionnaire data has resulted in the production of a mapping sentence for the social value of, and attitudes towards, environmental concern. In this section, further analyses will be

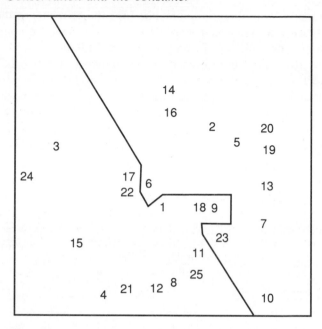

Figure 8.9 Projection of the SSA of the money pledged to environmental concern questionnaire, showing partitioning of the physical scale facet

performed upon the same data. These analyses will be performed in order to show the relationships between elements within the modes of expression facet.

Data will first be summarised through the calculation of mean scores. It was originally planned to calculate means for the same facet elements within each mode of expression. However, SSA revealed different facets to be present in the different expression modes. For example, in the case of both the importance and the effectiveness modes, a facet that divided actions into either social or ecological conservation was present. This facet was not present for the other modes. Similarly, for the two involvement modes, an action type facet was present. However, this facet was not present in the cognitive modes. It was therefore decided to calculate comparable mean scores. It was important to produce comparable means in order to allow the investigation of the relationships between cognitive and behavioural modes of expression and other facets from the mapping sentence. To enable this, mean scores were also calculated for the four expression modes (see Figure 7.1).

Mean scores were therefore calculated for the elements of the life area and scale facets (which were present in the SSAs of cognitive expression modes) for each of the four modes of expression. A mean score was also calculated for each of the elements of the 'behaviour mode facet' (instrumental = time and money; cognitive = importance and effectiveness). The facet elements for which mean scores were calculated, along with their respective mean scores, are listed in Table 8.1.

The data contained in Table 8.1 is further broken down in Tables 8.2 to 8.5a. In Table 8.2 the mean scores are presented for each of the questions in the questionnaire by each of the modes of expression. Questions are arranged in descending order of their mean scores. Table 8.3 presents a breakdown of behaviour mode facet by physical scale facet elements. In Table 8.4 the mean scores are presented for each of the behaviour mode facet elements in combination with each of the life area facet elements.

Table 8.5a shows the mean scores for the elements of the life area and scale facets as they combine within the questionnaire. Each combination of life area and physical scale facet elements is presented for each of the behaviour mode facet elements. It should be noted that no combinations of the local and ecological facet elements were present in the questionnaire.

The mean scores for the three facets of behaviour mode, physical

Table 8.1 Facet element mean scores

Facet/Element	Mean score
BEHAVIOUR MODE	
Importance	3.13
Effectiveness	1.76
Time	1.41
Money	0.65
LIFE AREA	
Social conservation	1.70
Ecological conservation	1.92
PHYSICAL SCALE	
Local	1.58
National	1.84
International	1.80
Global	2.10
Ethical	1.68

Table 8.2 Mean scores for each question by behaviour mode

Question (with questionnaire number)	MODE			
	Importance	Effectiveness	Time	Money
Saving unspoilt areas (9)	4.0	1.6	1.7	1.2
Halt atmospheric destruction (1)	4.0	1.2	1.7	1.2
Reduce rainforest destruction (18)	4.0	1.2	1.8	0.8
Protect animals worldwide (11)	3.9	2.3	1.6	1.0
Support 3rd world agri' dev' (4)	3.8	2.1	1.6	1.0
Protect British wildlife (23)	3.6	2.3	1.6	0.9
Develop local nature reserves (7)	3.5	2.2	1.3	0.6
Lead reduction policy (19)	3.5	2.0	1.6	1.0
Concern for environmental issues (17)	3.4	2.2	1.5	0.8
Halt EEC food mountains (21)	3.4	1.1	1.6	0.9
Save British countryside (13)	3.3	2.5	1.6	0.9
Children's nature experiences (14)	3.3	2.0	1.2	0.6
Halt international animal trade (25)	3.3	1.8	1.5	0.1
Control development in GB (6)	3.3	1.7	1.2	0.4
Care for all living things (22)	3.3	1.5	1.4	0.6
Reduce world population growth (24)	3.3	1.3	1.1	0.5
Industrial exploitation (8)	3.3	1.2	1.1	0.5
International fishing policy (10)	2.9	2.0	1.0	0.4
Destructive GB farming (2)	2.9	1.6	1.0	0.4
City traffic levels (5)	2.8	1.3	1.1	0.4
Global family (3)	2.8	0.7	1.2	0.4
Protecting villages (20)	2.6	1.8	1.0	0.4
Campaigning for animal rights (12)	2.4	2.0	1.0	0.6
Encouraging city wildlife (16)	2.3	1.5	0.9	0.3
3rd world mineral exploitation (15)	2.3	1.0	0.9	0.4

scale and life area have all been calculated. These scores are presented in Tables 8.1 to 8.5a, both as mean scores for each of these elements and as mean scores for elements in facet combinations. The data in these tables will now be commented upon in respect to each of the three facets noted above.

Behaviour mode facet

Table 8.1 shows the mean scores for each of the four elements of the behaviour mode facet. This shows that respondents clearly felt that

Table 8.3 Mean scores for behaviour mode by life area

Behaviour mode	Life area	Mean
IMPORTANT	ecological	3.46
	social	3.08
EFFECTIVE	social	1.82
	ecological	1.79
TIME	ecological	1.52
	social	1.30
MONEY	ecological	0.94
	social	0.62

Table 8.4 Mean scores for behaviour mode by physical scale

Behaviour mode	Physical scale	Mean score
IMPORTANT	global	3.92
	international	3.21
	ethical	3.07
	national	3.07
	local	2.85
EFFECTIVE	national	2.07
	local	1.82
	international	1.71
	ethical	1.64
	global	1.56
TIME	global	1.72
	national	1.45
	international	1.42
	ethical	1.37
	local	1.16
MONEY	global	1.21
	international	0.86
	national	0.75
	ethical	0.67
	local	0.50

most environmental issues were of importance (mean scores = 3.29).
They also expressed a belief that most environmental actions were
ineffective (mean score = 1.76). Respondents were relatively
unwilling to pledge either their time or their money to environmental

Table 8.5a Mean scores for combinations of physical scale with life area by behaviour mode

Behaviour mode	Life area with physical scale	Mean score
IMPORTANT	GE	4.04
	IS	3.56
	GS	3.37
	NE	3.37
	NS	3.16
	ES	3.12
	EE	3.11
	LS	3.07
	IE	2.96
EFFECTIVE	NE	2.16
	LS	1.91
	NS	1.87
	IS	1.77
	EE	1.69
	IE	1.66
	GE	1.62
	ES	1.58
	GS	1.33
TIME	GE	1.83
	IS	1.65
	NE	1.43
	EE	1.36
	ES	1.32
	IE	1.26
	GS	1.25
	NS	1.24
	LS	1.11
MONEY	GE	1.33
	IS	1.03
	NE	0.77
	IE	0.74
	EE	0.72
	GS	0.69
	LS	0.63
	ES	0.58
	NS	0.45

Key to facet element codes: EE = ethical + ecological, ES = ethical + social, GE = global + ecological, GS = global + social, IE = international + ecological, IS = international + social, NE = national + ecological, NS = national + social, LS = local + social

Table 8.5b Mean scores for combinations of ecological/social life areas

Behaviour mode	Life area	Ecological	Social
IMPORTANT	ethical	3.11	3.17
	global	4.04	3.37
	international	2.96	3.56
	local		3.07
	national	3.37	3.16
EFFECTIVE	ethical	1.69	1.56
	global	1.62	1.33
	international	1.66	1.77
	local		1.91
	national	2.16	1.87
TIME	ethical	31.36	1.32
	global	41.83	1.25
	international	1.26	1.65
	local		1.11
	national	1.43	1.24
MONEY	ethical	0.72	0.58
	global	1.33	0.69
	international	0.74	1.03
	local		0.63
	national	0.77	0.45

conservation activities (mean time score = 1.41; mean money score = 0.80).

Table 8.2 shows the mean scores for each of the questionnaire's twenty-five questions for each of the modes of behavioural expression. From this it can be seen that the activities and issues rated to be of the greatest importance were those that were rated as being of low effectiveness. The same was true of those areas assessed to be of low importance. Areas and issues judged to be of moderately high importance were assessed to be of most effectiveness.

It can be seen from the data presented in Table 8.4 that a positive monotonic relationship existed between the three scales of importance, time pledge and money pledge. Those issues areas assessed by respondents as being of greatest importance were likely to receive the greatest levels of time and money pledges. If an area of environmental conservation is seen to be important by respondents, then it is more likely that a greater level of support will be pledged to this area of conservation activity (relative to other areas of conservation). The effectiveness scale was not positively related to the other three scales; perceived effectiveness not appearing to be related to expressed willingness to become involved in conservation activities. However, the effect of perceiving an environmental issue area to be effective may be seen to be playing a minor role in influencing involvement pledges if viewed in combination with perceived importance. Table 8.6 illustrates this effect. In order to produce this table the mean scores given in Table 8.2 were first divided into quartile groups, independently for each behaviour mode. The top 25 per cent of each of these groups taken separately, were assigned to a 'high' response category. The bottom 25 per cent of each group were assigned to a 'low' category, whilst the mid 50 per cent were assigned to a middle category. To simplify any relationships present in the data matrix so formed, the three category groups were each assigned a symbol; high = +, middle = 0 and low = − . The resulting symbol matrix is shown in Table 8.6.

The symbols in column five of Table 8.6 are included to simplify the relationships between the elements of the modalities of behaviour facet. Four relationships exist and these are listed a to d. There were the following number of cases described by each of the relationships: a = 6, b = 13, c = 4, d = 2. These symbols show the importance variable to have an important relationship with involvement pledges. In all cases where the importance of an environmental conservation action or issue is perceived to be high, involvement pledges fall within the high or mid ranges. In twelve cases, when importance was rated as low or mid range, involvement pledges were low. In two cases, importance was rated as low whilst involvement was high. The above relationships may be interpreted in the following manner. If an area or issue within environmental conservation is perceived as being of importance, and actions within this area are assessed to be effective, then pledged involvement will be relatively high. Involvement pledge will also be relatively high if perceived importance is high but effectiveness is seen to be low. However, pledges of both time and monetary involvement (contributions) will be low if importance is seen to be low and effectiveness is low, medium or high.

These relationships are also present when the mean scores of physical scale and the mean scores of the life area facets are related to the elements of the behaviour modality facet (Tables 8.3, 8.4). This leads to the hypothesis that cognitive assessments of importance are the primary factor in motivating pledges to become involved in activities that are supportive of environmental conservation.

Table 8.6 Matrix of score symbols comparing cognitive modes and involvement modes

Question number	MODE				
	IMP	EFF	TIME	MONEY	CODE
9	+	0	+	+	c
1	+	−	+	+	c
18	+	−	+	+	c
11	+	+	+	+	a
4	+	+	+	+	a
23	+	+	+	+	a
7	+	+	0	0	a
19	+	+	+	+	a
17	+	+	+	+	a
21	+	−	+	+	c
13	0	+	+	+	b
14	0	+	−	0	d
25	0	+	+	+	d
6	0	0	−	0	b
22	0	−	−	0	b
24	0	−	−	−	b
8	0	−	−	−	b
10	−	+	−	−	b
2	−	0	−	−	b
5	0	−	−	−	b
3	−	−	−	−	b
20	−	+	−	−	b
12	−	+	−	−	b
16	−	−	−	−	b
15	−	−	−	−	b

Codes: a = if IMP = '+' and EFF = '+', then TIME = '+' and MONEY = '+',
b = if IMP = '−' or '0' and EFF = '+' or '0' or '−',
then TIME = '−' and MONEY = '−' or '0'.
c = if IMP = '+' and EFF = '−' or '0', then TIME = '+'
or '0' and MONEY = '+' or '0'.
d = if IMP = '0' and EFF = '+', then TIME = '+' and MONEY = '+'.

Life area facet

Having considered the modality of behaviour facet, attention is now addressed to the life area facet. Ecological conservation received a higher score than social conservation, when these were summated across all four behaviour modality elements. In terms of their importance, ecological conservation issues were judged to be of greater importance than social conservation issues. There were no differences between the assessments of the effectiveness of the two life areas, and respondents were more willing to pledge to become involved (both cognitively and behaviourally) with ecological concerns (Table 8.3). This again demonstrates how assessments of the importance of environmental issues are closely associated with involvement.

Physical scale facet

The mean scores for the elements of the physical scale facet across all modalities were (in descending magnitude): global, national, international, ethical and local scales of conservation (Table 8.1). Table 8.4 presents the mean scores for each physical scale facet element broken down by behaviour modality. It can be seen that global conservation was assessed to be of the greatest importance and also to attract the most pledges of involvement. Conversely, local conservation was assessed as least important amongst the conservation issues, and received the lowest level of involvement pledges. The same relationship is present in nearly all of the remaining three scale elements.

Combined facet relationships

Table 8.5a lists the mean scores for each combination of the physical scale facet elements and the life area facet elements, by the elements of the behaviour modality facet. From this table it is apparent that the importance assessments are closely related to expressions of involvement; global/ecological and international/social element combinations being consistently rated as being of greater importance and receiving pledges of greater levels of involvement.

Table 8.5b breaks the same data down by ecological and social life areas. From this it can be seen that ecological conservation and global activities are seen to be of greater importance and to receive the highest pledge levels, whilst national conservation is seen as most ecologically effective. For social conservation, international efforts are rated as most important and receive highest pledge levels, whilst local conservation is rated most effective.

In the following chapter the results of the questionnaire studies, along with the results from the repertory grid interviews, are discussed and related to existing social science environmental concern literature. These results are also compared with social values research which has adopted a facet theory approach.

9 The structure of environmental concern

Environmental and applied social psychology draw upon many different approaches in their research (e.g., Bell, Fisher and Loomis, 1976). Facet theory is one approach which has been employed. This has been used as it provides a technique for the analysis of complex, multivariate events. In this chapter the results of the facet analyses presented in the preceding chapters are discussed as these relate to both strands of research which motivated the multivariate investigation of environmental concern:

1 facet theory approach to the study of social values
2 environmental concern research

In the first chapter a series of hypotheses was stated, and in the chapters that followed, the theoretical bases for the hypotheses were given. This resulted in a series of studies being designed and implemented in order to test these hypotheses. The hypotheses that were investigated were embodied in the facets of the mapping sentences used to design each of the studies. Canter (1985b) comments in some detail upon the procedure of developing facet research projects. He cites the development of an initial mapping sentence as the first objective of this form of research. However, he also notes the diverse ways in which a mapping sentence may be developed.

> The initial mapping sentence may be developed from any of a mixture of sources. If the area of research has already been thoroughly studied within a facet framework . . . then already established mapping sentences will exist which can be raided from the particular purpose that the researcher has in mind.
>
> (Canter, 1985b: 266)

In this research the mapping sentence for social values (Levy, 1986) was adapted to the specific context of environmental concern. This modification was undertaken in order to illustrate the psychological processes associated with the social value of environmental concern. It was also performed to allow answers to be made to questions about the dimensionality of environmental concern.

In order to achieve the above aims, it was necessary to 'contextualise' the mapping sentence. This was achieved through open-ended repertory grid interviews. This form of study is often useful in initiating a facet investigation.

> In many cases researchers find that exploratory data collection helps them to give the literature some organisation. This may be through open-ended interviews, field observations, or any of a number of common exploratory techniques which help to identify the likely critical facets in an area of concern. The researcher is, in essence, making a preliminary attempt to establish a category scheme which would help to explain established or anticipated variations in responses or observations.
>
> (Canter, 1985b: 266)

The exploration of the content area was undertaken in the initial stages of the present research. The results that arose from this exploration, and the mapping sentence produced, have already been presented. In the current chapter these results are discussed as they provide answers to questions regarding the dimensionality of environmental concern and research into social values.

The results from all studies that have been conducted will be presented in a single table, allowing the reader to compare results from the separate studies, and an overall mapping sentence will then be proposed for the content area. The facets listed in this will account for the variation in the results from all of the studies, and it will therefore depict the entire semantic domain of environmental concern. Having established an overall mapping sentence for the content area of the research, more detailed relationships in the data will be discussed. The specific roles each of the elements of the ordered facets performed in structuring evaluations will be reviewed. The Partial Order Scalogram Analysis of elements of facets for evaluating environmental hazards will be related to the overall findings of the research. The discussion will then proceed to consider the effect each facet, and its elements, had in shaping specific aspects of environmental concern. This will be followed by a review of the findings of this research as these relate to the literature on environmental concern. The discussion will conclude by considering the overall implications of the research. Attention will also be paid to the cumulative findings of the results. From the results, answers may now be forwarded to the hypotheses that motivated the research. These answers are in the form of an overall model (mapping sentence) for the social value and attitudes of environmental concern and the facets and facet elements contained therein.

THE DIMENSIONALITY OF ENVIRONMENTAL CONCERN

The investigation of environmental concern reported in the literature has taken many forms (as discussed in Chapter 4). As a result of the different measures used to generate research instruments, several authors have questioned the dimensionality of environmental concern. Some of the contemporary research in this area has moved away from a unidimensional design for its research instruments. The investigations by Van Liere and Dunlap (1981) and Cotgrove (1982) are examples of multidimensional conceptualisations and designs to research.

The individual studies reported in this book have led to the development of a multivariate descriptive model being proposed for attitudes and social values associated with environmental concern. A mapping sentence, and the facets contained within this, has been presented for each of the studies that have been conducted. During this discussion these facets are reviewed and are presented in a manner allowing the comparison between studies of the facets in their results. A facet model, including all domain and background facets, will then be posited in the form of an overall mapping sentence. The development of this will now be discussed.

THE DEVELOPMENT OF A MAPPING SENTENCE MODEL OF ENVIRONMENTAL CONCERN

In this research, multiple hypotheses were stated regarding the structure of environmental concern attitudes and social values, in the form of a mapping sentence. This mapping sentence was used to design questionnaire studies and to interpret and analyse subsequent data. This mapping sentence was derived from two sources: (a) existing mapping sentences present in facet theory literature on social value and attitude, and (b) exploratory studies that developed a mapping sentence for the structure of individual understanding and personal values associated with environmental conservation activities.

A summary of the structure of attitudes and values of environmental concern

The results of the Similarity Structure Analysis of all of the research studies have been presented in the result sections of the book. The structure of assessments which has been displayed through the facet studies is now to be summarised to enable the commonalties and pertinent differences present between studies to be readily observed. Initially, a common structure for environmental concern values will be established as an overall mapping sentence. Subsequently, the variations present in this structure between the different studies conducted during this research, will be considered in relation to the overall mapping sentence.

In Table 9.1 the facets and facet elements that were present for each of the studies are listed, enabling the results from each of the individual studies to be compared. This clearly illustrates several points which help answer the original hypotheses of the research. This table is a listing of facets of the evaluation of environmental concern issues and actions and does not constitute a mapping sentence, as no linkages are proposed between the facets of the studies. Furthermore, the context, subjects and response ranges are not listed. The 'contextualisation' of facets through their inclusion in a mapping sentence greatly affects the psychological significance of the facets. The development of an overall mapping sentence will illustrate this point at a later stage of this discussion. The results (Table 9.1) report only the associations between environmental concern and cognitive variables. No socio-demographic variables were included in the study as variation has consistently been found in the associations between socio-demographic and environmental concern measures (Van Liere and Dunlap, 1981; Cotgrove, 1982). The aim of the present research was to develop clear models of environmental concern. This model could (in future research) be investigated to reveal its socio-demographic correlates. In developing a model of environmental concern, Cotgrove (1982) makes the important point that: 'analysis shows that cognitive variables have substantial direct effects on environmental concern. . . . These variables are also the most consistent predictors of environmental concern' (Cotgrove, 1982: 134).

FACETS OF ENVIRONMENTAL CONCERN

Table 9.1 provides a list of the cognitive facets or dimensions that have been discovered within each of the studies. It has been possible for each study to be categorised by no more than four of these facets. However, the context of the study had considerable influence upon the precise psychological significance of each facet.

The interrelationships present between each of the facets is specified in the overall mapping sentence for environmental concern in Figure 9.1. This mapping sentence clearly specifies all facets of the research domain. For any one of the studies in this thesis, facets and facet elements were chosen for inclusion in the research design as they related to the context of the survey. A mapping sentence is defined as a 'verbal statement of the domain and of the range of a mapping including connectives between the facets as in ordinary language' (Shye, 1978a: 413). This was not explicit in all of the surveys described by the overall mapping sentence.

This research has developed and proposed this template or classification system in the form of an overall mapping sentence. This systematically accounts for the variation amongst the correlation coefficients between each pairing of the variables that have been used to assess respondents' expressions of concern for the quality of the natural environment. It is both the conclusion of the present research and a template for developing future research. The mapping sentence provides a taxonomy which, if used in future research design, will enable environmental concern research to address more directly the specific areas of environmental concern that are of most interest to that research.

Each of the facets in Figure 9.1 are now independently considered as they relate to the study in which they were present, and to the overall structure of environmental concern.

Behaviour (expression) modality

This facet was specified as facet 'a' in the overall mapping sentence. During the present research, respondents were required to make a cognitive assessment in their evaluations of environmental concern. Levy and Guttman (1985) have stated that: 'The assessment itself of importance may be regarded as a cognitive behaviour of a person or group' (Levy and Guttman, 1985: 206).

A behaviour modality facet could have been included which had elements representative of other behaviour modalities. For instance,

Table 9.1 Facets and facet elements by research study

1	Social Educational Ecological (e1)	Ethical Global International National Local (f)	More Less (h)	More Less (c)
2	Social Educational Ecological (e1)	For itself For a greater (d)		More Less (c)
3	Social Ecological (e1)	No present Future Present (g)	Central Peripheral (h)	More Less (c)
4	Social Pollution Waste Depletion (e1)	UK (f)	Central Peripheral (h)	Central Peripheral (c)

5	Modality
	Cognitive
	  (important)
	  (effective)
	Instrumental
	(i)			

6	Habitat
	Species
	Moral/ethical
	(e2)
		Global
		British
		International
		(f)
				Central
				  (for itself)
				Peripheral
				  (for a greater)
				(c)

7	Habitat Species Development (e2)	Global International National Local Ethical (f)		Central Peripheral (c)
8	Protection Control Development (e3)	Own ends Influences (d)		Central Peripheral Benefit (c)
9	Protection Control Development (e3)	Small scale Large scale (f)		Own ends Influences (d)

Table 9.1 Continued

Key:
1 = Exploratory Repertory Grid Study/Analysis 1
2 = Exploratory Repertory Grid Study/Analysis 2
3 = Environmental Hazard Study/Analysis
4 = Environmental Urgency Study/Analysis
5 = General Environmental Concern Study/Analysis
6 = Conservation Importance Study/Analysis
7 = Conservation Effectiveness Study/Analysis
8 = Time Pledge to Conservation Study/Analysis
9 = Monetary Pledge to Conservation Study/Analysis

c = environmental relevance facet
d = purpose facet
e1, e2, e3 = life area facet
f = physical scale facet
g = time effect facet
h = personal relevance facet
i = behaviour modality facet

Note: The precise element for each of the studies is shown by the elements listed in the cells in the matrix

in investigating environmental concern, more overt 'behaviours' could have been included. Examples of this behaviour facet element would have been attendance at meetings organised by the environmental movement, purchasing chlorofluorocarbon-free aerosols, installing catalytic converters to motor cars, etc. A person performing the specified behaviour could then have been deemed to be environmentally concerned. Indeed, by adopting such an approach, a more accurate measure of a person's 'real life' commitment to environmental protection may have been assembled than that achieved by cognitive reports of support. However, this may not have occurred as a person's reasons for committing behaviours cannot be judged from overt actions. A person may attend a meeting of Friends of the Earth because their boyfriend or girlfriend attends; may have purchased a given aerosol because it was the cheapest available; or have had a catalytic converter fitted because of their employing company's policy. To discover intent, a person must be questioned in some way as to the motives for his/her actions:

> the ultimate explanation of human behaviour lies in examining man's undertakings, the lines of enquiry he initiates, and the strategies he employs, rather than analysing the logical pattern and impact of events with which he collides. Until one has grasped the nature of man's undertakings, he can scarcely hope to make sense out of the muscular movements he observes.
>
> (Kelly, 1969: 6)

Person (x) being a   (conservation employee)
(member of the public)
(undergraduate student)

a
in a (cognitive)   modality of expression,
(affective)
(behaviour)

b
assesses the environmental concern   (issue goal)
(action)

c
which is of (central)   environmental relevance
(peripheral)

d   **(e1)**
for (its own)   purpose in (social)
(a greater)   (educational)
(ecological)
 – waste
 – pollution
 – depletion

(e2)   **(e3)**
or (habitat/area)   or (protective) life areas
(species/animals)   (controlling)
(morals/ethics)   (developing)

f   **g**
at the (local)   scale, having a (present)
(national)   (future)
(international)   (no future)
(global)
(ethical)

h
time effect, of (central)   personal relevance,
(peripheral)

i
and express their concern in a (cognitive)   modality,
(instrumental)

R
as being (very great)
to   in terms of the content of evaluation.
(very little)

Figure 9.1 Overall mapping sentence for environmental concern
Note: Facet e had three alternative parts (e1, e2, e3). Only one of these facet configurations occurred in any one of the research studies

In the present research it was not the intention to assemble a list of actions that were supportive of the aims of environmental conservation. Instead it was intended that the cognitions through which respondents understood environmental conservation, and were therefore concerned for the quality of the natural environment, were to be investigated. Consequently, cognitive measures, rather than affective measures or measures of overt behaviour, were employed in all of the studies. It should be noted, however, that overt behaviours could have been specified and included in this research. In doing so, variation amongst responses may have been observed which related to this inclusion of this element from the modality of behaviour facet.

Life area

The life area facet was present in all of the studies undertaken during this research. Furthermore, the structure of this facet was approximately similar in each of its appearances. The element arrangement was circular with each of the elements of the facet corresponding to different directions from a common origin. However, in the environmental hazard questionnaire study only two elements of this facet were included. Consequently, a dichotomous configuration of elements occurred. However, the arrangement of items within elements suggested circularity.

A circular arrangement was present for all occurrences of the life area facet. Facets with this type of structure are deemed to be playing polarising roles (Levy and Guttman, 1985). In the present research each region corresponded to the life area that was the primary target of a specified environmental conservation action or issue. With these types of assessments being embodied within the facet, it is of little surprise that the precise type of elements present in this facet varied a great deal between studies, the specific elements of each of the life area facets being dependent upon the domain of the research. Similarity of the underlying form of elements was present for most of the studies, with life area being divided into two regions, human and ecological, which represented the main life areas that were affected by, or were the cause of, the activity or issue specified.

Respondents differentiated consistently between environmental activities by using this facet. For each of the studies, respondents assigned questionnaire or repertory grid items to a life area element. The precise psychological meaning of the facet and its elements varied according to the substantive content of a study. This is shown in Table 9.1. When respondents were questioned about the personal value of an environmental conservation activity or issue (studies 1 to 4, Table 9.1) the life area elements of social and ecological were present. When respondents were from the 'knowledgeable' sample of environmental conservation employees, a subdivision of educational conservation was also present. This element fell between the ecological and social elements. This positioning showed education to link activities that were aimed at protecting the environment for its own sake and saving the environment for human beings. It also is demonstrative of the context of the research in these studies. In these studies, conservation activities rather than conservation issues formed the subject matter. It would appear from these findings that education is more readily construed as an activity than as an issue of environmental concern.

In the seriousness of environmental hazards questionnaire survey, the social/ecological dichotomy was present. This was also present in the analysis of the urgency of environmental issues questionnaire. However, in this latter case, the ecological element subdivided into three distinct types of issue: pollution, waste and resource depletion. In studies 6 and 7 (the importance and effectiveness surveys) another set of elements was present for the life area facet. These were the same in both of these two studies. The three elements of the facet were: habitat, species and morals. Again these elements reflect an underlying human/ecological dimension. The facet elements of habitat and species are identifiable as embodying ecological considerations. Conversely, the ethics (morals) element was a specific form of the human or social element of this facet. Finally, in the two studies that viewed the instrumentality modalities of time and money pledges to environmental goals (studies 8 and 9) a different element set was present. These elements were of protection, control and development. It is interesting to note that for these two studies, the human/ecological distinction was less obvious and may not have been the psychological variable which produced the dichotomy which was present in the print-out from the analysis.

From the presence of a life area facet in eight of the nine studies (the facet was only missing in the general environmental concern study), it would appear that this form of qualitative assessment was intrinsic in the evaluation of environmental concern. The variation in the elements of this facet show it is the facet which, in effect, defines the orientation of research towards the assessment of environmental concern.

If the social value or social attitudes towards environmental conservation actions and issues is being assessed, respondents categorise conservation in terms of its affecting human or ecological life areas. When importance and effectiveness of environmental conservation actions are evaluated, this facet specifies the areas of environmental concern that will benefit from the actions. When people are approached and asked directly to support environmental conservation activities, this facet then specifies the type of behaviours for which support is being requested.

These findings have important implications for the design of environmental concern research. They show how the presence of variation in the issues addressed within a research instrument, or variation in the substantive issues addressed between surveys, will significantly affect the responses that are collected (this variation will have important affects upon the comparability and cumulativeness of findings). This provides support for the variation in substantive issue dimension in the model proposed by Van Liere and Dunlap (1981), through which they explained the differences in environmental concern research findings. This finding also issues a warning to researchers who have assembled a battery of environmental-concern-related questions and included these within a single questionnaire (e.g., Maloney, Ward and Braucht, 1975). Adopting an approach that includes different life areas within a single study instrument may result in variation in the subsequent data which is reflective of the different life area elements present. Moreover, the existence of an underlying 'contextualised' human/ecological division in evaluations would suggest that researchers should include these two elements (in their contextualised format) in their investigation of specific environmental concerns. This approach would be recommended in both academic research and in applied surveys attempting to gauge responses from a social grouping to environmental development and changes, or the conservation of the natural environment.

The human/ecological life area facet also lends support to the notion that a broad range of issues fall under the 'environmental' heading. This finding to some extent justifies the diverse subject matter which social scientists have studied within investigations of environmental concern, for instance: technological impact and the risks associated with this (Fischoff *et al.*, 1978; Fischoff, Slovic and Lichtenstein 1979; Kates, 1972); social values and ecological values (Buss and Craik, 1984; Disch, 1970; Caldwell, 1970; Campbell and Wade, 1972; Craik, 1969, 1970; Dunlap, 1975a, 1976; Dunlap, Gale and Rutherford, 1973; Dunlap, Grineeks and Rokeach, 1981; Harry, 1977; Johoda and Freeman, 1978; Malkis and Grasmick, 1977; Pirages and Ehrlich, 1974; Barbour, 1973; Harman, 1977; Henderson, 1976; Daly, 1973; Yankelovich, 1972; Dunlap and Van Liere,

1978b); environmental legislation (Dillman and Christenson, 1972; Weigel, Woolston and Gendelman, 1977); the environmental movement (Albrecht, 1976; Dunlap, Van Liere and Dillman, 1979; Hornback, 1974; Buttel and Flinn, 1974; Cotgrove and Duff, 1980); political orientations and affiliation (Dunlap, 1975b; Buttel and Flinn, 1976c; Dunlap and Allen, 1976; Ray, 1980; Lowe and Rudig, 1986). All of the above research areas may be usefully included within the social element of a study of environmental concern.

The life area facet has been found to be present in all previous investigations using a facet theory approach in the study of social values (Levy and Guttman, 1974a, 1974b, 1976, 1981a, 1981b, 1981c, 1985; Levy, 1986) and in studies of attitudes (Guttman, 1973), well-being (Levy and Guttman, 1975) and socio-political involvement and protest (Levy, 1978, 1979). For example, Levy (1986) discovered a polarised (circularly arranged) life area facet to be present in her investigations of Israeli social values. This element structure was evident in analyses of values as guiding principles, personal well-being values, social values and their execution, fundamental problem values, and socio-political values. The life area facets in all of these studies also categorised life area in a contextualised manner which was analogous to the present results.

The differentiation process which is present in the life area facet has been found to be the type of differentiation process present in many other life area facets within a wide variety of different contexts (e.g., Marsden and Laumann, 1978; Levy and Guttman, 1975; Canter and Walker, 1980). Levy (1985) provides a thorough review of this facet. She notes how a second facet modifying the life area facet is often a necessary component in a social research study. The inclusion of this facet allows the researcher to 'focus' the life area being addressed by a questionnaire item. This modification is achieved by conjointly requiring a second (modular) evaluation to be made of the life area's polarised differentiations.

In many of the results from the present surveys, the life area facet was modified by a second facet. This was either discovered (as in the exploratory studies) or included in the research design (all other studies). Two types of modulating facets (modifying facets) were found during data analysis and these are now discussed.

Environmental relevance

The environmental relevance facet (facet c in the overall mapping sentence) appeared on seven occasions in SSA. The facet had the same structural format on six of these appearances. On these six occasions the facet structured evaluations as a modulating facet. This form of facet structure has elements that are centrally and peripherally positioned. The facet appeared once with a different structure. On this occasion items were arranged along a straight line. When this facet possessed a modulating structure, the elements were of a single type. Elements were a central region element reflecting items of central relevance, and an outer region comprising items which were of more peripheral relevance. These placements were achieved through the facet causing some items to be 'displaced' from the circularity of arrangement. Some items are 'pulled' towards the centre of the plot because they possess a similarity in terms of the judgements present in the modifying facet. As the two facets are found in the same plot of smallest space, the evaluations each possess are intimately related to each other. The two-dimensional plot of the life area and environmental relevance facets showed the life area facet to be partitioned into circularly arranged sections where each section represents a particular life area of environmental concern. In the same plot, a centrally placed circle was found to divide the items; the more central being of more environmental relevance.

The two-facet layout is not unusual in facet theory analyses. Shye (1982) compiled expert opinion upon the impact on environmental quality of a nuclear power plant. When interpreting the position of items in her resulting similarity analyses, Shye stated:

> the picture conforms to what has been more generally noted in previous studies, namely the fields, domains or life areas tend to be circularly ordered. . . . The distance of a plotted item . . . from the centre of the map is determined by the extent to which that item belongs exclusively to its sector.
>
> (Shye, 1982: 296)

It is possible for Shye to form this conclusion as an item which has some level of affinity with sectors of the analysis, other than its own, will tend to be located closer to these other sectors. The geometric position implied by this is centrality (Shye, 1982). Levy (1976a) and others (e.g., Levy and Guttman, 1974a) discovered within the domain of social values and social satisfaction a life area of circularly arranged regions which were modified by a modulating facet. In the current research this modulating facet was present in all studies except the monetary pledge and general environmental concern studies.

Personal relevance

The facet of personal relevance was the second facet of the analyses which had a modifying effect upon evaluations. This modular facet of personal relevance (facet h in the overall mapping sentence) caused the assessments present in the life area facet to be modified. Essentially, its structure was similar to that of the environmental relevance facet (facet c) and many of the above points made about the facet of environmental relevance apply to this facet also. The facet of personal relevance was present in three of the studies (personal repertory grid, environmental hazards and urgency surveys). The facet structure was similar in each of these studies and modified the judgement criteria present in the life area facet. The facet had two separately identifiable regions: central and peripheral. Centrality was afforded to those hazards, issues and activities with which respondents had the greatest extent of personal contact. The peripheral element comprised those items that were experienced, by the sample, through less direct contact.

The two modulating facets of personal and environmental relevance brought a sense of importance or value to environmental concern judgements. However, as this facet was found in the same plot as the life area facet, importance is not assigned to environmental concern overall, but to each of the elements of the life area facet. The facet allows there to be central and peripheral components of each of the judgements embodied in the life area elements. Furthermore, whilst the life area facet may possess a similar structure between different studies, the different substantive issues addressed cause the precise content of the facet elements to change. Moreover, the form of the commitment required from respondents also changed between studies. This is shown in the different response ranges and issue types.

The modulating facets found in analysing the results of the present series of research studies appeared particularly sensitive to these changes in issue and range specification; the modality facet logically represented such changes in its structure. This may be illustrated by considering the environmental relevance facet's elements in the instrumental modality study of time pledged to environmental activities. Central regions of the environmental relevance facet were formed by items which respondents evaluated would benefit most from their personal 'involvement' (an instrumental activity); whereas, in the studies requiring cognitive evaluations, central regions were comprised of items perceived as being of central relevance (a cognitive activity). The sensitivity of modulating facets should be noted, and should be taken into account when designing research instruments.

Behaviour modality

This second behaviour modality facet (facet i in the overall mapping sentence) was included in all of the research surveys. However, in all studies except one (the general environmental concern study) this facet possessed only one specified element. Constantly specifying one element from a facet in a design has the effect of holding constant the variation due to this facet. Consequently, partitioning of regions for the facet was only present in the one study in which multiple elements were specified.

In the overall mapping sentence the behaviour modality facet has two specified elements: cognitive and instrumental. This is derived from the mapping sentence for social values (Levy, 1986) which was used as a template for the present research design. Throughout all the research that has been reported, these two modes were superordinate facet categories with a total of four subordinate elements. The four elements so formed were used in the design of all questionnaires. The subcategories that were used in the final stage of the project were: important, effective, (cognitive), time, money, (instrumental). The response ranges of seriousness and urgency, importance, effectiveness and repertory grid evaluations used in research instruments are ranges all from the cognitive element of the behaviour modality facet. The two involvement pledge studies were both of instrumental modality.

It was decided to include one individual subcategory from the cognitive or the instrumental element within each subsection (importance, effectiveness, time, money) of the general environmental concern questionnaire. This was done in order to simplify the format of questions and to make them easily understandable to respondents. The design of the questionnaire viewing overall environmental concern was such that direct comparison was possible between the two modalities (four elements) of expression of environmental concern.

The behaviour modality facet appears to be structurally simplistic. However, the effects it has upon the cognitive assessments within a research domain may be complex: 'the behavioural modality facet can play different roles under different circumstances, depending upon the nature of order of the content facets of the design' (Levy and Guttman, 1985:89).

The complexity of the effect that this facet had upon responses was illustrated by the coefficients between the four elements. All of the ranges of the four modes were specified from positive to negative towards an action or issue. However, the correlations were not always positive and the directionality of the relationship was not always constant between mode elements. When all four modality facet elements were included in an analysis, the polytonic relationship between elements of this facet effectively masked variation attributable to the other facets.

This finding has two important implications within environmental concern research:

1 Items within a single survey should be carefully selected with similar response modalities.
2 Caution should be employed when interpreting the results of multiple response modality studies.

Goal

The goal facet is present in the overall mapping sentence as facet b. A structure emerged for two of the studies (group repertory grids and time pledge questionnaire) which dichotomised items. The one region was made up of items that were important in their own right; the other region contained those aimed at achieving a greater goal or achieving goals through influence. This implies that the goal of environmental concern should be recognised in research design. It is common practice in environmental concern research to include not only items that achieve ends which are important in their own right but also items that achieve important ends through influence (e.g., McKechnie, 1974; Milbrath, 1984). This facet may account for much of the inconsistency between environmental concern measures found by Van Liere and Dunlap (1981).

Physical scale

A facet was present in five studies which reflected physical scale (facet f in the overall mapping sentence). This represented the physical scale of the conservational or environmental action or issue being investigated. The precise structure of the judgements embodied in this facet varied considerably between the studies in which it was present. In each instance of its occurrence this facet was present in a separate plot of similarity structure analysis to any of the already noted facets. In one study in which this facet was specified, only one element was delineated. In the questionnaire investigation of the urgency of environmental issues, all issues specified were of urgency within the context of the United Kingdom. Consequently, no partitioning occurred in analysis for this facet. The effects of specifying one element of a content facet have already been discussed and will not be further commented upon.

In the analyses of the two studies viewing individual assessments using repertory grids, and in the effectiveness of actions questionnaire, a similar structure was present for the scale facet. In both of these studies this facet had five elements. This structure represented the four physical scales of global, international, national and local conservation. The findings from the questionnaire investigating the importance of conservation activities and issues were similar to these, but the local and national scale elements were collapsed into a single British element. In all three of these analyses the facet formed a second life area facet. The elements were circularly arranged with elements circularly arranged around a common origin.

For each of the three circular arrangements of this facet, a second modifying facet was also present in the same SSA plot. For the individualistic repertory grid study, the modifying facet was one of personal relevance. For both of the importance and effectiveness studies, the modulating facet was one of environmental relevance. It has already been commented upon how the two elements of local and national conservation were combined within a single circularly ordered region in the analysis of importance. The two elements were in fact present but formed a single region in terms of the life area facet. The reason for this was due to the effects of the modifying facet. The national element was placed centrally within the British region; the local element was placed peripherally. This demonstrates that the sample of respondents assessed the national items that were included to be of greater environmental relevance than those items that reflected a local life area. A differently formatted scale facet was present in analyses of monetary pledges. In this a scale facet was present with two elements of large scale and small scale. These findings show the overall context of a research study (the mapping sentence used in its design) to affect significantly the manner in which respondents evaluate the scale of the actions and issues involved.

In previous research viewing social values (e.g., Levy, 1986), a facet of physical scale has not been included in the research design. In each of these studies, value was studied at the national scale. Consequently, scale has not been present in analyses. However, in the present research, a specific social value has been investigated rather than the broad concept of 'social values'. If other specific social values are delineated for facet investigation, it may be expected that this facet will also be pertinent in design and analysis. Levy (1979) conducted a research project that viewed political involvement. Whilst she did not include a scale facet in her design, it is interesting to note that all involvement items were of a national scale except for two. These two items reflected political issues at a larger physical scale. The coefficients between these two items were extremely high (0.82). This may suggest the presence of scale discrimination present in evaluation. This, however, is a question for future research.

A facet of physical scale has, however, been found to be useful in the design of place evaluation research (Donald, 1985). This is of interest as the multidimensional nature of evaluation in this study area was one of the reasons for employing a facet design in the present research. In place evaluation and experience studies, different physical scales have been discovered; the precise nature of this facet being related to the place under investigation and the sample's purpose within this setting. For instance, Hackett (1985) included a facet of physical scale in an evaluative study of an international airport. The same questions about the design of the airport were given to three separate samples of airport users: passengers, visitors and staff. SSA of data from the three samples revealed a scale or a level of interaction facet to be present for two of the samples. However, the psychological processes involved were of a very different kind for the two samples.

> We originally proposed a scale of interaction facet. This was found to be present in visitors responses . . . but not in other groups. Visitor division was found to be in terms of the terminal, the location, and the gallery. Passengers . . . were found to employ a level of interaction facet, with staff revealing no structure along this dimension.
>
> (Hackett, 1985: 55–56)

Hackett interpreted these findings to support the claim of Donald (1985). Hackett stated that: 'when no clear single goal can be identified then the level of interaction will be in terms of environmental scale' (Hackett, 1985: 56).

In the present investigation of social values and attitudes, a similar relationship may have existed between the content area and the presence in analyses of a scale facet. For instance, the physical scale facet was present in the evaluation of importance and effectiveness of environmental concern activities. However, when evaluation was changed from these two forms of cognitive evaluation to behavioural pledges, the scale facet did not appear. Instead, in both of these cases a purpose facet was present. This facet will be discussed in detail in the next section. However, for a clear purpose to be identified, a clear, and perhaps single goal must also be identifiable. In pledging their own time and money, it may be proposed that respondents indeed possessed this clarity. Whereas, in the theoretical cognitive assessments, purpose was less well defined.

This is an important finding in this context of social value research as it has direct consequences upon the design of attitude research, social values research and environmental concern research. Different behavioural modalities cannot be employed as equivalent and comparable measures of environmental concern. Reasons for this statement have already been noted. However, the presence of two different types of facets (scale and purpose) which are dependent, to some extent, upon the modality of assessment gives more support to this contention. A further scale facet was present in one analysis. This was a time scale of effect facet.

Time effect

Similarity Structure Analysis of the data from the environmental hazard questionnaire revealed a structure for a time scale of effect facet. This facet had a linear structure and caused hazard issues to be arranged along a straight line. This line had at one end hazards which are having an effect at present time. Progressing along the line, the next element was one of hazards that respondents judged to pose a serious future hazard. The final element was one of items assessed to have little or no serious effect. On its one occurrence, this facet appeared alone in a plot. The fact that this facet appeared separately suggests that the evaluative criteria it embodies are relatively independent processes.

The facet approach literature concerning social values has not previously included a time scale facet in its design, neither has one been reported in exploratory facet analyses in other research areas. Consequently, this facet cannot be related to previous research. Furthermore, in the present studies, the environmental hazards questionnaire was the only study to possess this facet, so little can be stated about it. Its presence in the format specified above states clearly the way in which respondents evaluated the time scale of effect. Future research could usefully benefit from designing investigations into other environmental topics which include these, and perhaps other, time scale elements. From the elements that comprise this facet, it can be seen that this facet was intimately linked to the perceived seriousness of the environmental hazard. This is not surprising as the range into which responses were gathered was a range of perceived seriousness. It does, however, reiterate the claim that the scale facet is sensitive to the form of the response that will be gathered in a survey. The physical scale facet has now been presented. None the less, it has already been noted that a facet of purpose was present in some analyses. Furthermore, this facet may constitute a scale facet in the contexts of the research in which it occurred. This facet will now be considered.

Purpose

The final content facet to be discussed is the facet of action or issue purpose. This facet occurred three times in the nine analyses. The facet was present for the studies requiring the instrumental involvement of money and time and in the group repertory grid study. On all occasions it dichotomised involvement items into actions that achieved their own ends, and actions that were for a greater or more superordinate purpose. The facet appeared on a separate plot of analysis in the time pledge study and the group repertory grid study. However, with monetary pledges this ordered facet interacted with the life area facet to form a duplex structure (Brown, 1985).

In the time pledge and group repertory grid study, respondents were being asked to evaluate their own levels of time involved with each of the specified environmental concerns. In both of these situations, the evaluations performed were independent of other assessments that respondents made. However, with the monetary pledge commitment, respondents' judgements of purpose were intimately related to the type of activity their involvement was supporting. The presence of these differences in the judgements which are made further supports the hypothesis that all measures of environmental concern are not equivalent. An ordered facet which causes the structuring of responses in terms of instrumentality or cognition has been found to be present in facet research into socio-political involvement (e.g., Levy, 1978, 1979). However, this facet was an involvement modality facet which modified the life area of the specified issue. Consequently, the present ordered facet of action purpose cannot be directly compared to existing research. A facet that contains the purpose of a value or involvement represents an important extension of the mapping sentences which were used to generate the present research.

Background facets

A background facet which was included in each study was one of respondent type. This is specified in the overall mapping sentence as p. This facet has three elements, which reflect the three different samples used in the surveys. These were: students, members of the general public and conservation employees. Each of the studies contained a sample from only one of these groups. As a consequence of this design, and the different measurement instruments used in each investigation, no comments regarding the variation in responses due to background facets can be made. However, this was not the intention of the research.

PARTIAL ORDERING OF ELEMENTS

The facet elements from the Similarity Structure Analysis were subjected to further analysis. This was undertaken in order to reveal the joint ordering which was present in assessments of the seriousness of environmental hazards. This particular study was chosen for this form of analysis for several reasons, which were presented in the results section. Furthermore, to perform POSA upon all data sets would have been unduly time-consuming and may well have produced confusing findings beyond the scope of the present investigation. The environmental hazard study that was selected contained a dichotomised life area facet and a linear scale facet (such facets being applicable to POSA). The structure of this POSA may not be present in all of the studies. Indeed, as the similarity structure varied between studies, partial ordering would also be expected to differ. A researcher is therefore required to perform a POSA of his/her own data. What is achieved through the current POSA is the demonstration of the technique's usefulness in allowing further statements to be made about a data set. These statements allow individuals to be identified with respect to their response profile in an investigation. The POSA that has been performed demonstrates this to be a useful analysis procedure in environmental concern research.

All Partial Order Scalogram Analyses plot the quantitative and qualitative dimensions of the research content. The Hasse diagram in Figure 7.10 specifies the quantitative dimension from very serious to not very serious (this is the response range of the investigation).

Plotted at 90 degrees to this is the qualitative dimension. Respondents located at the one end of this dimension were those who assessed all life areas of hazard to be serious (both human/social and ecological). These respondents also tended to be relatively unconcerned about hazards that had no present or future effects. Positioned at the other extreme of this dimension are respondents who rated the human and ecological effects as being of low levels of seriousness, and who perceived as very serious future hazard effects, and who scored highly upon the no present effects element. From this it is possible to state that respondents tended to fall into two structural categories. The first category of respondents perceived as serious all hazards which may be considered to be 'here and now' hazards; whilst the second group was more concerned with the possible future effects of hazards. The two groupings described are not typical of all respondents from the sample. However, the qualitative and quantitative dimensions described in this analysis are the only dimensions which discriminate systematically between individuals. Whilst some respondents will be characterised by the dimension, others will be represented less perfectly. Furthermore, the facet elements that are specified in the Hasse diagram systematically structure responses. Other facet elements were discovered to be playing less important or less consistent roles.

The important points to be noted from this POSA are as follows. The identified facets, and their respective elements, are important dimensions or criteria along which respondents may be differentiated. This differentiation may be of a qualitative or a quantitative kind. Through the use of POSA, responses are not simply used to understand the content area of an evaluation (as is done with SSA). In these analyses, respondents may be typified within the context of the research area in terms of their actual scores upon each of the facets within the research area. These findings allow further support to be given to the facets identified in the Similarity Structure Analysis. Thereby, these results support the multidimensional hypothesis of environmental concern and the hypotheses of the facet and facet elements proposed for environmental hazard attitudes.

Having discussed the findings in terms of their facet structure, the questions regarding the dimensionality of environmental concern, posed at the start of the research, can now be addressed.

FACET ELEMENTS OF ENVIRONMENTAL CONCERN

The results of Similarity Structure Analyses have revealed facets (or dimensions) of environmental concern. Partial Order Scalogram

Analysis of the element scores, from one study, have further supported the multivariate descriptive model proposed in an overall mapping sentence. This multidimensional descriptive model of environmental concern has important implications in environmental concern research design. The mean scores for facet elements further illustrate this need for careful design which takes into account the variation due to these facets. Mean scores have been calculated and presented in Chapter 8 (Tables 8.1 to 8.6). The presentation of these scores has enabled some interesting relationships between elements of the facet model to emerge. Statements have been made about these relationships in Chapter 8. Some of these will now be reiterated as they apply to the design of research to investigate environmental concern.

Table 8.1 shows that the overall importance of environmental concern issues and activities is rated quite highly, whilst effectiveness is rated somewhat lower. Respondents were also more willing to pledge money than time. This order of the behaviour modality facet elements (important – effective – time – money) was present in all analyses. Effectiveness is to a large extent negatively related to all other modalities. This is illustrated in Tables 8.3 and 8.4. In these two tables the life area elements are broken down by behaviour modality (Table 8.3), as are the scale elements in Table 8.4.

Table 8.3 shows the life area element of ecological conservation to be rated more highly than the social conservation element, in the importance modality and the two instrumental modalities. However, the order is reversed by altering the modality to effectiveness. Table 8.4 shows a similar effect due to the specification of effectiveness as the modality facet element in reference to physical scale elements. The elements of importance and the two instrumental modalities are not identical, but a degree of commonalty exists. The modality of effectiveness conversely has a meaning that is reversed relative to the other modalities. Table 8.5a presents a breakdown of mean scores for a three-way combination of scale, life area and modality facet elements. From this table it can be seen that the reversed relationship between the effectiveness modality and other modalities is less consistent. A similarity between the importance modality and the two instrumental modalities does, however, still exist (although this is less perfect than in the previously presented tables). Several important points can be made from these relationships of element order. It should however be noted that in order to characterise an individual as being higher or lower than other respondents across modalities, Z transformations of scores need to be performed.

From the comparisons of mean scores, it is important to note that the degree of support for environmental concern given by respondents varied according to the measurement taken. Also, by changing the range of responses it is possible to reverse the psychological meaning of a scale. Furthermore, as more facets were included within a comparison of mean scores, the relationship between any two facets of the evaluation became less predictive in its nature. These findings have important implications upon the design of environmental concern research. They imply that the researcher must take great care in designing observations and in clearly specifying response ranges. It also illustrates the point that as more complex research items are defined, the internal consistency of observations is likely to be reduced. These caveats do not invalidate the study of complex behaviours associated with environmental concern, neither do they remove the possibility of employing multiple response ranges in research. Their implication is that research must be aware of these findings. From the findings of this research, a simple solution which will allow research design to conform to these standards would be to use and adapt the mapping sentence in Figure 9.1. A further important point made by the mean score analyses is that a specified facet (for instance, the behavioural modality facet) can have direct substantial affects upon the data gathered. However, in research into complex multivariate events, the effect of any given variable, facet or dimension will be mediated by all other facets, variables, etc. included within a design. Without carefully specifying all facets in a design, variation within a data set cannot be thoroughly understood. In the context of environmental concern, the facets of the overall mapping sentence (Figure 9.1) need to be clearly specified in relation to the specific environmental concern context of a study.

Having discussed the facet structure of environmental concern and the implications of this structure for research design, the next section will consider the dimensionality of the research area.

THE DIMENSIONALITY OF ENVIRONMENTAL CONCERN (CONCLUSIONS)

The initial question which motivated this research was 'How many dimensions are present in environmental concern attitudes, and what is this, or what are these, dimensions?' A different question has been posed in the literature which has developed out of an uncertainty of the dimensionality of environmental concern. This has been explicitly stated as, 'Do all measures of environmental concern measure the same underlying concept?' Van Liere and Dunlap (1981) reviewed this and concluded that measures were measuring differentially the concept of environmental concern. They concluded by stating: 'further research is needed to clearly establish the boundaries of the concept of Environmental Concern' (Van Liere and Dunlap, 1981: 670).

The findings from the present research have investigated the dimensions of environmental concern. These (it may be argued) form the dimensions, at the extreme ends of which may be found these boundaries. The location of these boundaries is a matter for future research; the facets provide the design for this enquiry.

There has been disagreement regarding the dimensional structure of environmental concern in the literature (de Haven-Smith, 1988). Psychological research has usually stopped short of directly investigating the dimensions of environmental concern. Instead, imprecise statements have been made about unidimensional hypotheses (Tognacci *et al.*, 1972) or multidimensional structures (Van Liere and Dunlap, 1981; Cotgrove, 1982) being the most appropriate solutions. The doubts that have been expressed regarding the unidimensional hypothesis have usually been in the form of questions such as, 'Will the environmentally concerned individual be equally concerned with all environmental issues?' (de Haven-Smith, 1988). Some research has found that there is a strong positive relationship between all measures of environmental concern issues (e.g., Tognacci *et al.*, 1972). However, other research has found this to be missing (e.g., Van Liere and Dunlap, 1981). These latter findings have led to the hypothesis being forwarded by some authors that support for environmental actions is issue-specific (Connerly, 1986).

Cotgrove's (1982) data supported the existence of a three-dimensional structure being present in environmental concern attitudes. The dimensions Cotgrove (1982) proposed were of damage, shortage and nature. However, the dimensions that were suggested were each composed of relatively few representative items. Furthermore, no precise statements were made about two important characteristics of the dimensions: neither the psychological nature of the proposed dimensions nor the interrelationships between the dimensions were specified. Both of these have been major tasks of the present research.

This research has addressed several different substantive types of environmental concern. Studies were designed so as to employ different environmental concern measures in order to answer the question of whether different types of environmental concern measure are equivalent. To state this more explicitly, researchers have asked, in a variety of ways, the question: 'Do all (or different) measures of environmental concern measure the same underlying environmental concern concept and to a similar degree and in a comparable manner?' (Weigel and Weigel, 1978; Van Liere and Dunlap, 1981).

The theoretical model developed by Van Liere and Dunlap (1981) to account for intermeasure variation was also investigated in the present research. The results found considerable support for the authors' two dimensions. These authors claimed that if the two dimensions were not held constant between different environmental concern studies, then these differences in research instruments would account for variations in research findings. The two hypothesised dimensions were based first upon variation in the substantive content of research (the incorporation of different environmental issues within a single research instrument). Second, they identified a dimension that embodied variations in the theoretical conceptualisations which had been used to develop measurement items (the scaling procedures and the range into which responses were gathered). The claim that variation in the findings of environmental concern research is due to differences in the measurement scales used (reviewed by Van Liere and Dunlap, 1981) is supported in the present research. This is shown by the differences in facet structure which were present in assessments and which were due to the range into which responses were mapped. The hypothesis that another cause of variation is due to substantive issue variance is also upheld. Support for this claim is illustrated by the presence of a content 'facet structure' for environmental concern.

The research therefore supports Van Liere and Dunlap's two hypotheses. These are that environmental concern is multidimensional and that differences in the results from a number of research studies are due to substantive and theoretical variations in research design. However, the present research continues beyond a conclusion that simply denotes the presence of this variance. It is now possible to state that variation will be present along the specified facets of the overall mapping sentence (Figure 9.1): substantive variation is due to nine facets. In all studies (except the general study) a polar life area facet was present. This facet was often accompanied by a separately differentiated scale facet. The evaluation criteria present in these facets were often modified by assessments of the personal and/or environmental importance of the specified environmental concern action or issue. The structures discovered have been discussed in detail above, as they pertain to specific studies. It is interesting to note that this four-facet structure was common (though often in a modified form) to many of the results.

The specification of the findings of the research in Table 9.1 includes a listing of all of the facets of assessment that were present in each study. It has therefore been clearly demonstrated that the range along which responses are gathered, together with the modality of behaviour which is being assessed, have very important effects upon the data gathered. The different ranges and modalities that may be employed are differentially related to environmental concern. As a consequence of these findings, it may be claimed that any study that intermixes different substantive issues (modalities) or theoretical conceptions (ranges) may produce results which, at best, do not form a component with a cumulative body of environmental concern literature.

The findings from the present research would also advise caution in adopting standardised measurement approaches. This is due to the different structures that emerged for the different assessments of environmental concern. By unsympathetically using a standardised assessment package, in the context of environmental concern monitoring, a structure could easily be imposed upon the data by the researcher. This could, of course, be true of the findings of the present study. However, it is hoped that through the adaptation of the approach, imposition of structure has been kept to a minimum.

It is clear from the data presented in Table 9.1 that there are several dimensions to environmental concern. The precise number of dimensions is dependent upon the precise context of the environmental concern attitudes and social values being investigated. However, most environmental concern issues and activities can be accurately depicted using up to four selected facets from the overall mapping sentence. The behaviour modality of responses will also become important in a research study in which affective responses are included. Furthermore, the facets that should be included in a study, their structure and the elements of a facet, are all dependent upon several factors. These factors are the precise issues, actions and design of the research. The claims made above are supported by the variation in the number and type of facets, and facet elements present for each of the nine studies (these are contained in the cells of Table 9.1).

Several researchers have been criticised for not using comparable criteria to indicate environmental concern (Van Liere and Dunlap,

1978). The results of the present research suggest that there is a diverse nature to this concern. However, diversity is predictable using the facets of the overall mapping sentence and applying these appropriately to a specified research setting. Consequently, it would be appropriate to develop a standardised questionnaire for the investigation of environmental concern using the overall mapping sentence.

It should be noted that careful specification of both content facets and mapping range are necessary as context influences the format of these facets. Therefore, an alternate approach to environmental concern research would be to use the overall mapping sentence to design instruments specific to each environmental concern investigation. The employment of the overall mapping sentence in research development would ensure two features being present in research. First, the research would clearly address the semantic area of environmental concern which the researcher was wishing to investigate. Second, the results produced in this way would be directly comparable with other environmental concern research employing this design. Consequently, the findings of studies would be cumulative.

Both the literature on facet theory design (Canter, 1982b, 1983) and the findings of the present research would suggest that facet theory approach could be beneficially employed to guide future environmental concern research. This would impel the researcher to produce standard instruments by requiring them to develop and modify the mapping sentence developed within their own research design (as has been done in Hackett and Florence, 1991).

The ability of mapping sentences to co-ordinate research in applied fields has been previously documented (Levy, 1979; Schlesinger, 1978).

> A mapping sentence is frequently both the start and the conclusion of a research project. It is not necessary that a mapping sentence identical to the one which helps initiate the project will also be produced at its end. Indeed, one may think about a piece of facet research as a process of refinement, elaboration, and validation of a mapping sentence.
>
> (Canter, 1985b: 260)

In the present research a mapping sentence has been developed as a conclusion. The overall mapping sentence and the individual mapping sentences for each study have been refined, elaborated and validated as they are appropriate to the study of the social value of environmental concern. Through using the overall mapping sentence in future investigations of environmental concern, the mapping sentence would be further modified and developed by researchers to the specific context of their investigations. The present research provides a starting point in further multidimensional investigations.

10 Conclusion

At the outset of this book one of the original stated aims was to initiate the multivariate investigation of environmental concern. Research has been undertaken in order to explore this concern in a wide variety of psychological contexts. This has culminated in the development of an overall mapping sentence. From the results presented, a number of interesting and important conclusions may be drawn. In the following sections the main conclusions will be presented of the individual facets of the research, and from the overall mapping sentence.

The initial stages of this research were exploratory and the facets identified in these studies were facets of content. In the sections and studies that followed, this content area was investigated further, in terms of its attitude, social value and involvement components. These studies in effect allowed environmental concern to be investigated 'in context'. The dichotomy of content and context is of course artificial: content being dependent upon context, and vice versa. In the concluding sections below, the content facets will initially be presented as a model of environmental concern.

MODEL OF ENVIRONMENTAL CONCERN

Facets of content

As the area of the research had not previously been the subject of facet research, no mapping sentence existed to guide research design. Consequently, the first two studies conducted did not use a mapping sentence in their development, execution or interpretation. Instead, they formed an 'in-depth' investigation into the semantic content of environmental concern. This resulted in the identification of three main facets of content: life area, physical scale and relevance. Other facets were added in later studies.

Life area

The facet of life area was discovered to be present in each of the exploratory studies. Furthermore, the structure of this facet and the elements that composed it were similar in both. The discovery of a life area facet was of little surprise as this form of facet has been discovered in many other faceted investigations (e.g., Levy and Guttman, 1981a, 1981b, 1981c). In the exploratory studies the facet was found to be composed of three elements. These were of social conservation, educational conservation and ecological conservation. These elements were circularly arranged, showing the differentiations between elements to involve respondents in radially differentiated forms of assessment with the circular order reflected the target of an environmental concern activity or issue. Issues that were assessed as being aimed to benefit humans (e.g., provisions of green spaces, cleaning cities) occupied one position in the circle. Along one boundary an opposite position was formed by actions and issues that were primarily ecological (e.g., saving blue whales (for their own sake)). Sandwiched between these two elements of life area was found educational conservation, which appeared to link the former two elements. The arrangement of elements showed respondents to clearly identify different environmental concern issues and activities along this continuum. This structure of life area was included in all research instruments used in the subsequent questionnaire studies. However, analysis of these studies revealed different cognitive structures to be pertinent when environmental concern attitudes, values and involvement were investigated.

Two studies of environmental concern attitudes were conducted. These viewed the urgency of environmental issues and the seriousness of environmental hazards. In both of these, the same underlying social–ecological polar dimension was present. This structure was modified by the context of the enquiry. Neither assessments of hazard seriousness nor issue urgency were perceived to possess an educational element. Furthermore, the ecological element of the urgency survey was subdivided into the three regions of: wastes, pollution and depletion. This illustrates that the precise subject that is being investigated, and the type of evaluations which respondents are required to make, will significantly affect responses.

This point is further supported by the analyses of the four

remaining questionnaire studies of the importance and the effectiveness of environmental concern, and the degree of expressed willingness towards involvement. In the first two of these analyses, the life area facet took a structure that reflected the social–ecological arrangement. However, the precise elements of this facet were of habitat, species and morals. The difference in the elements that were present was due to respondents having to make value assessments along different response ranges. This effect was also present when respondents were asked to pledge involvement. The life area of involvement changed quite drastically from the structure of life area which has so far been presented. In both involvement surveys, the life area facet had elements of protection, control and development. These elements differentiate the types of actions with which respondents were being asked to become involved.

From the above findings two important claims may be made, both of which have an effect upon environmental concern research. First, the presence of this facet in all of the individual analyses of the studies undertaken show this to be a very pertinent facet of environmental concern attitudes, values and involvement. As a consequence of this pertinence, future environmental concern research should specify the life area facet in its design. Second, the variation in the precise nature of the elements that composed the facet between different studies suggest that great care should be taken in specifying the elements of this facet. A social–ecological division was present in most analyses. However, variations occurred due to both the substantive content and the response range of the research. A second facet of the content of environmental concern is that of its physical scale.

Physical scale

This facet was present in the individual exploratory repertory grid study and the importance, effectiveness and monetary pledge questionnaire. In all cases the facet had elements that reflected the geographic scale of an environmental action or issue. The precise elements of this facet differed between studies, in a similar way to the life area facet. In the analyses of the individual repertory grid, and the importance and effectiveness questionnaires, four or five facet elements were present. However, in assessments of monetary pledges, only two elements were present. This demonstrates that respondents making cognitive assessments made fine differentiations of the activities and issues they were assessing. However, in the case of instrumental assessments, discriminations were less refined. The validity and implications of this statement is a subject for future research. Furthermore, cognitive evaluations were circularly arranged, whilst the instrumental evaluation was modular. This demonstrates that involvement is an instrumental activity which involves different assessments to those present in purely cognitive appraisals. The inclusion within a research instrument of both cognitive and instrumental assessment ranges, or the comparison of questionnaires with different ranges, will be confounded in terms of the physical scale of respondents' assessments.

It should also be noted that the physical scale facet was not discovered within both exploratory studies, nor included within each design. This may, however, be a confusing finding as a single element (a single scale) may have been present in these studies. The presence of this facet in several of the analyses does show this to be an important source of variation in research data. Consequently, the physical scale facet should be explicitly stated in subsequent environmental concern research design.

The sections above have both presented polar facets (and in one case a linearly ordered facet). These polar facets have been found to differentiate qualitatively responses to questions about environmental concern. A further facet present in nearly all studies was a facet of environmental relevance.

Environmental relevance

On all but one of the occurrences of this facet it was found to possess a modulating structure. This is the structure of a facet which is found in a plot to have centrally and peripherally placed elements. Items that comprise the central region are more similar to other items in an analysis in reference to the modulator. It is also often the case with a modulating facet that it is discovered in the same plot of SSA as a polar facet. It is therefore possible to state that the centrally located items are classified by the two facets concurrently.

Environmental relevance had the tendency to occur in a modulating facet format. The presence of this facet in research design is of great importance, as modulation is a form of modification. This facet was found to modify the assessments of both the life area and the physical scale facets. What this means in effect is that the life area and physical scale of environmental concern are polar (circularly arranged) distinctions which must be specified in research design. However, each element of both of these life area facets has items that respondents deemed to be of central or peripheral environmental relevance. This implies that the design of environmental concern research should enquire about the life area and scale of concern, both at different levels of environmental relevance. The structure of this facet was relatively constant. The structure did alter in two cases. In the questionnaire survey of problem urgency, the facet had central and peripheral elements. However, the facet appeared in a plot of its own and did not modify other assessments. In the seriousness study, the facet took a totally different structure. On this occasion the facet was linear with elements arranged from greater to lesser environmental relevance. These findings show that in certain circumstances, the facet of environmental relevance can play an independent role in structuring responses. Therefore, the researcher should carefully specify the role this facet plays within the design of attitude assessments: in many instances it may not be appropriate to ask questions of environmental relevance without first specifying relevance towards what (life area or action scale).

Personal relevance

The facet of personal relevance was essentially of the same structure, and possessed the same elements, as the environmental relevance facet. Therefore, the statements made for this previously discussed facet apply. Each time this facet was present, its structure was modular. Furthermore, the facet always modified the polar regions of the life area facet. This implies that subjects often referred the life area of an action or issue which was being addressed 'to themselves'.

Perhaps the point of greatest importance in regard to this facet was that it was present in the same analysis as the environmental relevance facet. This shows that relevance can be accorded conjointly in terms of both the environmental and the personal. This necessitates research to consider both relevance facets in design. It also shows that the personal relevance of environmental concern should be investigated in terms of specific life areas.

Time

A facet that represented time scale was included in one study; namely, attitudes towards environmental hazards. SSA of this data showed this facet to play an independent role in structuring responses along a linear dimension. The elements of this facet are of particular interest. Placed at one end of the linear order were items assessed to be serious hazards at the present time. At the other end were located items assessed not to be serious environmental hazards at the present time. Sandwiched between these poles were items which were evaluated as presenting future environmental hazards.

The presence of this facet necessitates that care should be taken in designing and interpreting research that includes multiple time scale elements. However, the facet was only included in the one study. Therefore, further research is needed to investigate the universality of this facet in structuring environmental concern attitudes. The unusual elements of this facet may represent the elements of time scale evaluations across environmental concern in general. Alternatively, the elements may be specific to the present study. These too are questions for future research.

Purpose

The purpose of concern facet was present in the analysis of the two instrumental studies of environmental concern. In both of these analyses, the structure of this facet formed two parallel regions. In the one region, items were contained that achieved an environmental goal in themselves (were undertaken for their own ends) whilst the other element comprised items that achieved goals through indirect means (influence). The presence of this facet in the analysis of the two instrumental studies is of importance to design. It implies that not only is an instrumental act different in its level of overt expression, but also the criteria that are used to evaluate the effectiveness (or other forms of evaluation) of instrumentallity differ to those used in cognitive evaluations. The purpose of instrumental involvement is here being used as an assessment criterion.

Researchers must therefore employ careful design which takes into account the modality of concern expression (cognitive or instrumental). Design must also be aware of the effect of the modality upon the presence of a purpose facet. Furthermore, it would appear that instrumental studies should include a facet of purpose in their specification.

Behaviour (expression) modality

Within the overall mapping sentence for environmental concerns two modality facets are present. The first of these represents the modality of the behaviour to be gathered in a study (cognitive, affective, behaviour). All of the studies were of the cognitive type. This facet will therefore not be discussed further. However, it should be noted that future research could be designed which investigated other modalities of environmental concern. For instance, conservation actions could be observed and these observations related to other facets of the overall mapping sentence (Figure 9.1). This would investigate the usefulness of this taxonomy in guiding research into more overt behaviours which are related to environmental concern.

Behaviour (involvement) modality

The second of the behaviour modality facets specified the modality of concern. The facet elements were of cognitive and instrumental behaviours. The facet was not concerned with the modality of the behaviour which was to be gathered, but with the modality of involvement.

This facet was employed differently to any of the other facets used in designing the present research. Different elements from this facet were not included within the same research instrument. Instead, each research study was designed around one of the elements. All instruments were of a cognitive modality excepting the questionnaires of time and monetary pledge. The questionnaire studies (studies 6 to 9 in Table 9.1) included identical items but two studies were of a cognitive modality (studies 6 and 7) and two were of an instrumental modality (studies 8 and 9). The reasons for adopting this design have already been noted.

Analyses have shown that this facet is of considerable importance in structuring assessments of environmental concern. The instrumental and cognitive elements have been seen to have significant effects upon the structure of other facets of assessment. The structure of this facet has been commented upon as it relates to the facet of purpose. Indeed, these two facets are very similar to each other. The purpose facet, however, classifies items in terms of their scale of purpose (e.g., activities that are undertaken for their own ends, and activities undertaken for more superordinate ends). The modality facet, in contrast, divides actions and issues into assessments of cognitive and instrumental 'behaviours'. Moreover, the structure of the purpose facet is to a large extent dependent upon the modality of assessments. The bipartite division of modality has been expanded to include 'specific forms' of each modality. The results have shown this to produce psychological dimensions which may be negatively related to each other. It is therefore obvious that this facet requires careful consideration and inclusion in the design and analysis of observations.

Goal

This facet specified environmental concern as being of environmental issue or environmental action. The facet was derived from the mapping sentence for social values (Figure 5.1). However, in the present research none of the studies contained both elements from this facet. None the less, this is a facet which would benefit from inclusion within future research into environmental concern. Having briefly reviewed all of the facets and facet elements of environmental concern research design, the model formed by the facets in combination is now considered.

The model of environmental concern in general

A number of general conclusions may be drawn about the facet model of environmental concern developed in this book. It is clear that a general model for environmental concern has been established in the form of an overall mapping sentence. Mapping sentences have also been developed for each of the research studies. From this it is apparent that no more than four facets define variation within any one study. Furthermore, this is a generalisable and coherent structure. This generalisability is evident from the nine analyses that have been presented. The evidence presented therefore represents a significant increase in the understanding of environmental concern.

The overall mapping sentence, and the ways in which it has been applied to specific environmental concern research, has been discussed. The generality of the template it provides suggests a wide number of possibilities for its future use. The model the mapping sentence forms may be used to investigate further environmental concern (this has been suggested in earlier sections). This is also the case with concern that is expressed through behavioural modalities other than cognitive. Repertory grid and questionnaire methods have been used and both have produced data supportive of the mapping sentence. Other data collection methods (such as secondary sources, e.g., society membership) could be used separately and with verbal collection methods. Furthermore, the mapping sentence could be employed to reinterpret many of the findings of environmental concern research in the literature.

The use of the mapping sentence could also facilitate the

comparison of different research projects. The differences between projects could be of many different kinds. For example, using the mapping sentence template, assessments could be made of different environmental issues, and solutions to these issues within a single population. This would allow the direct comparison of alternative future scenarios. A variation upon this would be to investigate the same (or different) issues and/or concerns across different populations. The standard framework provided by the mapping sentence would allow comparability of results. There is a need to continue research by applying the mapping sentence to other environmental concerns with different respondent samples. In doing this, the utility of the existing structure will be tested and adaptations and extensions made. The model represents a first attempt at developing a framework for environmental attitudes (e.g., Hackett, 1987a, 1987b, 1989, 1992a, 1992b, 1992c). Attention should therefore be directed at replicating this model, which subsequently may be expanded.

Background variables

The mapping sentence could also be used to design studies investigating the association between environmental concern and background variables. One such study is at present being analysed. This has used the environmental hazard and urgency questionnaires, and differences are emerging due to respondents' gender. Many other background variables could be investigated in this way. The use of this research template would result in directly comparable results. This may help to resolve many of the differences in associations between environmental concern and socio-demographic variables reported in the literature.

MODEL OF ENVIRONMENTAL CONCERN AND SOCIAL VALUES AND ATTITUDES

One of the explicit aims of the research was to relate environmental concern to social values and attitudes. Through the use of what was termed at the start of this chapter 'context facets', this aim has been achieved. A mapping sentence, and thereby understanding, has been produced for environmental concern as a personal and social value and attitude. Furthermore, variation in respondents' understanding of this concern has been seen to be influenced by the context of the enquiry. In general it can be concluded that a useful descriptive structural model of environmental concern values and attitudes has been produced. The integration of facets from mapping sentences for social values has allowed environmental concern to be investigated as it is personally valued.

EXTENSIONS OF THE MODEL

The results form an answer to many of the problems that have beset the environmental concern research literature. More importantly, the findings form a starting point for future research in this and allied areas. The mapping sentence has already been used to design a study concerned with Third World issues. The results from the analysis of this study lent support to the mapping sentence in this analogous semantic area (Phipps, 1988). The ability of the mapping sentence to help design investigations of Third World issues illustrates the existence of a great potential for future research, as whilst these issues are similar to environmental concern in that they embody a social issue, they differ in many ways. To adapt the general mapping sentence for environmental concern to this research area successfully, suggests that the sentence may be adapted to address and investigate other social problems. Furthermore, the mapping sentence could be used to ask applied questions and help to provide answers to environmental problems. An example of this would be the development of community forests (Countryside Commission, 1989b). Questions could be developed based upon the facet structure of this research. In doing this it would be possible to assess the impact, and attitudes about potential impacts, of these forest developments (and other types of development projects) in a manner that is meaningful to respondents.

SUMMARY OF THE AIMS

The conclusion of this research will be in the form of a recapitulation of the research aims that motivated the current work. The overall aim of this research was to develop a multivariate description of environmental concern in the form of a mapping sentence. This has clearly been achieved. Furthermore, the model so produced provides a template for future research into environmental concern and possibly into other social issue areas. A second aim of the research was to resolve the conflicting hypotheses regarding the multi-dimensional or unidimensional structure of environmental concern. This would appear to have been resolved in favour of the multivariate depiction, with the dimensions identified as facets in several contexts.

However, further research is needed before greater confidence can be stated regarding dimensionality. The mapping sentence has been used to represent different behavioural modes of the expression of environmental concern. Personal and social attitudes of urgency, seriousness, the value, the effectiveness, and levels of involvement with environmental concern, as well as a variety of different contexts of concern (hazards, environmental problems, etc.) have all been considered – this being the third aim of the research. In achieving the above objectives, the research has fulfilled its fourth aim, namely to extend facet theory research of social values and attitudes into this new research domain. The final aim was to adapt, to the environmental concern context, the published mapping sentences used in the generation of the research instruments. These have been modified to fit the context of the current research. This has provided support for each mapping sentence as a multivariate descriptive instrument within the specified content areas. Furthermore, achieving this has allowed the production of appropriate research instruments. The results of this have been the development of a multivariate description of environmental concern.

These aims, and the findings they have generated, represent the most comprehensive multivariate investigation of environmental concern so far undertaken. The findings represent a significant advance in both environmental concern research and in facet theory approach to investigations of values and attitudes. The mapping sentence taxonomy provides a template for the research domain. This may be modified and adapted to allow future environmental concern research, such as environmentally conscious consumer behaviour (Hackett, 1992a, 1992b, 1992c; Hackett and Florence, 1991), to be viewed, and thus to extend further the initial stages of understanding that has been developed.

Appendices

APPENDIX A.1 LIST OF GRID ELEMENTS (INDIVIDUAL REPERTORY GRID STUDY)

Elements

Awareness

Morals of conservation and ethics.

Education.

Man and nature ethics.

Ecological morals.

Green morals.

Information services.

Campaigning.

Advertising.

Worldview/thoughtfulness.

Rural conservation.

Political role.

Pressure groups.

Green sites and nature as people's choice.

People involved in nature.

Government involved in nature conservation.

Economic role.

Preservation of gene stock.

Practical ground work.

British conservation.

National conservation.

Conservation in your area.

Local conservation.

Single-issue groups.

Conservation to preserve ecology and species.

Organisation and administration of conservation.

Large-scale projects.

Small-scale projects.

Rural and urban conservation.

Nature's beauty.

Emotions.

Nature's intrinsic value.

Healthy living.

Lifestyle.

Self-sufficiency.

Commercial aspects.

Social problems.

Habitat protection.

Species protection.

Personal or individual involvement.

Personal effect.

Personally motivated.

Ineffective.

Group related.

Mental work.
Involvement of external
  agencies.
Exploitative, anti-conservation.
Essential.
Direct action/influence.
Indirect action/influence.
Effective/significant.
Doing/active.
Initiating agency.
Excludes public.
Informed choices and responses.
Emotional choices.
Responses.
Conservation studies.
Man's effect on the environment.
Global effects/wider concern.
Global management/wider
  action.
Long-term action/effect.
Short-term action/effect.
Narrow/personal concern.
Conservation related.
Conservation as elitist/scientific.
Produces pollution.
Is fulfilling.
Isn't fulfilling.

Just human.
Socially useful.
Ethical consideration.
Disregards ethics.
Sustainable.
Primary issue.
Superficial conservation.
Open mind to conservation.
External agencies working in
  conservation.
Involves whole life.
Small part of life.
Nature conservation solves social
  problems.
People give nature conservation
  their mandate.
Conservation without mandate.
Receives publicity.
Receives no publicity.
Behind the scenes.
Progressive area where influence
  is occurring.
Dead end for conservation.
Children involved.
Children not involved.
Conservation as a model.

APPENDIX A.2 STANDARD REPERTORY GRID AND INSTRUCTIONS (GROUP REPERTORY GRID STUDY)

ENVIRONMENTAL CONSERVATION RESPONSE GRID

PLEASE READ THESE INSTRUCTIONS CAREFULLY.

Please complete all scales. All information given will be treated totally confidentially. Please complete this form without the aid of other people, i.e. friends or work colleagues etc. – IT IS YOUR RESPONSE THAT IS WANTED, AND WHICH IS OF VALUE TO US.

In the GRID that follows, you will see printed along the top of each sheet, a series of 19 actions or *AREAS* of work associated with environmental conservation. Printed down the right- and left-hand sides of each sheet are a series of 48 *SCALES*.

The statement on the left-hand side of each pair of words is one end of a SCALE. The right-hand statement opposite this is the other end of this SCALE; it is the opposite or contrasting statement to the right-hand statement.

What you have to do is to look at both ends of the first scale and think what this scale means to you. Then look at the AREAS along the top of the sheet – decide which one of these AREAS is most or best described or represented by the statement on the LEFT-HAND side of this scale.

When you have done this, write a number 1 in the box on the SCALE directly beneath the AREA you decided. For instance, if you decided that AREA number 3 was the one that you most felt fitted the LEFT-HAND end of this SCALE then you would have written a number 1 beneath this AREA – as in the stage 1 diagram below.

When you have done this, then decide which of the remaining AREAS best fits or is represented by the RIGHT-HAND SCALE which is opposite the LEFT-HAND SCALE you were just looking at. Give this a score of 19.

For instance, in our example, the RIGHT-HAND SCALE is 'An area in which I have had no personal involvement'. If you decided that AREA number 6 best fitted this SCALE end, then you would write number 19 beneath it.

The next stage is to decide which of the remaining AREAS along the top of the sheet is the one which is the next best described or represented by the LEFT-HAND SCALE. You then give this a score of 2 in its box on the SCALE beneath the chosen AREA.

Then chose the next AREA most like the RIGHT-HAND SCALE and give this a score of 18.
Carry on doing this, finding the AREA next most associated with the LEFT- and RIGHT-HAND scales and giving them the next score until you have given each AREA a score from 1 to 19 along this SCALE.

When you have finished you should find that the AREAS that you have numbered 16, 17, 18, 19, are the ones that you feel are most associated with the description at the RIGHT-HAND end of the SCALE. The AREAS you have numbered 1, 2, 3, 4 are best described by the LEFT-HAND SCALE description, and the AREAS numbered 7, 8, 9, 10, 11 are equally well described by both SCALE ends.

When you have done this, move down to the next SCALE. Read the two SCALE ends and rate the 19 AREAS in terms of their 'closeness' to the RIGHT- and LEFT-HAND SCALE ENDS (as you did before). You will now have another line of numbers 1 to 19 written along this second SCALE.

Continue doing this until you have done this for each of the 48 SCALES on the 7 pages.

Thank you for taking the time to complete this grid–

Paul Hackett
University of Aston

APPENDIX A.2 STANDARD REPERTORY GRID FOLLOWS

Areas / Left-hand scales	Small-physical scale projects involving small-scale organisational actions. (1)	Green politics. (2)	Rural nature conservation. (3)	Nature's beauty and intrinsic value – emotions. (4)	National or British nature conservation strategies. (5)	Advertising and campaigning. (6)	Large-physical scale projects involving large-scale organisational actions. (7)	'Single-issue' groups and nature conservation. (8)	Awareness creation and education. (9)	Preservation and protection of the natural environment. (10)
1 An area in which I have had personal involvement.										
2 An area that involves mental or intellectual work.										
3 An area that involves urban nature conservation.										
4 An area that involves large-scale projects.										
5 An area that involves habitat protection.										
6 An area that receives publicity.										
7 An area that is personally fulfilling.										
8 Involves direct nature conservation with direct effects.										
9 Actions in this area have a personal effect.										
10 Involves nature conservation studies and research.										
11 A primary area or issue for nature conservation.										
12 Nature conservation which involves the ethics of nature conservation.										

Nature conservation political role – pressure groups.	Urban nature conservation.	Lifestyle issues – healthy, self-sufficient living.	Government actions and nature conservation policies.	Community and local involvement in local 'green' areas.	Species protection.	Global/ecosphere conservation.	Ecological ethics and morals behind environmental conservation.	Habitat protection.	Environmental conservation response grid
									PAGE 1 of 5
11	12	13	14	15	16	17	18	19	Right-hand scales
									An area in which I have no personal involvement.
									An area that involves physical or practical work.
									An area that does not involve urban nature conservation.
									An area that involves small-scale projects.
									An area not involving habitat protection.
									A behind-the-scenes nature conservation activity – receives no publicity.
									An area that is not personally fulfilling.
									Involves indirect nature conservation action with indirect effects.
									Actions in this area have no personal effect.
									Involves practical work.
									A secondary area or issue for nature conservation.
									Nature conservation which pays little regard to nature conservation ethics.

Areas / Left-hand scales	Small-physical scale projects involving small-scale organisational actions.	Green politics.	Rural nature conservation.	Nature's beauty and intrinsic value – emotions.	National or British nature conservation strategies.	Advertising and campaigning.	Large-physical scale projects involving large-scale organisational actions.	'Single-issue' groups and nature conservation.	Awareness creation and education.	Preservation and protection of the natural environment.
	1	2	3	4	5	6	7	8	9	10
13 An area that involves long-term actions and effects.										
14 An area that uses existing sites as models for nature conservation.										
15 Involves the whole of a person's life.										
16 An area that involves species protection.										
17 An area that is directly related to nature conservation.										
18 An area involving green politics.										
19 An area that involves campaigning and advertising.										
20 An area that is economically beneficial to nature conservation.										
21 An area involving national nature conservation strategy.										
22 I would feel personally motivated to become involved in this area.										
23 Nature conservation which involves the general public										

Nature conservation political role – pressure groups.	Urban nature conservation.	Lifestyle issues – healthy, self-sufficient living.	Government actions and nature conservation policies.	Community and local involvement in local 'green' areas.	Species protection.	Global/ecosphere conservation.	Ecological ethics and morals behind environmental conservation.	Habitat protection.	PAGE 2 of 5
11	12	13	14	15	16	17	18	19	Right-hand scales
									An area that involves short-term actions and effects.
									Involves site creation.
									Involves just a small part of a person's life.
									An area that does not involve the protection of species.
									An area that is indirectly related to nature conservation.
									An area not involving green politics.
									Does not involve advertising and campaigning in this area.
									An area that is not economically beneficial to nature conservation.
									An area not involving national nature conservation stratergy.
									I would not feel personally motivated to become involved in this area.
									An area of nature conservation that excludes the general public – elitist, scientific.

Left-hand scales	Small-physical scale projects involving small-scale organisational actions.	Green politics.	Rural nature conservation.	Nature's beauty and intrinsic value – emotions.	National or British nature conservation strategies.	Advertising and campaigning.	Large-physical scale projects involving large-scale organisational actions.	'Single-issue' groups and nature conservation.	Awareness creation and education.	Preservation and protection of the natural environment.
Areas →	1	2	3	4	5	6	7	8	9	10
24 Ecology and nature are the areas of concern.										
25 An area of nature conservation which receives public support.										
26 An area within nature conservation that has an open mind to nature conservation.										
27 An area involving rural nature conservation.										
28 An area where nature conservation is concerned with environmental and nature preservation.										
29 An area involving single-issue groups.										
30 Nature conservation takes a political role in this area.										
31 Involves nature conservation for the sake of nature.										
32 An area where nature conservation is making progress.										
33 Socially useful nature conservation helps to solve social problems.										

Nature conservation political role – pressure groups.	Urban nature conservation.	Lifestyle issues – healthy, self-sufficient living.	Government actions and nature conservation policies.	Community and local involvement in local 'green' areas.	Species protection.	Global/ecosphere conservation.	Ecological ethics and morals behind environmental conservation.	Habitat protection.	PAGE 3 of 5
11	12	13	14	15	16	17	18	19	Right-hand scales
									Concern is just for humans in these areas.
									An area of nature conservation that receives little public support.
									An area within nature conservation that has a closed mind to nature conservation.
									An area that does not involve rural nature conservation.
									An area where nature conservation pays little concern to nature and environmental preservation.
									An area that involves a wider concern.
									In this area nature conservation does not take a political role.
									Involves nature as being seen to have a value only in terms of its usefulness to human beings.
									An area where nature conservation is making little progress.
									Nature conservation that solves ecological problems.

Left-hand scales	Small-physical scale projects involving small-scale organisational actions.	Green politics.	Rural nature conservation.	Nature's beauty and intrinsic value – emotions.	National or British nature conservation strategies.	Advertising and campaigning.	Large-physical scale projects involving large-scale organisational actions.	'Single-issue' groups and nature conservation.	Awareness creation and education.	Preservation and protection of the natural environment.
Areas	1	2	3	4	5	6	7	8	9	10
34 Nature consevation choices are made on the basis of 'sound' – 'rational' evidence.										
35 An area that is effective in nature conservation terms.										
36 An area that involves work done by an individual.										
37 Nature conservation that has a global 'wide' effect and area of concern – 'global management'.										
38 Involves organisations existing solely for nature conservation.										
39 An area that involves children.										
40 Involves healthy living – self-sufficient living.										
41 An area in which the local community is involved in nature conservation.										
42 An area in which global/ecosphere is involved.										
43 An area that has an economic role outside of nature conservation.										

Nature conservation political role – pressure groups.	Urban nature conservation.	Lifestyle issues – healthy, self-sufficient living.	Government actions and nature conservation policies.	Community and local involvement in local 'green' areas.	Species protection.	Global/ecosphere conservation.	Ecological ethics and morals behind environmental conservation.	Habitat protection.	PAGE 4 of 5
11	12	13	14	15	16	17	18	19	Right-hand scales
									Nature conservation that involves emotional responses.
									An area that is of little effect in nature conservation terms.
									Involves work that is done by or related to nature conservation 'groups'.
									Local nature conservation having a narrow area of effect and concern – 'local management'.
									Involves external agencies working in nature conservation.
									An area that does not involve children.
									Does not necessarily involve healthy living – self-sufficient living.
									Involves no local community involvement in nature conservation.
									An area that has a narrower physical scale of concern.
									An area that has no economic role outside of nature conservation.

Areas Left-hand scales	Small-physical scale projects involving small-scale organisational actions.	Green politics.	Rural nature conservation.	Nature's beauty and intrinsic value – emotions.	National or British nature conservation strategies.	Advertising and campaigning.	Large-physical scale projects involving large-scale organisational actions.	'Single-issue' groups and nature conservation.	Awareness creation and education.	Preservation and protection of the natural environment.
	1	2	3	4	5	6	7	8	9	10
44 An area where government actions and policies are involved in nature conservation.										
45 An area involving awareness creation.										
46 An area involving nature conservation responding to bad effects/influences in the environment.										
47 An area involving solely nature conservation groups.										
48 An area which is of importance to nature conservation in terms of it achieving its overall aims.										

Nature conservation political role – pressure groups.	Urban nature conservation.	Lifestyle issues – healthy, self-sufficient living.	Government actions and nature conservation policies.	Community and local involvement in local 'green' areas.	Species protection.	Global/ecosphere conservation.	Ecological ethics and morals behind environmental conservation.	Habitat protection.	PAGE 5 of 5
11	12	13	14	15	16	17	18	19	Right-hand scales
									An area within nature conservation not involving government actions and policies.
									An area not involving awareness creation.
									An area where nature conservation is the initiator of the action.
									An area involving agencies external to nature conservation.
									An area of little importance to nature conservation in terms of achieving its overall aims.

APPENDIX A.3 SERIOUSNESS OF ENVIRONMENTAL HAZARDS QUESTIONNAIRE

Environmental pollution assessment form: A

> **Instructions**
> Below is a statement, please read this and then look at each type of pollution. For each of these put a tick under how serious you think each of these is.

Gender   Male ☐   Female ☐

Work   Employed ☐   Unemployed ☐   Student ☐   Retired ☐

Age   0–20 ☐   21–35 ☐   36–50 ☐   51–64 ☐   65+ ☐

How serious an effect on our environment do you think each of these things has?

	Very serious	Quite serious	Not very serious	Not at all serious
Noise from aircraft				
Lead from petrol				
Industrial waste in the rivers and seas				
Waste from nuclear power stations				
Industrial fumes in the air				
Noise and dirt from traffic				

APPENDIX A.4 URGENCY OF ENVIRONMENTAL PROBLEMS QUESTIONNAIRE

Environmental pollution assessment form: B

Instructions

Below you will again see a statement. This time will you please read this and put a tick under how 'urgent' you think each problem is.

In each case   1 = not at all urgent
                   2 = not very urgent
                   3 = not urgent
                   4 = neither urgent nor non-urgent
                   5 = slightly urgent
                   6 = urgent
                   7 = very urgent

How urgent are the following environmental problems?

	Not at all urgent					Very urgent	
	1	2	3	4	5	6	7
Noise							
Air pollution							
Water pollution							
Over-population							
Solid waste disposal							
Toxic waste							
Nuclear waste							
Destruction of land and townscape							
Repletion of natural resources							
Energy							

THANK YOU
Paul Hackett

APPENDIX A.5 GENERAL ENVIRONMENTAL CONCERN QUESTIONNAIRE

HOW EFFECTIVE DO YOU THINK ENVIRONMENTAL/ NATURE CONSERVATION HAS BEEN IN EACH OF THE FOLLOWING AREAS OF ENVIRONMENTAL/NATURE CONSERVATION?

For each of the statements that follow, decide how effective the activities of environmental/nature conservation have been in this area. The numbers on the scale below show how effective environmental/nature conservation may have been. 0 is the least effective, the higher the number the more effective is has been, up to 5 which is the highest level of effectiveness possible. When you have decided how effective it has been in an area or activity, write the number you have chosen in the CHOICE column in line with the statement. Please do this for all the statements.

	slightly effective		effective			
not at all effective	0 . . . . 1 . . . . 2 . . . . 3 . . . . 4 5					completely effective
		moderately effective		very effective		

CHOICE

Halting damage and destruction of the atmosphere, damage to the ozone layer, acid rain, etc.   _____

Highlighting farming practices that may be destructive to the British countryside.   _____

Encouraging human beings to see themselves as members of one global family.   _____

Supporting agricultural development in developing countries.   _____

Controlling traffic levels in cities.   _____

Regulating industrial and housing development in the British countryside.   _____

Developing local nature areas/green sites in inner cities.   _____

Regulating industry's rights to exploit the earth's natural resources.   _____

Saving unspoilt areas, such as: polar regions, tropical forests, the oceans, etc. _____

Regulating international fishing policy. _____

Protecting animal species worldwide. _____

Campaigning for animal rights. _____

Saving habitats and beautiful countryside areas in Great Britain. _____

Facilitating school children's experiences of nature. _____

Campaigning against the exploitation of mineral resources in developing countries. _____

Encouraging wildlife in cities. _____

Encouraging concern for all environmental issues. _____

Reducing the destruction of tropical rain forests. _____

Petitioning for national policy which controls the levels of lead emissions from car exhausts. _____

Protecting village greens and ponds. _____

Petitioning against the existence of EEC food mountains. _____

Encouraging caring towards all living things. _____

Protecting Britain's wildlife. _____

Reducing world population growth. _____

Halting the international trade in animals, e.g.: tortoises, budgerigars, animal fur, whale products, etc. _____

TO WHAT EXTENT WOULD YOU BE WILLING TO BECOME PERSONALLY INVOLVED IN EACH OF THE FOLLOWING AREAS OF ENVIRONMENTAL/NATURE CONSERVATION?

For each of the statements that follow, decide how much you would be willing to become involved with the area or activity addressed by the statement. The numbers on the scale below show how much you may become involved. 0 is the least amount of personal involvement, the higher the number the more involvement, up to 5 which is the highest level of personal involvement possible. When you have decided how involved you would be willing to become, write the number you have chosen in the CHOICE column in line with the statement. Please do this for all the statements.

	sign a		distribute		
would not	petition		leaflets		take other
become	0.......1.......2.......3.......4.......5	direct
involved		write to		join		personal
		MP/papers		protest	action.
				march	

CHOICE

Halting damage and destruction of the atmosphere, damage to the ozone layer, acid rain, etc.

_____

Highlighting farming practices that may be destructive to the British countryside.

_____

Encouraging human beings to see themselves as members of one global family.

_____

Supporting agricultural development in developing countries.

_____

Controlling traffic levels in cities.

_____

Regulating industrial and housing development in the British countryside.

_____

Developing local nature areas/green sites in inner cities.

_____

Regulating industry's rights to exploit the earth's natural resources.

_____

Saving unspoilt areas, such as: polar regions, tropical forests, the oceans, etc.

_____

Regulating international fishing policy.

_____

Protecting animal species worldwide.

_____

Campaigning for animal rights.

_____

Saving habitats and beautiful countryside areas in Great Britain.

_____

Facilitating school children's experiences of nature.

_____

Campaigning against the exploitation of mineral resources in developing countries.

_____

Encouraging wildlife in cities. _____

Encouraging concern for all environmental issues. _____

Reducing the destruction of tropical rain forests. _____

Petitioning for national policy which controls the levels
of lead emissions from car exhausts. _____

Protecting village greens and ponds. _____

Petitioning against the existence of EEC food mountains. _____

Encouraging caring towards all living things. _____

Protecting Britain's wildlife. _____

Reducing world population growth. _____

Halting the international trade in animals, e.g.: tortoises,
budgerigars, animal fur, whale products, etc. _____

LISTED BELOW IS A SERIES OF AREA IN WHICH ENVIRONMENTAL/NATURE CONSERVATION IS ACTIVE. HOW MUCH MONEY WOULD YOU BE PERSONALLY WILLING TO DONATE TO EACH OF THESE AREAS?

For each of the statements that follow decide how much of your money you would be willing to give to environmental/nature conservation activity in this area. The numbers on the scale below show how much money you may give. Nothing (0) is the least you may give, rising in £5 steps to £25 or more, which is the most you can give. When you have decided how much money you are willing to give to this area or activity, write the amount you have chosen in the CHOICE column in line with the statement. Please do this for all statements.

£0....£5....£10....£15....£20....£25+

CHOICE

Halting damage and destruction of the atmosphere,
damage to the ozone layer, acid rain, etc. _____

Highlighting farming practices that may be destructive to
the British countryside. _____

Encouraging human beings to see themselves as
members of one global family. _____

Supporting agricultural development in developing
countries.

Controlling traffic levels in cities. _____

Regulating industrial and housing development in the
British countryside. _____

Developing local nature areas/green sites in inner cities. _____

Regulating industry's rights to exploit the earth's natural
resources. _____

Saving unspoilt areas, such as: polar regions, tropical
forests, the oceans, etc. _____

Regulating international fishing policy. _____

Protecting animal species worldwide. _____

Campaigning for animal rights. _____

Saving habitats and beautiful countryside areas in Great
Britain. _____

Facilitating school children's experiences of nature. _____

Campaigning against the exploitation of mineral
resources in developing countries. _____

Encouraging wildlife in cities. _____

Encouraging concern for all environmental issues. _____

Reducing the destruction of tropical rain forests. _____

Petitioning for national policy which controls the levels
of lead emissions from car exhausts. _____

Protecting village greens and ponds. _____

Petitioning against the existence of EEC food mountains. _____

Encouraging caring towards all living things. _____

Protecting Britain's wildlife. _____

Reducing world population growth. _____

Halting the international trade in animals, e.g.: tortoises,
budgerigars, animal fur, whale products, etc. _____

References

Albrecht, S. L. (1976) 'Legacy of the environmental movement', *Environment and Behavior*, 8: 148–168.

Albrecht, S. L., Bultena, G., Moilberg, E. and Nowak, P. (1982) 'The new environmental paradigm scale', *Journal of Environmental Education*, 13: 39–43.

Albrecht, S. L., Hardin, C.W. and Mause, A. L. (1975) 'Population' in Mause, A. L. (ed.) *Social Problems as Social Movements*, Philadelphia: Lippincott.

Allen, G. H. (1972) 'How deep is environmental awareness?' *Journal of Environmental Education*, 3: 1–3.

Allen, R. (1980) *How to Save the World*, London: Kogan Page.

Amar, R. (1989) 'Demonstration of the Hebrew University Data Analysis Package (HUDAP)', paper presented at the Second International Facet Theory Conference, University of Surrey, 4–6 July.

Amelang, M., Teppe, K., Vagt, G. and Wendt, W. (1977) 'Mitteilung über einige Schritte der Entwicklung einer Skala zum Umweltbewusstsein', *Diagnostica*, 23, 86–88.

Arbuthnot, J. (1977) 'The roles of attitudinal and personality variables in the prediction of environmental behavior and knowledge', *Environment and Behavior*, 9 (2): 217–232.

Arbuthnot, J. and Lingg, S. (1975) 'A comparison of French and American environmental behaviors, knowledge, and attitudes', *Journal of Psychology*, 10: 275–281.

Arcury, T. A., Scollay, S. J. and Johnson, T. P. (1987) 'Sex differences in environmental concern and knowledge: The case of acid rain', *Sex Roles*, 16: 463–472.

Barbour, I. G. (ed.) (1973) *Western Man and Environmental Ethics*, Reading, Mass.: Addison-Wesley.

Barker, M. J. C. (1986) *Directory for the Environment: Organisations in Britain and Ireland 1986–7*, London: Routledge Kegan Paul.

Barr, J. (1971) *The Environmental Handbook*, London: Ballantine.

Bart, W. M. (1972) 'A hierarchy among attitudes toward animals', *Journal of Environmental Education*, 3: 4–6.

Beail, N. (ed.) (1985) *Repertory Grid Techniques and Personal Constructs*, London: Croom Helm.

Bell, P. A., Fisher, J. D. and Loomis, R. J. (1976) *Environmental Psychology*, London: W. B. Saunders Company.

'Blueprint for Survival' (1972) in *The Ecologist*, 2 (1).

Blunden, J. and Curry, N. (eds) (1985a) *The Changing Countryside*, Beckenham: Croom Helm.

———————— (1985b) *The Countryside Handbook*, Beckenham: Croom Helm.

———————— (1988) *A Future for Our Countryside*, Oxford: Basil Blackwell.

Borden, R. J. and Francis, J. L. (1978) 'Who cares about ecology? Personality and sex differences', *Journal of Personality*, 46: 190–204.

Borg, I. (1978) 'A comparison of different studies of life quality', *Zeitschrift-für-Sozialpsychologie*, 9 (2): 152–164.

———————— (1979) 'Some basic concepts in facet theory', in Lingoes, J. C., Roskam, E. E. and Borg, I. (eds) *Geometric Representations of Relational Data*, Ann Arbor, Michigan: Mathesis Press.

———————— (ed.) (1981) *Multidimensional Data Representations: When and Why*, Ann Arbor, Michigan: Mathesis Press.

Borg, I. and Lingoes, J. (1987) *Multidimensional Similarity Structure Analysis*, New York: Springer Verlag.

Borg, I. and Shye, S. (in press) *Facet Theory: The Method and Its Applications*, Newbury Park, CA: Sage.

Borman, F. H., and Kellert, S. R. (1991) *Ecology, Economics, Ethics: The Broken Circle*, New Haven and London: Yale University Press.

Bradby, H. (ed.) (1990) *Dirty Words: Writings on the History and Culture of Pollution*, London: Earthscan.

Braithwaite, V. A. (1977) 'The structure of attitudes to Domesday issues', *Australian Psychologist*, 12: 167–174.

Brandt Commission Report (1987) *North–South: A Programme for Survival*, London: Pan Books.

Braun, A. (1983) *Umwelterziehung zwischen Anspruch und Wirklichkeit*, Frankfurt: Haag & Herchen.

Brown, J. (1985) 'An introduction to the use of facet theory', in Canter, D. (ed.) *Facet Theory: Approaches to Social Research*, New York: Spring Verlag.

———————— (1991) *State of the World 1991*, London: Earthscan.

Brown, J., Lee, T. and Henderson, J. (1983) 'Public perception of nuclear power', paper presented at the London Conference of the British Psychological Society, 19–20 December.

Brown, L. R. (1982) 'Can we learn to live better on less?', *International Wildlife*, 12(1): 31–35.

Bruhn, M. (1979) 'Das soziale Bewusstsein von Konsumenten', in Meffert, H., Steffenhagen, H., and Freter, W.(eds) *Konsumverhalten und Information*, Wiesbaden: Betriebswirtschaftlicher Verlag Dr. Th. Gabler KG.

Bruvold, W. H. (1974) 'Attitudes towards science and accompanying beliefs', *Journal of Social Psychology*, 9: 264–274.

Bunyard, P. and Grenville-Morgan, F. (1987) *The Green Alternative Guide to Good Living*, London: Methuen.

Buss, D. M. and Craik, K. H. (1984) 'Contemporary world views: personal and policy implications', *Journal of Applied Social Psychology*, 13(3): 259–280.

Buttell, F. H. and Flinn, W. L. (1974) 'The structure of support for the environmental movement', *Rural Sociology*, 39: 56–69.

———— (1976a) 'The politics and environmental concern: the impact of party identification and political ideology on environmental attitudes', *Environment and Behavior*, 10: 17–36.

———— (1976b) 'Economic growth versus the environment: survey evidence', *Social Science Quarterly*, 57: 410–420.

———— (1976c) 'Environmental politics: the structuring of partisan and ideological cleavages in mass environmental attitudes', *Sociological Quarterly*, 17: 477–490.

Buttell, F. H. and Johnson, D. E. (1977) 'Dimensions of environmental concern, factor structure, correlates, and implications for research', *Journal of Environmental Education*, 9: 49–64.

Button, J. (ed.) (1988a) *Green Pages: A Directory of Natural Products, Services, Resources and Ideas*, London: McDonald & Co.

———— (1988b) *A Dictionary of Green Ideas*, London: Routledge.

Caldwell, L. K. (1970) 'Authority and responsibility for environmental administration', *Annals of the American Academy of Political and Social Sciences*, 389: 107–115.

Camerson, P. (1972) 'Sound pollution, noise pollution and health: community parameters', *Journal of Applied Psychology*, 56: 67–74.

Campbell, R. R. and Wade, J. L. (1972) 'Value systems', in Campbell, R. R. and Wade, J. L. (eds) *Society and Environment: the Coming Collision*, Boston, Mass.: Allyn & Bacon.

Canter, D. (1982a) 'Facet theory', in *International Encyclopedia of Psychiatry, Psychology, Psychoanalysis and Neurology*, New York: Aesculapius Publishers.

———— (1982b) 'Facet approach to social research', *Perceptual and Motor Skills*, 55: 143–154.

———— (1983) 'The potential of facet theory for applied social psychology', *Quality and Quantity*, 17: 35–67.

———— (ed.)(1985a) *Facet Theory: Approaches to Social Research*, New York: Springer Verlag.

———— (1985b) 'How to be a facet researcher', in Canter, D. (ed.) *Facet Theory: Approaches to Social Research*, New York: Springer Verlag.

Canter, D. and Donald, I. (1985) 'Selection and progress of scientific officers', final report to the Recruitment Research Unit, University of Surrey.

Canter, D. and Kenny, C. (1981) 'The multivariate structure of design evaluation: a cylindrex of nurses' conceptualisations', *Multivariate Behavior Research*, 16: 215–235.

Canter, D. and Rees, K. (1982) 'A multivariate model of housing satisfaction', *Internal Review of Applied Psychology*, 31: 145–151.

Canter, D. and Walker, E. (1980) 'Environmental role and conceptualisations of housing', *Journal of Architectural Research*, 7: 30–35.

Capra, F. (1982) *The Turning Point*, London: Fontana.

Carson, R. (1971) *Silent Spring*, Harmondsworth: Penguin.

———— (1991) *The Sea*, London: Paladin.

Caufield, C. (1982) *Tropical Moist Forests*, London: Earthscan.

CEC (1980) *Factors Influencing Ownership, Tenancy, Mobility, and Use of Farmland in the United Kingdom*, Luxembourg: Office of Official Publications of the European Communities.

Clark, R. (1991) *Water: The International Crisis*, London: Earthscan.

Clark, R. N., Burgess, R. L. and Hendee, J. C. (1972) 'The development of anti-litter behavior in a forest campground', *Journal of Applied Behavior Analysis*, 7: 377–383.

Cone, D. and Hayes, S. C. (1984) *Environmental Problems, Behavioural Solutions*, Monterey, CA.: Brooks/Cole Publishing Co.

Cone, D., Parham, I. A. and Feinstein, D. B. (1972) 'The effects of environmental cleanliness and model's behavior on littering in young children', paper presented at the meeting of the Eastern Psychological Association, Boston, April 1972.

Connerly, C. E. (1986) 'Growth management concern: the impact of its definition on support for local growth controls', *Environment and Behavior*, 18: 707–732.

Conroy, C. and Litvinoff, M. (eds) (1988) *The Greening of Aid: Sustainable Livelihoods in Practice*, London: Earthscan.

Constantini, E. and Hanf, K. (1972) 'Environmental concern and Lake Tahoe: a study in elite perceptions, backgrounds and attitudes', *Environment and Behavior*, 4: 209–242.

Converse, P. E. (1964) 'The nature of belief systems in mass publics', in Apter, D. E. (ed.) *Ideology and Discontent*, New York: Free Press.

Conway, G. R. and Pretty, J. N. (1991) *Unwelcome Harvest: Agriculture and Pollution*, London: Earthscan.

Cook, G. (ed.) (1990) *The Future of Antarctica: Exploration versus Preservation*, Manchester and New York: Manchester University Press.

Coombes, C. (1964) *Theory of Data*, New York: Wiley.

Cotgrove, S. (1982) *Catastrophe or Cornucopia: the Environment, Politics and the Future*, New York: Wiley.

Cotgrove, S. and Duff, A. (1980) 'Environmentalism, middle class radicalism and politics', *Journal of Applied Social Psychology*, 13 (3): 259–280.

Council on Environmental Quality (1970) First annual report, Washington DC: Government Printing Office.

—————— (1971) Second annual report, Washington DC: Government Printing Office.

Countryside Commission (1984) *National Countryside Recreation Survey: 1984*, CCP 201, Cheltenham: Countryside Commission.

—————— (1985) 'City sanctuaries', *Countryside Commission News*, 17, Sept./Oct.: 5.

—————— (1986a) *National Countryside Recreation Survey 1984*, Cheltenham: Countryside Commission.

—————— (1986b) *Access to the Countryside for Recreation and Sport*, CCP 217, Cheltenham: Countryside Commission.

—————— (1986c) 'Recreation 2000: ideas invited for leisure policy review', *Countryside Commission News*, 18.

—————— (1987) 'Enjoying the countryside: a consultation paper on future policies', CCP 225, Countryside Commission, Cheltenham.

—— (1988) 'At work in the countryside', CCP 257, Countryside Commission, Cheltenham.

—— (1989a) 'Putting pollution on the agenda: Commission comment', *Countryside Commission News*, 35, Jan./Feb.

—— (1989b) 'Forests for the Community', *Countryside Commission News*, 38: 4–5.

Craik, K. H. (1969) 'Assessing environmental dispositions', paper presented to the annual American Psychological Association meeting, Washington, 4 September.

—— (1970) 'The environmental dispositions of environmental decision makers', *Annals of the American Academy*.

Craik, K. H. and McKechnie, G. E. (1977) 'Personality and environment', *Environment and Behavior*, 9: 155–168.

Daly, H. E. (ed.) (1973) *Towards a Steady-State Economy*, San Francisco: W. H. Freeman.

Dancer, S. (1985) 'On the multi-dimensional structure of self-esteem: facet analysis of Rosenberg's self esteem scale', in Canter, D. (ed.) *Facet Theory: Approaches to Social Research*, New York: Springer Verlag.

—— (1989) 'Analysis of the stability of structure of a measure of attitudes towards abortion from 1977 to 1985', paper presented at the Second International Facet Theory Conference, University of Surrey, 4–6 July.

Davidson, J. (1988) *How Green is Your City?*, London: Bedford Square Press.

Davis, J. (1989) *Cleobury Mortimer: The Past in Pictures*, Stottsdon: Pen and Think Publishing Co.

de Groot, I. (1967) 'Trends in public attitudes towards pollution', *Journal of Air Pollution Control*, 17: 679–681.

de Haven-Smith, L. (1988) 'Environmental belief systems: public opinion on land use regulation in Florida', *Environment and Behavior*, 20 (3): 276–299.

Dillman, D. A. and Christenson, J. A. (1972) 'The public value for pollution control', in Burch, W. R. jnr, Cheek, N. N. jnr, and Taylor, L. (eds), *Social Behavior, Natural Resources and the Environment*, New York: Harper & Row.

Disch, R. (ed.) (1970) *The Ecological Conscience: Values for Survival*, Englewood Cliff, NJ.: Prentice-Hall.

Dispoto, R. G. (1977) 'Interrelationships among measures of environmental activity, emotionality and knowledge', *Educational and Psychological Measurement*, 37: 451–459.

Ditton, R. B. and Goodale, T. L. (1974) 'Water quality perceptions and attitudes', *Journal of Environmental Education*, 6: 21–27.

DocTer Institute (1987) *European Environmental Yearbook 1987*, London: DocTer International Institute for Environmental Studies.

DOE (Department of Environment) (1987) *Digest of Environmental and Water Statistics*, 9, London: Department of the Environment.

—— (1988) *Digest of Environmental and Water Statistics*, *10*, London: Department of the Environment.

Donald, I. (1983) 'The multivariate structure of office evaluation', unpublished Master's dissertation, University of Surrey.

—— (1985) 'The cylindrex of place evaluation', in Canter, D. (ed.) (1985)

Facet Theory: Approaches to Social Research, New York: Springer Verlag.

———— (1987) 'Office evaluation and its organisational context: A facet study', unpublished Ph.D. thesis: University of Aston in Birmingham.

———— (1989) 'From architectural evaluation to organisational theory', paper presented at the Second International Facet Theory Conference, University of Surrey, 4–6 July.

Dunlap, R. E. (1975a) 'Sociological and social psychological perspectives on environmental issues: a bibliography', *Exchange Bibliography 916*, Monticello, Ill.: Council of Planning Librarians.

———— (1975b) 'The impact of political orientation on environmental attitudes and actions', *Environment and Behavior*, 7: 428–454.

———— (1976) 'Understanding opposition to the environmental movement: the importance of dominant American values', paper presented at the annual meeting of the Society for the Study of Social Problems.

Dunlap, R. E. and Allen, M. P. (1976) 'Partisan differences on environmental issues: a congressional roll-call analysis', *Western Political Quarterly*, 29: 384–397.

Dunlap, R. E. and Van Liere, K. D. (1978a) *Environmental Concern: A Bibliography of Empirical Studies and Brief Appraisal of the Literature*, Public Administration Series Bibliography P-44, Monticello, Ill.: Vance Bibliographies.

———————— (1978b) 'The new environmental paradigm', *Journal of Environmental Education*, 9 (4): 10–19.

———————— (1985) 'Commitment to the dominant social paradigm and concern for environmental quality', *Social Science Quarterly*, 85(4): 1013–1023.

Dunlap, R. E., Gale, R. P. and Rutherford, B. N. (1973) 'Concern for environmental rights among college students', *American Journal of Economics and Sociology*, 27: 106–119.

Dunlap, R. E., Grineeks, J. K. and Rokeach, M. (1981) 'Human values and pro-environmental behaviors', in Conn, W. D. (ed.) *Energy and Material Resources: Attitudes, Values and Public Policy*, Boulder, Col.: Westview.

Dunlap, R. E., Van Liere, K. D. and Dillman, D. A. (1979) 'Evidence of decline in public concern with environmental quality', *Rural Sociology*, 44: 204–212.

du Toit, S. H. C., Steyn, A. G. W. and Stumpf, R. H. (1986) *Graphical Exploratory Data Analysis*, New York: Springer Verlag.

Earthscan (1984) *Cropland or Wasteland: the Problems and Promises of Irrigation*, London: Earthscan briefing document 38.

Eckholm, E. (1982) *Down to Earth*, London: Pluto Press.

Ehrlich, P. (1968) *The Population Bomb*, London: Ballantine.

———— (1981) *Extinction: The Causes and Consequence of the Disappearance of Species*, London: Victor Gollancz Ltd.

Elizur, D. and Guttman, L. (1976) 'The structure of attitudes towards work and technological change within an organisation', *Administrative Science Quarterly*, 21: 611–622.

Elkington, J. and Hailes, J. (1988) *The Green Consumer Guide: From Shampoo to Champagne – High Street Shopping For a Better Environment*, London: Gollancz Ltd.

Erickson, D. L. (1971) 'Attitudes and communications about wildlife', *Journal of Environmental Education*, 2: 17–20.

Everett, P. B., Hayward, S. C. and Meyers, S. W. (1974) 'The effects of token reinforcement procedure on bus ridership', *Journal of Applied Behavioural Analysis*, 7: 1–9.

Fairweather, G. W. (1972) 'Social change and survival', in Clemente, C. L. (ed.) *Environmental Quality: Now or Never*, East Lansing, Michigan: Michigan State University.

FAO (Food and Agricultural Organisation) (1979) *A Review of the State of the World Fishery Resources. 13th Session.*, Rome: FAO.

———— (1982) *Tropical Forest Resources*, Rome: FAO Forestry paper.

Fischoff, B., Slovic, P. and Lichtenstein, S. (1979) 'Weighing the risks', *Environment*, 21: 17–20, 32–38.

Fischoff, B., Slovic, P., Lichtenstein, S., Read, S. and Combs, B. (1978) 'How safe is safe enough? A psychometric study of attitudes towards risks and benefits', *Policy Science*, 8: 127–152.

Foa, U. G. (1958) 'The continguity principles in the structure of interpersonal relations', *Human Relations*, 11: 229–237.

Fransella, F. and Bannister, D. (1970) *Inquiring Man: The Psychology of Personal Constructs*, Harmondsworth: Penguin Books.

———————— (1977) *A Manual of Repertory Grid Technique*, New York: Academic Press.

Fraser Darling, F. (1969) *Wilderness and Plenty: Reith Lecture 1969*, London: British Broadcasting Corporation.

Gaisford, M. (1992) 'Farmers' plan is well on course', *Farmer's Weekly*, 116 (23): 72–73.

Global 2000 Report to the President (1982), Harmondsworth: Penguin.

Goldman, R. D., Platt, B. B. and Kaplan, R. B. (1973) 'Dimensions of attitudes toward technology', *Journal of Applied Psychology*, 57: 184–187.

Goldsmith, E. and Hildyard, N. (eds) (1986) *Green Britain or Industrial Wasteland?*, Cambridge: Polity Press.

———————— (eds) (1989) *The Earth Report: Monitoring the Battle for the Environment*, London: Mitchell Beazley.

Goodman, R. F. and Clary, B. B. (1976) 'Community attitudes and action in response to airport noise', *Environment and Behavior*, 8: 441–470.

Grainger, A. (1982) *Desertification*, London: Earthscan.

Gribbin, J. (1988) *The Hole in the Sky: Man's Threat to the Ozone Layer*, London: Corgi.

Grossman, G. H. and Potter, H. R. (1977a) 'A longitudinal analysis of environmental concern: evidence from natural surveys', paper presented at the annual meeting of the American Sociological Association, Chicago.

———————— (1977b) 'A trend analysis of competing models of environmental attitudes', Working paper Pt 127, Institute for the Study of Social Change, Department of Sociology and Social Anthropology, Purdue University.

Gullard, J. (1975) 'The harvest of the sea', in Murdock, W. W. (ed.), *Resources, Pollution and Society*, Sunderland: Massachusetts.

Gupta, A. (1988) *Ecology and Development in the Third World*, London and New York: Routledge.

Guttman, L. (1954) 'A new approach to factor analysis: the radix', in

Laarfeld, P. F. (ed.), *Mathematical Thinking in the Social Sciences*, New York: Free Press.

—— (1973) in Gratch, H. (ed.), *25 years of Social Research in Israel*, Jerusalem: Jerusalem Academic Press.

—— (1982) 'What is not what in theory construction', in Hanser, R. M., Mechanic, D. and Hauer, A. (eds), *Social Structure and Behavior*, New York: Academic Press.

Gwynn, R. (1987) *Way of the Sea: the Use and Abuse of the Oceans*, Bideford: Green Books.

Hackett, P. M. W. (1985) 'Birmingham International Airport user evaluation: a faceted appraisal', unpublished dissertation: University of Aston in Birmingham.

—— (1986) 'Sandwell Valley Nature Reserve evaluation study', unpublished dissertation, Milton Keynes: Open University.

—— (1987a) 'A structural model of environmental conservation: some initial findings', Doctoral Working Paper Series, 109, University of Aston in Birmingham.

—— (1987b) 'Personal constructs and nature conservation', *Constructs*, 5(1): 3–4.

—— (1989) 'A proposed strategy for the investigation of motivation for and outcome from orthodontic treatment', unpublished report, University College Cardiff.

—— (1992a) 'The understanding of environmental concern', *Social Behavior and Personality*, 20: 3.

—— (1992b) 'Thinking green – acting green: conservationists' workplace values', paper presented at the Third International Conference on Work and Organisational Values: An Empirical and Theoretical State of the Art Review. International Society for the Study of Work and Organisational Values, Karlovy Vary, Czechoslocakia, 12–15 July.

—— (1992c) 'Consumers' environmental concern values: understanding the structure of contemporary green worldviews', paper presented at the Association of Consumer Research European Conference, Amsterdam, The Netherlands, 11–14 June.

—— (1992d) 'The understanding of environmental concern', *Social Behavior and Personality*, 20 (2): 143–148.

—— (1992e) 'The Childe in the Countryside: Colin Ward', *Landscape Research*, 17 (2): 95.

Hackett, P. M. W. and Florence, S. J. (1991) 'The Facet Theoretical Analysis of green consumer values: theoretical implications and empirical findings', paper presented at the First International Workshop on Values and Lifestyle Research in Marketing, European Institute for Advanced Studies in Management, Brussels, 14–15 October.

Hackett, P. M. W., Kenealy, P., Shaw, W. and Frude, N. (1989) 'Beauty's in the mouth of the beholden: motivation for orthodontic treatment for maloclusion', paper presented at the Second International Facet Theory Conference, University of Surrey, 4–6 July.

Hackett, P. M. W., Shaw, W. and Kenealy, P. (1993) 'A multivariate descriptive model of motivation for orthodontic treatment', *Multivariate Behavior Research*, 28 (1): 41–62.

Hake, D. F. and Fox, R. M. (1978) 'Promoting gasoline conservation: the effects of reinforcement schedules, a leader and self recording', *Behavior Modification*, 2: 229–369.

Halliday, T. (1980) *Vanishing Birds*, Harmondsworth: Penguin.

Harman, W. H. (1977) 'The coming transformation', *The Futurist*, 11: 106–112.

Harrelson, L. E., Jordan, J. E. and Horn, H. (1972) 'An application of Guttman facet theory to the study of attitudes toward the mentally retarded in Germany', *Journal of Psychology*, 80: 323–335.

Harris, L. and Associates (1970) *The Public's View of Environmental Problems in the State of Washington*, New York: Louis Harris and Associates.

Harris, L. (1988) in *The Times*, 24 September 1988.

Harry, J. (1977) 'Work and leisure: situational attitudes', *Pacific Sociological Review*, 14: 302–309.

Hay, C. G. (1977) 'The environment and the public: what the polls tell us', *Australian and New Zealand Journal of Sociology*, 13: 242–247.

Heale, B. (1986) 'Psychology of the environment', *Bulletin of the British Psychological Society*, 39: 63.

Heberlein, T. A. and Black, J. S. (1976) 'Attitudinal specificity and the prediction of behavior in a field setting', *Journal of Personality and Social Psychology*, 33: 474–479.

Henderson, H. (1976) 'Ideological paradigms and myths: changes in our own operative social values', *Liberal Education*, 62: 143–157.

Hinrichsen, L. (1989) 'Acid rain and forest decline', in Goldsmith, E. and Hildyard, N. (eds) *The Earth Report: Monitoring the Battle for the Environment*, London: Mitchell Beazley.

Holdgate, M. W. (1979) cited in Royal Commission on Environmental Pollution (1984) Tenth Report, London: HMSO.

Holdgate, M. W., Kassas, M. and White, G. F. (1982) (eds) *The World Environment, 1972–1982*, Dublin: Tycooly.

Hornback, K. E. (1974) 'Orbits of opinion: the role of age in the environmental movement', unpublished Ph.D. dissertation, Department of Sociology, Michigan State University.

Horvat, R. E. and Voekler, A. M. (1976) 'Using a Likert Scale to measure environmental responsibility', *Journal of Environmental Education*, 8: 36–47.

House of Commons Select Committee (in press) *The Effects of Pesticides on Human Health*, London: HMSO.

HRH the Prince Philip (1989) 'Living off the land: the 1989 Richard Dimbleby Lecture', *The Listener*, 121, 3104: 4–7.

ICIDI (Independent Commission on International Development Issues) (1980) *North–South: a Programme for Survival*, London: Pan Books.

IUCN (International Union for the Conservation of Nature), UNEP (United Nations Environmental Programme) and WWF (World Wildlife Fund) (1988) *World Conservation Strategy*, Gland: IUCN.

Iwata, O. (1977) 'Some attitudinal determinants of environmental concern', *Journal of Social Psychology*, 103: 321–322.

Johoda, M. and Freeman, C. (eds) (1978) *World Futures: The Great Debate*, Oxford: Martin Robertson.

Jollans, J. L. (1985) *Fertilizers in UK Farming*, CAS Report 9, Reading: Centre for Agricultural Strategies.

Jowell, R., Witherspoon, S. and Brook, L. (eds) (1984) *British Social Attitudes: The 1984 Report*, London: Gower.

——————— (eds) (1985) *British Social Attitudes: The 1985 Report*, London: Gower.

——————— (eds) (1986) *British Social Attitudes: The 1986 Report*, London: Gower.

——————— (eds) (1987) *British Social Attitudes: The 1987 Report*, London: Gower.

——————— (eds) (1988) *British Social Attitudes: The 5th Report, 1988/ 1989 Edition*, London: Gower.

Kates, R. W. (ed.) (1972) *Managing Technological Hazards: Research Needs and Opportunities*, Boulder: University of Colorado, Institute of Behavioural Sciences.

Kelly, G. (1955) *The Psychology of Personal Constructs, Volumes 1 and 2*, New York: Norton.

——————— (1969) 'Man's construction of his alternatives', in Maher, B. (ed.) *Clinical Psychology and Personality: Selected Papers of George Kelly*, London: Wiley.

Kelly, P. (1985) *Fighting for Hope*, London: Chatto and Windus, The Hogarth Press.

Kenny, C. and Canter, D. (1981) 'A facet structure of nurses' evaluation of ward design', *Journal of Occupational Psychology*, 54: 93–105.

Kessel, D. (1984) 'Environmental problems questionnaire', reported in: The Royal Commission on Environmental Pollution, 10th Report, London: HMSO.

King, A. and Clifford, S. (1985) *Holding your Ground*, Hounslow: Temple Smith.

Kley, J. and Fietkau, H. J. (1979) 'Verhaltenswirksame variablen des Umweltbewusstseins', *Psychologie und Praxis*, 23: 13–22.

Koenig, D. J. (1975) 'Additional research on environmental activism', *Environment and Behavior*, 7: 472–485.

Kohlenberg, R. J., Barach, R., Martin, C. and Anschell, S. (1976) 'Experimental analysis of the effects of price and feedback on residential electricity consumption', unpublished manuscript.

Krause, F., Bach, W. and Koomeg, J. (1990) *Energy Policy in the Greenhouse: From Warming Fate to Warming Limit*, London: Earthscan.

Kronus, C. L. and Van Es, J. C. (1976) 'The practice of environmental quality behavior', *Journal of Environmental Education*, 8: 19–25.

Langeheine, R. and Lehmann, J. (1986) *Die Bedeutung der Erziehung für das Umweltbewusstsein*, Keil: University of Keil, Institut für Pedagogik der Naturwissenschaften.

Leggett, J. (ed.) (1990) *Global Warming: The Greenpeace Report*, Oxford: Oxford University Press.

Levy, S. (1976a) *The Multivariate Structure of Well Being*, Jerusalem: Israel Institute of Applied Social Research.

——————— (1976b) 'The use of the mapping sentence of coordinating theory and research: a cross-cultural example', *Quality and Quantity*, 10: 117–125.

——————— (1978) 'Involvement as a component of attitude: theory and political examples', in Shye, S. (ed.), *Theory Construction and Data Analysis in the Behavioural Sciences*, San Francisco: Jossey Bass.

—— (1979) 'The cylindrical structure of political involvement', *Social Indicators Research*, 6: 436–473.

—— (1981) 'Lawful roles of facets in social theories', in Borg, I. (ed.), *Multidimensional Data Representations: When and Why*, Ann Arbor, Michigan: Mathesis Press.

—— (1985) 'A faceted cross-cultural analysis of some core social values', in D. Canter (ed.) *Facet Theory: Approaches to Social Research*, New York: Springer Verlag.

—— (1986) *The Structure of Social Values*, Jerusalem: Israeli Institute of Applied Social Research.

Levy, S. and Guttman, L. (1974a) *The Desire to Remain in Israel*, Jerusalem: The Israel Institute of Applied Social Research.

——————— (1974b) *The Values and Attitudes of Israel High Street Youth*, Jerusalem: The Israel Institute of Applied Social Research.

——————— (1975) 'On the multivariate structure of well being', *Social Indicators Research*, 2: 361–388.

——————— (1976) *Values and Attitudes of Israel High School Youth – Second Research Project*, Jerusalem: The Israel Institute of Applied Social Research.

——————— (1981a) 'Two examples of value analysis: social control and amenities', in Borg, I. (ed.) *Multidimensional Data Representations: When and Why*, Ann Arbor, Michigan: Mathesis Press.

——————— (1981b) 'Structure and level of values for rewards and allocation criteria in several life areas', in Borg, I. (ed.), *Multidimensional Data Representations: When and Why*, Ann Arbor, Michigan: Mathesis Press.

——————— (1981c) *A Structural Analysis of Some Core Values and Their Cross-cultural Differences*, Jerusalem: The Israel Institute of Applied Social Research.

——————— (1985) 'A faceted cross-cultural analysis of some core social values', in Canter, D. (ed.), *Facet Theory: Approaches to Social Research*, New York: Springer Verlag.

Levy, S. and Meyer-Schweizer, R. (1989) 'Values and social problem indicators: an international comparative project with Louis Guttman', paper presented at the Second International Facet Theory Conference, University of Surrey, 4–6 July.

Lingoes, J. (1973) *The Guttman–Lingoes Nonparametric Program Series*, Ann Arbor, Michigan: Mathesis Press.

Lorr, M. and McNair, D. (1963) 'Interpersonal behavior circle', *Journal of Abnormal and Social Psychology*, 67: 63–75.

Lounsbury, J. W. and Tornatsky, L. G. (1977) 'A scale for assessing attitudes toward environmental quality', *Journal of Social Psychology*, 101: 299–305.

Lovelock, J. (1989) 'Man and Gaia', in Goldsmith, E. and Hildyard, N. (eds), *The Earth Report: Monitoring the Battle for Our Environment*, London: Mitchell Beazley.

Lowe, P. and Goyder, J. (1983) *Environmental Groups in Politics*, Resource Management Series 6, London: George Allen & Unwin.

Lowe, P. and Rudig, W. (1986) 'Political ecology and the social sciences – the state of art: a review article', *British Journal of Political Sciences*, 16: 513–550.

Lowenthal, D. (1972) 'Research in environmental perceptions and behavior', *Environment and Behavior*, 4: 333–342.

McCatcheon, L. E. (1974) 'Development and validation of a scale to measure attitudes towards population control', *Psychological Reports*, 34: 1235–1242.

McCormick, J. (1985a) *The User's Guide to the Environment*, London: Kogan Page.

———— (1985b) 'The international environmental movement, 1945–1980', Unpublished M.Phil. thesis, University of London.

———— (1985c) *Acid Earth: The Global Threat of Acid Pollution*, London: International Institute for Environment and Development.

McEvoy, J. (1972) 'The American concern with the environment', in Burch, W. jnr, Cheek, N. N. jnr and Taylor, L. (eds), *Social Behavior, Natural Resources and the Environment*, New York: Harper & Row.

McGrath, J. E. (1967) 'A multifaceted approach to classification of individual groups and organisations', in Indik, B. P. and Berrien, K. F. (eds) *People, Groups and Organisations*, New York: Columbia University.

McKechnie, G. E. (1974) *Environmental Response Inventory Manual*, Palo Alto: Consulting Psychologists' Press.

———— (1978) 'Environmental dispositions: concepts and measures', in McReyald, P. (ed.), *Advances in Psychological Measurement* (vol. IV), San Francisco: Jossey Bass.

Malkis, A. and Grasmick, H. G. (1977) 'Support for the ideology of the environmental movement', *Western Sociological Review*, 8: 25–47.

Maloney, M. P. and Ward, M. P. (1973) 'Ecology: let's hear it from the people', *American Psychologist*, 26: 583–586.

Maloney, M. P., Ward, M. P. and Braucht, G. N. (1975) 'A revised scale for the measurement of ecological attitudes and knowledge', *American Psychologist*, 30: 787–789.

Mannion, A. M. and Bowlby, S. R. (eds) (1992) *Environmental Issues in the 1990's*, Chicago: Wiley.

Manzo, L. C. and Weinstein, N. D. (1987) 'Behavioural commitment to environmental protection: a study of active and nonactive members of the Sierra Club', *Environment and Behavior*, 19 (6): 673–694.

Marsden, P. V. and Laumann, E. O. (1978) 'The social structure of religious groups: A replication and methodological critique', in Shye, S. (ed.) *Theory Construction and Data Analysis in the Behavioural Sciences*, New York: Jossey Bass.

Marsh, C. P. and Christenson, J. A. (1977) 'Support for economic growth and environmental protection 1973–1975', *Rural Sociology*, 42: 101–107.

Martinson, O. B. and Wilkening, E. A. (1975) 'A scale to measure awareness of environmental problems: structure and correlates', paper presented at the annual meeting of the Midwest Sociological Society, Chicago.

Meadows, D. H., Meadows, D. L., Randers, J. and Behrens, W. W. 3rd (1974) *The Limits to Growth*, New York: Universe Books.

———————— (1992) *Beyond the Limits: Global Collapse or a Sustainable Future?*, London: Earthscan.

Milbrath, L. W. (1984) *Environmentalist: Vanguard for a New Society*, Albany, New York: State University of New York Press.

────── (1985) 'Environmental beliefs: A tale of two countries', mimeographed report, State University of New York at Buffalo.

Miles, H. and Canter, D. (1976) 'Energy conservation in British universities', mimeo, University of Surrey.

Miller, F. A. and Tranter, R. B. (eds) (1988) *Public Perception of the Countryside*, CAS paper 18, Reading: Centre for Agricultural Strategy.

Millward, A. and Bradley, C. (1986) 'Successful green space – do we know it when we see it?', *Landscape Research*, 1 (2): 2–10.

Mindick, B. (1977) 'Attitudes toward population issues', in Oskamp, S. (ed.), *Attitudes and Opinions*, Englewood Cliffs, NJ: Prentice-Hall.

Mitchell, B. and Tinker, J. (1980) *Antarctica and its Resources*, London: Earthscan.

MORI (1987) *Public Attitudes to the Environment, a Research Study Conducted in April 1987 for the Friends of the Earth and the World Wildlife Fund*, London: MORI.

Morrison, P., Burnard, P. and Hackett, P. M. W. (1991) 'A smallest space analysis of nurses' perceptions of their interpersonal skills', *Counselling Psychology Quarterly*, 4 (2/3): 119–125.

Murch, A. W. (1974) 'Who cares about the environment? The nature and origins of environmental concern', in Murch, A. W. (ed.), *Environmental Concern*, New York: Harper & Row.

Murdock, S. H. and Schriner, E. C. (1977) 'Social and economic determinants of the level of support for evironmental protection and economic growth', paper presented at the Annual Meeting of the Rural Sociological Society, Madison, Wisconsin.

Myers, N. (1979) *The Sinking Ark*, New York: Pergamon Press.

────── (1980) *Conversion of Tropical Moist Forests*, Washington DC: National Academy of Sciences.

Natchez, P. B. (1985) *Images of Voting/Visions of Democracy*, New York: Basic Books.

National Trust (1989) Editorial in *The National Trust Magazine*, 56.

National Wildlife Federation (1972) *The US Public Considers its Environment: Survey II*, Washington, DC: National Wildlife Federation.

NOP (National Opinion Polls) (1987) 'Public attitudes to the environment', *Digest of Environmental Protection and Water Statistics*, 9: 54–61.

Nunnally, J. C. (1967) *Psychometric Theory*, New York: McGraw-Hill.

O'Riordan, T. (1971) 'The third American conservation movement: new implications for public policy', *American Studies*, 5: 155–171.

Parker, S. P. (1980) *Encyclopedia of Environmental Science*, (2nd edition), New York: McGraw-Hill.

Parrington, J. R. (1983) 'Asian dust: Seasonal transport to the Hawaiian Islands', *Science*, 8 April.

Payne, R. L., Fineman, S. and Wall, T. D. (1976) 'Organisational climate and job satisfaction: a conceptual synthesis', *Organisational Behavior and Human Performance*, 16: 45–62.

Pearce, D. (ed.) (1989) *Blueprint for a Green Economy*, London: Earthscan.

────── (ed.) (1991) *Blueprint 2: Greening the World Economy*, London: Earthscan.

Phillips, E. M. (1989) 'Use and abuse of the repertory grid: an approach', *The Psychologist* 2 (5): 194–198.

Phipps, A. (1988) 'Third World issues: a faceted study', unpublished dissertation, University of Aston in Birmingham.

Pierce, J. C. and Lovrich, N. P. jnr (1980) 'Belief systems concerning the environment: the general public, attentive publics, and state legislators', *Political Behavior*, 2: 259–286.

Pirages, D. C. and Ehrlich, P. R. (1974) *Ark II: Social Response to Environmental Imperatives*, San Francisco: W. H. Freeman.

Porritt, J. (1984) *Seeing Green: the Politics of Ecology Explained*, Oxford: Basil Blackwell.

——— (1986) 'Beyond environmentalism', in Goldsmith, E. and Hildyard, N. (eds), *Green Britain or Industrial Wasteland?* Cambridge: Polity Press.

——— (ed.) (1987) *Friends of the Earth Handbook*, London: McDonald & Co.

——— (1990) *Where on Earth are We Going?*, London: BBC Publications.

Porritt, J. and Warner, D. (1988) *The Coming of the Greens*, London: Fontana.

Powell, K. (1986) 'The destruction of Britain's urban heritage', in Goldsmith, E. and Hildyard, E. (eds) *Green Britain or Industrial Wasteland?*, Cambridge: Polity Press.

Pringle, S. L. (1976) 'Tropical moist forests in world demand, supply and trade', *Unasylva*, Nos 112–113.

Ray, J. J. (1974) 'Environmentalism as a trait', *The Planner*, 14: 52–62.

——— (1975) 'Measuring environmentalist attitudes', *Australian and New Zealand Journal of Sociology*, 11: 70–71.

——— (1980) 'The psychology of environmental concern: some Australian data', *Personality and Individual Differences*, 1: 161–163.

Rees, A. (1991) *The Pocket Green Book*, London: Zed Books Limited.

Rose, C. (1984) 'Wildlife: the battle for the British countryside', in Wilson, D. (ed.), *The Environmental Crisis*, London: Heinemann.

Roskam, E. (1981) 'Contributions of multidimensional scaling to social science research', in Borg, I. (ed.), *Multidimensional Data Representations: When and Why*, Ann Arbor, Michigan: Mathesis Press.

Royal Commission on Environmental Pollution (1984) Tenth Report, London: HMSO.

RSPB (Royal Society for the Protection of Birds), (1988), Editorial, *Birds*, 12 (3).

——— (1992) Editorial: 'Change for the Countryside', *Birds*, 14 (2).

Runkel, P. J. and McGrath, J. E. (1972) *Research on Human Behaviour: a Systemic Guide to Method*, New York: Holt Rinehart & Winston.

Salvat, B. (1979) 'Trouble in Paradise, part 2: coral reef parks and reserves', *Parks*, 4: 1–4.

Schahn, J. and Holzer, E. (1990) 'Studies of individual environmental concern: the role of knowledge, gender, and background variables', *Environment and Behavior*, 22 (6): 767–786.

Schlesinger, I. M. (1978) 'On some properties of mapping sentences', in Shye, S. (ed.), *Theory Construction and Data Analysis in the Behavioural Sciences*, London: Jossey Bass.

Schlesinger, I. M. and Guttman, L. (1969) 'Smallest space analysis of intelligence and achievement tests', *Psychological Bulletin*, 71: 95–100.

Scientific America (1991) *Energy for the Planet Earth: Readings from Scientific America*, New York: W.H. Freeman.

Scott, W. A. and Scott, R. (1965) *Values and Organisations*, San Francisco: Jossey Bass.

Sharma, N. C., Killvin, J. E. and Fliegel, F. C. (1975) 'Environmental pollution: is there enough public concern to lead to action?', *Environment and Behavior*, 7: 455–471.

Sheil, J. (1983) 'The historical perspective', in Warren, A. and Goldsmith, M.B. (eds), *Conservation in Perspective*, London: John Wiley.

Shoad, M. (1980) *The Theft of the Countryside*, London: Temple Smith.

Shye, S. (ed.) (1978a) *Theory Construction and Data Analysis in the Behavioral Science*, London: Jossey Bass.

—— (1978b) 'Partial order scalogram analysis', in Shye, S. (ed.), *Theory Construction and Data Analysis in the Behavioural Sciences*, London: Jossey Bass.

—— (1979) *A Systematic Facet-Theoretical Approach to the Study of Quality of Life*, Jerusalem: Israel Institute of Applied Social Research.

—— (1982) 'Compiling expert opinion on the impact on environmental quality of a nuclear power plant: an application of a systematic life quality model', *International Review of Applied Psychology*, 31: 285–302.

—— (1985a) 'Lawful roles of facets in social theories', in Canter, D. (ed.), *Facet Theory: Approaches to Social Research*, New York: Springer Verlag.

—— (1985b) 'Partial order scalogram analysis by base coordinates and lattice mapping of items by their scalogram roles', in Canter, D. (ed.), *Facet Theory: Approaches to Social Research*, New York: Springer Verlag.

—— (1985c) 'Smallest space analysis', in *The International Encyclopaedia of Education*, Oxford: Pergamon.

—— (1985d) 'Partial order scalogram analysis', in *The International Encyclopaedia of Education*, Oxford: Pergamon.

—— (1986) 'Multiple Scaling: The theory and application of partial order scalogram analysis', Amsterdam: North Holland.

Shye, S. and Elizur, D. (in press) *Introduction to Facet Theory*, Newbury Park, CA: Sage.

Simon, R. J. (1972) 'Public attitudes toward population and pollution', *Public Opinion Quarterly*, 36: 93–99.

Sinclaire, T. C. (1973) 'Environmentalism', in Cole, H. S. D. (ed.), *Thinking about the Future: a Critique to the Limits to Growth*, London: Chatto & Windus for Sussex University Press.

Slater, P. (1980) 'Construct systems in conflict', *International Journal of Man–Machine Studies*, 13 (1): 49–57.

Smith, K. (1992) *Environmental Hazards: Assessing Risk and Reducing Disaster*, London: Routledge.

Smyth, B. (1987) *City Wildspace*, London: Hilary Shipman.

Spretnak, C. (1986) *The Spiritual Dimension of Green Politics*, Santa Fe, New Mexico: Bear and Company.

Spretnak, C. and Capra, F. (1984) *Green Politics: the Global Promise*, London: Palladin.

Springer, J. F. and Constantini, E. (1974) 'Public opinion and the environment: an issue in search of a home', in Nafel, S. S. (ed.) *Environmental Politics*, New York: Praeger.

Steel, C. (1992) 'Tipping the balance for wildlife', *Natural World*, 34, Spring/Summer: 8.

Stokols, D. (ed.) (1973) 'Special issues on population research and environmental psychology', *Representative Research in Social Psychology*, 4.

—————— (1978) 'Environmental psychology', *Annual Review of Psychology*, 29: 253–295.

Svensson, G. (1984) 'Forest at risk', *Acid Rain*, Spring 1984: 27–38.

Tait, J., Lane, A. and Carr, S. (1988) *Practical Conservation: Site Assessment and Management Planning*, London: Open University in association with the Nature Conservancy Council.

Timberlake, L. (1989) 'The politics of food aid', in Goldsmith, E. and Hildyard, N. (eds) *The Earth Report: Monitoring the Battle for Our Environment*, London: Mitchell Beazley.

Tognacci, L. N., Weigel, R. H., Wideen, M. F. and Vernon, D. T. A. (1972) 'Environmental quality: how universal is public concern?', *Environment and Behavior*, 4: 73–86.

Tolba, M. K. (1984) *Desertification is Stoppable*, London: Earthscan.

Tremblay, K. R. jnr and Dunlap, R. E. (1978) 'Rural–urban residence and concern with environmental quality: a replication and extension', *Rural Sociology*, 43: 474–491.

Turner, K. and Jones, T. (eds) (1990) *Wetlands: Market and Intervention Failures: Four Case Studies*, London: Earthscan.

Tyson, P. (1992) *Acid Rain*, London: Chelsea House Publishers.

UKWCS (United Kingdom World Conservation Strategy), (1983) *The Conservation and Development programme for the United Kingdom: a Response to the World Conservation Strategy*, London: Kogan Page.

Ullrich, J. R. and Ullrich, M. F. (1976) 'A multidimension scaling analysis of perceived similarities of rivers in western Montana', *Perceptual and Motor Skills*, 43: 575–584.

UNEP (United Nations Environmental Program) (1990) *Environmental Data Report, Third Edition 1991/1992*, London: Blackwell.

Van Liere, K. D. and Dunlap, R. E. (1978) 'Environmental concern: consistency among its dimensions, conceptualisations and empirical correlates', paper presented at the annual meeting of the Pacific Sociological Association, Spokane, Washington.

—————— (1980) 'The social basis of environmental concern: a review of hypotheses, explanations and empirical evidence', *Public Opinion Quarterly*, 31: 103–106.

—————— (1981) 'Environmental concern: does it make a difference how it's measured?', *Environment and Behavior*, 13: 651–676.

Wall, G. (1973) 'Public response to air pollution in South Yorkshire, England', *Environment and Behavior*, 5: 219–248.

—————— (1974) 'Public response to air pollution in Sheffield, England', *International Journal of Environmental Studies*, 5: 259–270.

———— (1975) 'Attitudes toward air pollution: A bibliography of English language literature', *Exchange Bibliography*, No. 891, Monticello, Ill.: Council of Planning Librarians.

Ward, B. and Dubos, R. (1980) *Only One Earth*, Harmondsworth: Penguin.

Watkins, G. A. (1974) 'Developing a "water concern" scale', *Journal of Environmental Education*, 5: 54-58.

———— (1975) 'Scaling of attitudes toward population problems', *Journal of Environmental Education*, 6: 14–20.

WCED (World Commission on Environment and Development) (1988) *Our Common Future*, Oxford: Oxford University Press.

Webber, D. J. (1982) 'Is nuclear power just another environmental issues? An analysis of Californian voters', *Environment and Behavior*, 14: 72–83.

Weigel, R. H. (1977) 'Ideological and demographic correlates of proecological behavior', *Journal of Social Psychology*, 103: 39–47.

Weigel, R. H. and Weigel, J. (1978) 'Environmental concern: the development of a measure', *Environment and Behavior*, 10: 3–15.

Weigel, R. H., Woolston, V. L. and Gendelman, D. S. (1977) 'Psychological studies of pollution control: an annotated bibliography', Mimeography Department of Psychology, Amherst College, Amherst, Massachusetts.

Wellburn, A. (1988) *Air Pollution and Acid Rain: The Biological Impact*, New York: Longman Scientific and Technical.

Westmacott, R. and Worthington, T. (1984) *Agricultural Landscapes – a Second Look*, CCP 168, Cheltenham: Countryside Commission.

Westoby, J. (1983) 'Who's deforesting whom?', *IUCN Bulletin*, 4: 10–12.

WHO (World Health Organisation) (1984) *Urban Air Pollution 1973–1980*, Geneva: WHO.

Whitmore, T. C. and Sayer, J. A. (eds) (1992) *Tropical Deforestation and Species Extinction*, London: Chapman and Hall.

Williams-Ellis, C. (1928) cited in Nicholson, M., *The New Environmental Age*, Cambridge: Cambridge University Press.

Williams, R. M. jnr (1968) 'The concept of values', in *The International Encyclopedia of the Social Science*, vol. 16, New York: Macmillan Co. and Free Press.

Wilson, D. (ed.) (1984a) *The Environmental Crisis: a Handbook for All Friends of the Earth*, London: Heinemann Educational Books.

———— (1984b) *Pressure: The A–Z of Campaigning in Britain*, London: Heinemann Educational Books.

———— (1986) *Citizen Action: Taking Action into Your Own Community*, London: Longman Press.

Wilson, M. (1989) 'The development of architectural concepts', paper presented at the Second International Facet Theory Conference, University of Surrey, 4-6 July.

World Resources Institute (1990) *World Resources 1990/1991*, Oxford: Oxford University Press.

Worster, D. (1989) 'Man and the natural order', in Goldsmith, E. and Hildyard, N. (eds) *The Earth Report: Monitoring the Battle for Our Environment*, London: Mitchell Beazley.

WWF, Greenpeace and Friends of the Earth (1988) *The Green Gauntlet: Testing the Government's Commitment to the Environment*, London: World Wide Fund for Nature.

Yankelovich, D. (1972) 'The new naturalism', *Saturday Review*, 55: 32–37.

Young, K. (1988) 'Does the countryside matter?', *Countryside Commission News*, 34: 3.

Zarling, L. H. and Lloyd, K. E. (1978) 'A behavioural analysis of feedback to electrical consumers', unpublished manuscript.

Zeibland, S. (1986) 'Radical environmentalism and the petite bourgeoisie: a survey of whole and health food shop proprietors?', unpublished M.Sc. dissertation, University of Surrey.

Index